WOMEN HEALING EARTH

ECOLOGY AND JUSTICE
An Orbis Series on Global Ecology

The Orbis *Ecology and Justice Series* publishes books that seek to integrate an understanding of the Earth as an interconnected life system with concerns for just and sustainable systems that benefit the entire Earth. Books in the Series concentrate on ways to:
- reexamine the human-Earth relationship in the light of contemporary cosmological thought
- develop visions of common life marked by ecological integrity and social justice
- expand on the work of those who are developing such fields as eco-social ecology, bioregionalism, and animal rights
- promote inclusive participative strategies that enhance the struggle of the Earth's voiceless poor for justice
- deepen appreciation for and expand dialogue among religious traditions on the issue of ecology
- encourage spiritual discipline, social engagement, and the reform of religion and society toward these ends.

Viewing the present moment as a time for responsible creativity, the Series seeks authors who speak to ecojustice concerns and who bring into dialogue perspectives from the Christian community, from the world's other religions, from secular and scientific circles, and from new paradigms of thought and action.

Also in the Ecology and Justice Series

ECOLOGY AND JUSTICE SERIES

WOMEN HEALING EARTH

*Third World Women on Ecology,
Feminism, and Religion*

**Edited and with Introductions by
Rosemary Radford Ruether**

ORBIS BOOKS

Maryknoll, New York 10545

The Catholic Foreign Mission Society of America (Maryknoll) recruits and trains people for overseas missionary service. Through Orbis Books, Maryknoll aims to foster the international dialogue that is essential to mission. The books published, however, reflect the opinions of their authors and are not meant to represent the official position of the society.

Published by Orbis Books, Maryknoll, NY 10545-0308
Manufactured in the United States of America

Library of Congress Cataloging-in-Publication Data

Women healing earth : Third World women on ecology, feminism, and
   religion / edited and with introductions by Rosemary Radford
   Ruether.
     p. cm. — (Ecology and justice series)
   ISBN 1-57075-057-2 (alk. paper)
    1. Ecofeminism—Developing countries.   2. Feminist theory
—Developing countries.   3. Feminist theology—Developing countries.
4. Women and religion—Developing countries.   I. Ruether, Rosemary
Radford.   II. Series: Ecology and justice.
HQ1233.W595   1996
305.42'01—dc20

Printed on recycled paper

Contents

Introduction

ROSEMARY RADFORD RUETHER

This volume of essays by women in Latin America, Asia, and Africa on religion, ecology, and feminism presents an effort at cross-cultural communication and solidarity between women in the "First World" and women in those countries that are struggling against the effects of Western colonization. There are many reasons why I wish to bring together such a collection of essays.

First of all, as a Euro-American woman living in the United States, I have for thirty years been deeply concerned with the oppressive use of power by my own country against subjugated people in the "Third World." I feel in solidarity with their struggles for liberation. My own experience of "crossing worlds" between affluent and poor, white and people of "color," and between "first" and "third" world has been revelatory and transformative for my understanding and my life. By viewing the ruling classes of my country from the underside, its evils and lies are revealed and put in the context of a larger reality and call for justice.

Second, for many years, but particularly in the last five years, I have sought to explore the interconnections between ecology and feminism, the interconnections between the domination of women and the domination of nature, or "ecofeminism," and how religion interplays with this connection, in both positive and negative ways. How has religion reinforced such domination, and how might it be a resource for liberation from violence for both women and nature?[1]

My experience with the thought and work of women in the many countries where I have traveled for speaking and dialogue—India, Korea, the Philippines, Central and Latin America, South Africa and Zimbabwe—suggests to me that the way they integrate the feminist, ecological, and religious connections would be instructive for women interested in these connections in North America.

Yet this book is not only about making the voices of women in Asia, Africa, and Latin America audible to women of the North; it is also an opportunity for women in the South to put together their own perspectives and to communicate with and learn from one another. This work has been done in collaboration with the *Con-spirando* collective in Santiago, Chile, which networks Latin American women on ecofeminist theology and spirituality and publishes the journal on that subject, *Con-spirando*.[2] This group gathered and translated the essays from Latin America for this volume. We also plan to have the communication flow the other way. They will translate these essays into Spanish for a Latin American publication.

The women of the South who wrote these essays are also crossing worlds, learning from one another in "South-South" dialogue, and also crossing cultures and social contexts in their own societies. Two of our Latin American writers, Janet May and Judith Ress, are North American in origin but have lived for many years in Latin America, forging their own immersion into and solidarity with the Latin American context. Other writers come from more educationally and socially privileged classes and have committed themselves to solidarity with women of the poor in their societies.

Still other writers have emerged from indigenous local cultures and seek to reconnect with their own roots. Many writing from the South recognize the "mix" of their own reality, as both indigenous people and as people who have been colonized and incorporated into the colonizer's culture and religion. They write on women, religion, and nature as people "crossing worlds" within themselves.

There is no suggestion in this book that these essays represent an ecofeminist "movement" in the "Third World" parallel to ecofeminism in North America. One can hardly say that there is an ecofeminist "movement" in North America. Rather, there is a variety of movements dealing with ecological crises from several perspectives, and within those movements, there are women who make a conscious critique of the movements' androcentrism and seek to show the connections between women's domination and the domination of nature.[3]

Likewise in Asia, Africa, and Latin America there is not an "ecofeminist movement." Most of the writers in this volume don't use the term ecofeminist, although several do and make their own contextualization of its meaning in their reality. What connects these essays is not a conscious use of a particular ideology of how women and nature are connected but rather a complex reality of how women and nature have been exploited both by their own societies as well as by colonizing powers, how women function as the mediators of nature's benefits for their families, and in this context, as caretakers of nature.

Some authors are also interested in indigenous religions in their local heritages, which identified the sacrality of nature with the roles of women as mothers and caretakers of nature. How can this sacrality of nature as woman-like be reclaimed by women (and men) today to overcome patterns of desacralization, instrumentalization, and disregard for nature brought by Western colonizing culture—both through Christianity and through Western science and technology?

It may be useful to spend some time comparing the views of ecofeminism found in North America with the perspectives on women and nature found in these essays. Among Northern ecofeminists the connection between domination of women and domination of nature is generally made first on the cultural-symbolic level. One charts the way in which patriarchal culture has defined women as being "closer to nature," as being on the nature side of a nature-culture hierarchical split. This is shown in the way in which women have been identified with body, earth, sex, the flesh in its mortality, weakness, and "sin-proneness," vis à vis a masculinity identified with spirit, mind, and sovereign power over both women and nature as the property of ruling class males.

A second level of ecofeminist analysis goes beneath the cultural-symbolic level and explores the socio-economic underpinnings of how the domination of women's bodies and women's work interconnects with the exploitation of the land and animals as sources of labor and wealth. How have women as a gender group been colonized by patriarchy as a legal, economic, social, and political system? How does this colonization of women's bodies and labor function as the invisible substructure for the extraction of wealth for ruling class men?[4] How does the positioning of women as the caretakers of children, the garden-ers, weavers, cooks, cleaners, and waste managers for men in the family both inferiorize this work and identify women with a nonhuman world which is like-wise inferiorized?

From a Marxist-feminist perspective, the cultural-symbolic patterns linking women and nature are an ideological superstructure by which the system of economic and legal domination of women, land, and animals is justified and made to appear "natural" and inevitable within the total patriarchal cosmovision. Religion then comes in to reinforce this domination of women and nature as reflecting the will of God and the relation of God as supreme deified patriarchal male to the "world" that he "created" and rules.

Ecofeminists who stress this socio-economic analysis of the women-nature connection as gender exploitation also generally want to include an analysis of class and race hierarchy as well. Women are not a homogeneous group. We have to look at the total class structure of society—fused with race hierarchy—and see how gender hierarchy falls within this class-race hierarchy. This means that women of the ruling class have not only vastly different comforts than women of the poor but also that there are different ideological "images" of the ruling class white lady that separate her from the poor woman of color, the slave woman, the peasant woman.

However much the white lady may also have extensive duties and suffer abuse from the males in her family, her image is sublimated as the "angel in the house" and a display object of leisure, while the poor woman, the slave woman, the peasant woman is seen as more like an "animal," both as beast of burden and as the object of projection of debased carnality. The Eve-Mary split reflects this split image of woman in Christianity. For Christianity, all women suffer the punishment due to being daughters of Eve, but the "good woman" is redeemed by being "Mary-like." The incorporation of Mary-likeness into class ideology is revealed by its identification with "Our Lady" and hence with "ladies."[5]

Northern ecofeminists have not only been interested in analyzing the con-nections of women and nature as expressions of an ideology and a socio-eco-nomic system of exploitation by the male elite. Many have also been interested in how to take hold of this historical cultural connection of women and nature as a positive relation by which women can stand in solidarity with exploited nature, resist the violence done to nature and to themselves, and become healers of nature.

Some ecofeminists see this positive role of women as defenders and healers of nature in more practical terms. It is not that female humans are any more like land, animals, and plants than male humans; or stated another way, male humans are as much like animals, plants, and land as female humans. Rather women's social location as mediators of nature can be employed to resist exploitation and to care for the environmental community upon which their welfare and that of their families depend.

Other Northern ecofeminists see a more essential connection between women and nature. There is a deeper truth to the link between women and nature that has been distorted by patriarchy to exploit them both. Women are the life-givers, the nurturers, the ones in whom the seed of life grows. Women were and often remain the primary food gatherers, the inventors of agriculture. Their bodies are in mysterious tune with the cycles of the moon and the tides of the sea. It was by experiencing women as the life-givers, the birthers of children, the food-providers, that early humans made the image of the female the first personification of the divine, as the Goddess, the source of all life.[6]

Many of these essentialist ecofeminists connect this primacy of the Goddess with a primal story of human history. In this story, humans in the hunter-gatherer and gardener stages lived in egalitarian classless societies in a benign, nurturing relationship with one another and with the rest of nature. The social system of war, violence, and male domination came in with a series of invasions by patriarchal pastoralists from the Northern steppes sometime in the sixth through third millennia B.C.E. in the ancient Middle East, reshaping earlier egalitarian societies into those of militarized domination.[7]

These dominator societies also brought with them a concept of God as patriarchal warrior and ruler, outside of and disconnected with nature, which they used to suppress the earlier concept of the Goddess as immanent life within nature. For some who ascribe to this primal story of "fall" into patriarchy and patriarchal religion, the implication is that in order to heal ourselves and the earth we must reject patriarchal religions (usually seen specifically as Christianity) and return to the worship of the ancient Goddess. For women this means rediscovering the wonderful connections between the sacrality of nature as Great Goddess and the sacrality of our own sexuality and life-powers. To worship the Goddess as a woman is to reclaim these lost powers unjustly stolen from us by patriarchal religion.

Other women of Christian background do not take the discovery of the prehistoric Goddess as a call to a literal return to worship of her. Rather, they receive this discovery as a liberation from the ultimacy of the biblical/Christian image of the patriarchal god. As Judy Ress put it (in a communication to me of April 27, 1995), "some women who have gone through a process of realizing that there was an evolution in our root image of the Holy—i.e., that before God there was a more primal image of Goddess . . . look for new images more appropriate to how we now sense Ultimate Mystery."

My own view of this fall-from-paradise-into-patriarchy story is that it is a powerful contemporary myth, although one with ancient roots. By myth I do not mean that it is simply untrue but that it is a simplified and selective reflection (like all myths) of a complex process—a process (in this case) by which humans shaped patriarchal social and religious-ideological hierarchies and gradually suppressed earlier egalitarian societies, which were more interdependent with their bioregional environments.[8]

Moreover, I also think that when privileged Northern feminists lay hold of this story as their identity myth, it can lead to some illusions and irresponsibility. The story can be read by First World ecofeminists who choose to worship the Goddess as if they, simply by shifting their religious images and practices, can see themselves in direct continuity with the innocent victims of patriarchal conquest over ten thousand years. They don't have to examine and take responsibility for their actual social context as heirs and beneficiaries of this conquest as First World affluent people.

Many essentialist or matricentric Northern ecofeminists fail to make real connections between their own reality as privileged women and racism, classism, and impoverishment of nature. Relation with nature is thought of in psycho-spiritual terms as rituals of self-blessing, exultant experiences of the rising moon and the seasonal wonders. I don't disvalue such ceremonial reconnecting with our bodies and nature. I think they have a vital place in the healing of our consciousness from a culture of alienation.

But such psycho-spiritual reconnecting with women's bodies and nature can become a recreational self-indulgence for a privileged counter-cultural Northern elite if these are the *only* ideas and practices of ecofeminism; if the healing of our bodies and our imaginations as Euro-Americans is not connected concretely with the following realities of over-consumerism and waste: the top 20 percent of the world's human population enjoys 82 percent of the wealth while the other 80 percent scrapes along with 18 percent; and the poorest 20 percent of the world's people, over a *billion* people—disproportionately women and children—starve and die early from poisoned waters, soil, and air.

A Northern ecofeminism that is not primarily a cultural escapism for an affluent female elite must make concrete connections with women at the bottom of the social-economic system. We must recognize the ways in which the devastation of the earth is an integral part of an appropriation of the goods of the earth whereby a wealthy minority can enjoy strawberries in winter, winged to their glittering supermarkets by a global food procurement system, while those who pick and pack the strawberries lack the money for bread and are dying from pesticide poisoning.

I remember standing in a market in Mexico in January looking greedily at boxes of beautiful strawberries and wondering if I might be able to sneak some back through customs into the United States to my snow-covered home. A friend of mine, Gary McEoin, longtime journalist of Latin American liberation struggles, standing next to me, said softly, "Beautiful, aren't they? . . . and they

are covered with blood." To be an ecofeminist in my social context is to cultivate that kind of awareness about the invisible underside of the goods and services readily available to me.

I look for an important corrective to the myopias of the white affluent context from dialogue with women from Asia, Africa, and Latin America, as well
as from the struggles of racial-ethnic women and men against environmental
racism in the United States. I find that ecofeminism sounds significantly different when it comes from these class, racial, and global contexts.

This does not mean that women in Latin America, Asia, and Africa are not
concerned with much of the same range of themes as Northern ecofeminists. As
shall be seen in the essays in this volume, some of the writers are analyzing the
masculine-feminine *qua* culture-nature split as a part of their own cultural inheritance, particularly from a Christianity that colonized their people. Many
also see a special relationship of women with nature, both as mediators of nature for their families and as women who are somehow more in touch with
natural rhythms than males. Many also want to reach back before European
Christian colonization two hundred to five hundred years ago and reclaim the
sacrality of nature imaged as immanent divine female (even longer ago for
women in India dealing with the Aryan invasions that brought Hindu patriarchal caste hierarchy two thousand years ago).

To me there are two important differences when such themes are
contextualized by women from the Third World. First, women from Asia, Africa, and Latin America are much less likely to forget, unlike Northern women,
that the base line of domination of women and of nature is impoverishment; the
impoverishment of the majority of their people, particularly women and children, and the impoverishment of the land.

This interconnection of the impoverishment of women and the impoverishment of the land is not an abstract theory to be expressed in statistics, as it often
is for Northern women living in well-heated or cooled houses and vehicles.
Rather, it is present in concrete realities one lives and observes every day. Deforestation means women walk twice as far each day to gather wood. Drought
means women walk twice as far each day seeking water. Pollution means a
struggle for clean water largely unavailable to most of one's people; it means
children in shantytowns dying of dehydration from unclean water.

Second, although many women of Asia, Africa, and Latin America are deeply
interested in recovering patterns of spirituality and practice from a pre-Christian past, these spiritualities are those of their own indigenous roots. They are
not fetched in as an idealized story from long ago and far away with which one
has no cultural experience, but rather this pre-Christian indigenous past is still
present. It has been broken and silenced by colonialism and Christianization,
but it is still present in the contemporary indigenous people of one's own land,
descendants of one's own indigenous ancestors, or even as customs with which
the woman writer herself grew up in her earlier years.

This means that the spiritualities and practices of tribal peoples appear in
these women's accounts in their complexity and specificity. One cannot ideal-

ize these spiritualities and practices as references to a lost Eden when all was well. Things may indeed have been better than the cruel regime brought by the colonialists, but these traditions also preserve patterns that are problematic for women. They record males' fear of women that can only be overcome by conquest and domination, and their projections upon women of pollution taboos that limit women's activities.

Women of Asia, Africa, and Latin America who turn to their indigenous traditions have to evaluate not only what may be empowering and healing in these traditions but also what may express, in a different social and literary genre, oppression of women, just as they have to evaluate what is oppressive and what may be liberating in the religious and secular traditions into which they have been socialized by their conquerers.

Third World women are then less likely to make blanket oppositions between all things Western and Christian as evil and all things from their own culture as good, or vice versa. They are deabsolutizing Christianity to see it as one cultural resource for themselves alongside others that come to them from their earlier roots. They are practical ecumenists who cross cultures, speak Shona as well as English, and critically and creatively use elements that come to them from their several cultural legacies to enhance life for their people, especially for women and children at the bottom of the society.

Northern ecofeminists, I believe, can learn much from these essays to help us be more truthful and responsible and to enter into concrete alliances between our ideas and work in North America and those of women in the South. First we need to keep our own eyes on what for us is a less visible relationship between oppression of women and poverty (the poverty of the majority of people, especially women and children), the impoverishment of the soil, pollution of the air and water—these shrinking means of basic survival for those struggling to live in a subsistence economy under and marginalized from the dominant global system of power and profits. This means we also have to be more truthful about who we are in this system.

Second, we can learn to be less dogmatic and more creative about what is good and bad, usable and problematic, in our own cultural legacies. We too might look back at our indigenous roots in Celtic, Nordic, or Slavic Europe (careful to separate such searches from its misuse by European fascism) and find similar patterns of spirituality to that found in Africa, Asia, and Latin America. We can also mine our Greek, Hebrew, and Christian heritages, as well as our modern emancipatory traditions for usable insights.

We need to free ourselves from both our chauvinism and our escapism to play with what is liberating in our heritages (as well as appraising their problems), letting go of both the urge to inflate our identity as the one true way or to repudiate it as total toxic waste. We must question our urge to imagine we can jettison our own reality by appropriating the ideas and practices of indigenous peoples of other worlds to save us without having any real relationship to these people, as some Euroamericans have done toward the indigenous peoples of North America.[9]

In short, we need to deal modestly and truthfully but also transformatively with who we are, culturally and economically. We need to reject what is oppressive but also make creative syntheses of what is liberating in our heritages that can be in positive reciprocity with the very different but complementary syntheses being made by women who are both Shona and Christian in Zimbabwe, who are Christian, Buddhist, and Shamanist in Korea, who are Mayan and Methodist in Mexico. Only in this way can we begin to find how to be true friends and sisters with women—with people—of other worlds, no longer as oppressors trying to suppress other peoples' identities but also not as "white blanks" seeking to fill our own emptiness at the expense of others.

Notes

1. See Rosemary Ruether, *Gaia and God: Ecofeminist Theology of Earth Healing*, HarperSanFrancisco, 1992.

2. The *Con-spirando* collective and magazine can be contacted at Casilla 371-11, Correo Nunoa, Santiago, Chile

3. See *Reweaving the World: The Emergence of Ecofeminism*, edited by Irene Diamond and Gloria F. Orenstein, San Francisco: Sierra Club, 1990.

4. See Ynestra King, "Healing the Wounds: Feminism, Ecology and the Nature/Culture Split," in *Reweaving the World*, pp. 106-121.

5. See, for example, Rosemary Ruether, "The Cult of True Womanhood and Industrial Society," in *From Machismo to Mutuality*, edited by Rosemary R. Ruether and Eugene Bianchi, New York: Paulist Press, 1976, pp. 39-53.

6. See Charlene Spretnak, "Ecofeminism: Our Roots and Our Flowering," in *Reweaving the World*, pp. 3-14.

7. See Riane Eisler, *The Chalice and the Blade*. San Francisco, CA: Harper and Row, 1987.

8. See Ruether, *Gaia and God*, pp. 144-155.

9. See Andy Smith, "For All Those Who Were Indian in a Former Life," in *Ecofeminism and the Sacred*, edited by Carol J. Adams, New York: Continuum, 1993, pp. 168-171.

PART 1

LATIN AMERICA

In the Casa de Cultura in Leon, Nicaragua, there hangs a large painting of a Nicaraguan *mestizo* woman standing in an open field, the mountains ringing the landscape. Her hands are extended, palms up, and the veins of her wrists are slit. Her blood drips into the field. Ronald Reagan is perched on her shoulders, carrying a shotgun, while Henry Kissinger and George Schultz stand beside her dressed as court jesters. The painting is a devastatingly ironic commentary on the exploitation of the Nicaraguan land and people by the North American superpower.

The imagery goes deep into the Latin American psyche and history. The *mestizo* woman, fruit of the violent rape of the indigenous woman by the Spanish conquistador, symbolizes the raped and exploited people and land of Central and Latin America, whose life blood is drained to enrich colonists who continue to sit on top of her. The image recalls the title of what is perhaps the most powerful book on this history of extraction of wealth by outside and domestic exploiters: Eduardo Galeano's *Open Veins of Latin America: Five Centuries of the Pillage of a Continent*.

The writers of these essays on women and ecology in Central and Latin America stand in the context of this history. Women, particularly indigenous women, represent the poorest of the poor. But they also struggle to survive, to cultivate a patch of land, to sweep an earthen floor and beautify the entrance of a hovel with flowers in tin cans, to thriftily garner the resources available to them to feed and clothe their families.

Ivone Gebara, a Brazilian theologian who lives and works with the poorest of the poor in Northern Brazil, reflects from an ecofeminist perspective on what is usually seen as the most obscure and incomprehensible of the religious doctrines brought to Latin America by the Christian missionaries: the Trinity. Gebara opens her essay with a recognition of the awe typically felt by Latin Americans in the face of this most central and yet most unfathomable doctrine. Women particularly feel intimidated at the very thought that they might think about such a theological idea for themselves in the context of their own experience.

Yet Gebara goes on to insist that not only can the doctrine of the Trinity be made meaningful to the experience of women but that at its root the Trinity is about the underlying patterns of our daily experience. Moreover, the Trinity as a theory did not drop out of heaven; it was itself created by human beings to express their experience—their experience with the cosmos, the earth, one another and their own selves.

Human beings, the earth and the whole community of life on earth, and finally the entire cosmos exist and are sustained by one breath of Life, one matrix of life-giving relationality in which we live and move and have our being (Acts 17:28). We call this life-giving power *God*, but God is not a distant ruler with "three heads." Rather, God is the underlying font of being who upholds the life-process of all creation that continually wells up and is renewed. This life-process unfolds through a dynamic process of diversification, interrelationship, and communion. These same patterns of diversity, interrelation, and communion shape everything that is—the cosmos with its many stars and galaxies, to the rich variety of plants and animals on the earth, to the diversity of human cultures, to the interactions of two people with each other, and finally, to one's relationship to oneself as embodied spirit.

For Gebara, the Trinity as a way of understanding God is nothing more and nothing less than the way humans seek to capture and express this dynamic process by which life pours forth in all its variety of expressions, is sustained, interconnects and communes with all around it, and is continually renewed. Evil also exists in these relations, not as something willed by the creator and source of life but rather as a way humans interrupt this life process by seeking to control it, to lay hold of it as power and wealth for the few against the many. In so doing, distortion in the dynamic processes takes place and is manifest in violence, the impoverishment of people, and the destruction of the land.

The struggle for liberation is then basically the struggle to overcome these distorted relations, to renew human life in its context of relations among people, among people and the earth community and the whole universe, in loving and life-giving mutuality. Redemption is rooted in that *metanoia*, that change of mind or turning around that restores us to our positive interrelationality, which is rooted in the trinitarian dynamics of the life-process of God's creative love. By liberating God from the encapsulation in imagery of patriarchal domination, Latin American women and men can rediscover the real meaning of God as liberating life itself.

Mercedes Canas, an El Salvadorean sociologist, brings an ecofeminist critique to bear on the struggles for liberation of her own tiny, war-torn and environmentally-devastated country. She critiques the growing ecological establishment in El Salvador for its tendency to look on women only as a problem, as those who "cause" over-population and who need to learn to care for the environment as they scour the land for wood, water, and food for their families.

Canas makes clear that those who have impoverished El Salvador's people and stripped its soil and forests are not poor peasant women but are the same group of large landowners and industrialists who own most of the best land and use it for their own profits without regard for the land itself or its people. Poor women are the most exploited of the poor, and their exploitation has been closely connected with the exploitation of the land. But women are also leading the protest against this double exploitation.

Ecofeminism claims an alternative principle of relationship between men and women, humans and the land—a mutuality in which there is no hierarchy but rather an interconnected web of life. This life-giving relationality is not an abstract theory but it manifests the concrete way that poor women care for the land and their families, sustaining life rather than destroying it. The revolt of women is the revolt of the land itself against soul and body destroying domination, with its ultimate expression in endless war and uncontrolled death-squads. It is a revolt in favor of rerooting humans in those ways of relating to one another and the land that make life worth living, where "it is worth the trouble to have been born."

Gladys Parentelli, a Venezuelan feminist theologian, turns her attention to the poor women of her country and the myriad ways they sustain life in their everyday activities. These endless activities of poor women in sustaining life stand as a counter-reality to the history of five hundred years of colonial and neo-colonial exploitation that continues today in the endless bleeding of Latin American wealth by its domestic and foreign power-holders.

Women, particularly women of the poor, instinctively love life and act to conserve it, for it is the very means by which they not only sustain survival for themselves and their families, but also provide touches of redeeming beauty to daily life in the midst of a world of violence that disregards them and the land, laying rapacious hands on anything and everything that brings power and profit.

Janet May, a North American who has lived and worked as a missionary and teacher for twenty years in Central and Latin America, writes from her present context as a feminist pastoral theologian teaching at the *Seminario Biblico Latinoamericano* in San José, Costa Rica. Her essay reflects a dialogue among five women at the seminary, all of them "strangers" to Costa Rica. These five women reflect on their own multi-cultural reality as women living in and studying in Costa Rica, drawn from a plurality of ethnic and religious backgrounds. Elena Kelly is an Afro-indigenous Moravian Nicaraguan; Anastasia Mejia is a Maya Kiché Guatemalan; Silvia de Lima an Afro-Brazilian Catholic; Esther Camac a Peruvian Quechua Methodist, and Janet May a Euro-American Methodist.

As these five women explore multi-cultural dialogue with one another, but especially within the multiple levels of their own reality, they ask how they can claim all of this multiplicity in a creative and good way. The parts of their identity which have been most despised—their indigenous and African ancestry, the religions of their indigenous and African ancestors—become precious resources for life-giving creativity and joy, for themselves, their people, and their sense of relationship to the natural world around them. They also ask how they can claim liberating and women-affirming resources from their Christian identities, not against but in harmony with the insights that come from their violated but also life-sustaining African and indigenous mothers and grandmothers.

In the final essay in this section, Mary Judith Ress, one of the founders and editors of the *Con-spirando* collective and magazine in Chile, explores this relationship to the "dark grandmothers," the indigenous women from whose violated bodies sprang the "mixed" peoples of Latin America. As women in Latin America seek their own liberation as women, and also seek to protect the land continually devastated by those who use it only for profit, they turn back particularly to the cultures and cosmovision of their indigenous ancestors.

The voices of the indigenous peoples and their many cultures, silenced for five hundred years by an arrogant Christianity that saw in the spirituality of these cultures only demonic "idolatry," have begun to be heard again, particularly through the 1992 observances of the five-hundred-year anniversary of the conquest by Columbus in 1492. As indigenous people reclaim their voices and identities, as Nahuatl and Mayan, Quechua, Aymara, and Mapuche, their *mestizo* daughters (and sons) are awakening from their long shame and repudiation of their dark grandmothers.

Latin Americans are discovering in their indigenous ancestors a cosmovision of respect for life that can resist the devastation of their land and reclaim the inseparable inter-dependency of a people with its life community of animals and plants, air, water, mountains, lakes, and valleys. Christ will still have a place for many in Latin American spirituality, but others, especially indigenous people, are withdrawing from his sway, which in some sense never really "took" for them. The question is whether Christ can be converted to liberation, to defense of the life of the poor, incarnate in the *mestizo* reality.

Christ can be incarnate as a *mestizo*, converted to care for the people in and through their land, only when the *mestizo* Christ acknowledges that he is the son of a dark Indian woman. The God to whom Christ points us must not be a distant Spanish conquistador but a God who is as much mother as father, who (for Andean people) is *Pachamama*, the source and principle of life itself.

1

The Trinity and Human Experience

An Ecofeminist Approach

IVONE GEBARA[1]

Human beings are a part of the whole we call the Universe, a small region in time and space. They regard themselves, their ideas and their feelings as separate and apart from all the rest. It is something like an optical illusion in their consciousness. This illusion is a sort of prison; it restricts us to our personal aspirations and limits our affective life to a few people very close to us. Our task should be to free ourselves from this prison, opening up our circle of compassion in order to embrace all living creatures and all of nature in its beauty.

Albert Einstein[2]

When we hear the word Trinity, we immediately associate it with unfathomable mystery. It is part of our faith, but we have trouble relating to it. We've been told that our God is a Trinity who has overcome all loneliness and isolation. We've heard that it is the communion among Father, Son, and Holy Spirit, a beautiful and perfect sharing that we should imitate in our own relationships. Today, this "imitation" seems more and more difficult to understand. It seems to take place so far from ourselves: from our own flesh, our concerns, our limitations. In the final analysis it is a sharing among "persons" who are totally spiritual and perfect. It is, after all, a divine communion.

There is a real fear in all of us of daring to doubt certain ideas, of raising questions about things we were taught that have been set forth as truths we have to accept. Religious institutions often create this fear in us, fettering our ability to think critically about faith issues. The Trinity, and the words Father, Son, and Holy Spirit are like a code that needs to be broken and translated anew. They are symbols that refer to life experiences, but their symbolism has grown hazy and has been absolutized within a closed, eminently masculine and arcane theoretical system. I invite you to *dare to think*, above all because this is a decisive moment in our history, a moment full of difficult questions and institutional crises, a moment in which the very survival of life is at stake.

For all these reasons, the perspective I adopt in this reflection is *ecofeminism*. In simple and practical terms, I'd like to show that there is a need to rediscover and reflect on the truly universal aspects of life, on dimensions that reflect what the earth and the cosmos are telling us about themselves, and the things women are vehemently affirming with regard to their own dignity and that of all humanity.

Before I speak of the Trinity I'd like to say a few words about the wonder of being human. I want to remind you that human beings are a fruit of a long process, the evolution of life itself. Life evolved for thousands and thousands of years before the creation of the species to which we belong and which we call human. Within us, life continues to be created: it develops, folds back, and reveals itself in differing cultures and economic, political, social, and cultural organizations. Life itself led humanity to arise from within the whole creative evolutionary process, which is both earthly and cosmic.

The human race carries on this creative expression of life both in itself and in its works. Participating in the creative evolution of life, we re-create ourselves. This is manifest in our ability to reflect and love, in our ethical behavior, and in all the other capabilities that make us what we are.

Living within the context of nature as a whole, we have gradually accumulated significant learnings. We have responded, for example, to the challenge of rivers that stretched before us, separating one place from another: we learned to build bridges. To move on water we built boats, then ships. To cross great distances we built airplanes, and so on. We learned to closely examine our human experience, as well as the lives of insects, animals, and plants; and thus we found ways of living and developing our creativity as we responded to the challenges posed by each situation.

Our learning led us to discover the social causes of poverty, and then to formulate hypotheses aimed at explaining and interpreting history and responding with concrete actions. Our learning also led us to cultivate a sense of wonder and perplexity in the face of the astounding order that marks all of reality.

We ourselves continually re-create the life that is in us. Human culture, in its multiple artistic and literary expressions, bears witness to our admirable creativity. This creativity also exists, albeit in a different form, in the vegetable and animal worlds. We have often been taught, however, that these "other worlds" have little creativity. The real reason for this attitude is that we always think of creativity in human terms and judge everything else on that basis. It would be good, however, if human beings would stop once in a while and reflect on the creativity that is manifest in an orange seed: the memory present in this small, vital center; its ability to develop when conditions are favorable; its ability to adapt to different soils and situations; to become a tree; to produce flowers and fruit, and then once again seeds. The seed's creativity is surely not the same as human creativity, but it clearly participates in the ongoing and awesome creativity of the universe.

The seed planted in the depths of the earth goes through a complex process of transformation, of changes in life and in death, before it breaks through the soil's surface. And when we discover that the seed has become a small plant, we do not remember the entire, arduous process it went through in the bowels of the earth and in its own innermost recesses; neither do we remember its multiple interactions with all the forces of nature.

The same is true of human beings. The things we produce, even the most precious among them, sublime creations such as our religious beliefs, emanate from a long maturation process in which our concern for our immediate needs has always been present. Our extraordinary creativity acquired the ability to produce meanings capable of helping us live out this or that situation. But these meanings are not static realities; they are part of the dynamism of life, and thus they change as well. Of necessity, they undergo transformations in order to respond to life's demands and adapt to new situations as they arise.

The important thing, if we are going to be able to take the next step in our reflection, is to get a clear sense that the *human* meanings of things come from ourselves, as does the human meaning of the entire universe. It is we ourselves who construct our interpretations, our science, our wisdom, our knowledge. It is we ourselves who today affirm one thing and tomorrow correct what we have said. It is we who affirm the image of God as warrior-avenger or as tender and compassionate. It is we, in our ancestors and traditions, who have construed the Trinity as three distinct persons in one God; so too, we can change our way of portraying it as we develop new perceptions.

The Trinity is an expression of our history, of human history, which is both tragic and challenging; but it is a unified Trinity, as if in that unity we were expressing our own desire for harmony and communion with all that exists. It is a communion to which we aspire in the midst of tears, of the experience of pain and suffering, as if that Holy Trinity of which we speak was the expression of a world that is both plural and transformed, harmonized, in which all suffering and pain are overcome, separation and division overcome, every tear wiped away; and in the end God, that is, the One, Love, is all in all.

The Trinity brings multiplicity and the desire for unity into one single and unique movement, as if they were moments within the same breath. Trinity is a name we give to ourselves, a name that is the synthesis of our perception of our own existence. Trinity is a language we build in an attempt to express our awareness of being a multitude and at the same time a unity. Trinity is a word that points to our common origin, our shared substance, our universal breathing within the immense diversity that surrounds each and every one of us, each a unique and original creation, a path along the great road of life. Trinity is also a word about ourselves, about what we know and live out in our own flesh-and life-stories.

A baptism of fire is one we go through as a result of our inner faithfulness to ourselves. It is a reality that envelops us by virtue of our rediscovery of our deepest self. Within that rediscovery we are reborn in God; we are reborn to the earth, to the cosmos, to history, and to service in the construction of human relationships grounded in justice and mutual respect.

Today, if we are to recover the dynamism of the Trinity, we need to recover the dynamism of our own existence—even at the risk of not managing to formulate our ideas in clear and precise terms. Our great challenge is to accept the insecurity involved in discussing what is real and to seek only the security that comes from dealing with the here and now, with daily life, with our own experiences and with our questions, heeding that wise phrase from the Hebrew world, "sufficient to the day is its own task."

The Trinity, then, is not three separate persons living in a heaven we cannot locate. It is not three persons different from one another the way we differ as persons. The Father, Son, and Holy Spirit are not of divine stuff as opposed to our human stuff; rather, they are *relationships*, that is, relationships we human beings experience. These relationships are expressed in anthropomorphic style; but the expression is metaphorical and not primarily metaphysical. Within Christian experience, Father, Son, and Holy Spirit are symbolic expressions we use to speak of the profound intuition that all of us share, along with everything that exists, in the same divine breath of life.

Reconstructing the Meaning of the Trinity

We speak of "reconstruction" when a human relationship, a piece of land, a city, or even a society needs to remake itself, re-create itself, renew its relational life. Something has happened that has weakened an edifice, a relationship, a bond of friendship. In this sense I'd like to offer a somewhat tentative effort at rebuilding Trinitarian meanings—a reconstruction demanded by the present historical situation. I'd like to propose five reflections on this reconstruction: the Trinity in the cosmos; the Trinity on earth; the Trinity in relationships among peoples and cultures; the Trinity in human relationships; and the Trinity in every person.

The Trinity in the Cosmos

"This universe is a single multiform energetic unfolding of matter, mind, intelligence and life."[3] So says Brian Swimme, a North American astrophysicist who has worked hard to tell the story of the universe in empirical language. He tries to show that as we approach the end of this century, humanity has acquired the ability to tell the story of the universe itself. This is a fundamental step in coming to understand our shared history and in the effort to create a new relationship with the earth, the cosmos, and with all peoples.

At this point I merely want to draw your attention to the unique and multiform structure of the universe that in symbolic and metaphorical terms we could call a "Trinitarian" structure. By Trinitarian structure I mean the reality that constitutes the entire cosmos and all life forms, a reality marked at the same time by multiplicity and by unity, by the differences among all things and their interdependence.

Stars, galaxies, heavenly bodies, planets, satellites, the atmosphere, the seas, rivers, winds, rain, snow, mountains, volcanos—all are expressions of the multiple creativity of the universe; they are profoundly interdependent and interrelated. They are diversity and unity, existing and interrelating in a unique and single movement of continual creativity.

The Trinity on Earth

Plants, animals, forests, mountains, rivers, and seas form the most diverse combinations in the most remote and varied places. They attract one another, couple with one another, blend with one another, destroy one another, and re-create themselves in species of pale or exuberant colors. They grow and feed on one another's lives, transforming and adapting to one another, dying and rising in many ways within the complex life process to which we all belong. In its stunning mutations, the earth sometimes threatens us and sometimes awes us, sometimes makes us shiver and at other times inspires cries of joy. Spinning around the sun and on its own axis, the earth creates days and seasons and brings forth the most varied forms of life.

The Earth as Trinity: The Trinitarian earth is a movement of continuous creativity, unfolding processes of creation and destruction that are expressions of a single vital process. To grasp the immense creative force in which we are immersed and of which we are an integral part, we need only think of the succession of geological eras, the birth of the continents, the transformation of seas into deserts, the flowering of forests, and the emergence of manifold expressions of vegetable and animal life.

The Trinity in Relationships among Peoples and Cultures

Whites, blacks, indigenous peoples, Asiatics and *mestizos*, all with different languages, customs, statures and sexes, make up the awesome and diverse human symphony in which, once again, multiplicity and unity are constitutive expressions of the single vital process that sustains us all. Life, in its complex process of evolution, brings about the variety of human groups and invites us to contemplate the luxuriance of our diversity.

If we accept this diversity as part of the Trinitarian structure itself and take it seriously as the basic make-up of all beings, there is no way to justify the idea of any being's superiority or inferiority. What we have now is cosmic citizenship. We are merely "cosmics," terrestrials, members of the cosmos and of the earth; we need one another, and can exist only on the basis of a community of being, of interdependence among our differences.

I am convinced that if we were to try to develop this idea of cosmic citizenship, we could more easily overcome the different strains of racism, anti-racism, xenophobia, exclusion, violence, and sexism that are rife in our culture. A new sense of citizenship needs to be born and grow in us, without denying the national affiliations that are still part of our history.

The pluralism that makes us a human species is Trinity: it is the symbolic expression of a single and multiple reality that is an essential component of our living tissue. This plurality is essential if human life itself is to continue on, if the different races and cultures are to develop, support one another and enter into communion.

The Trinity in Human Relationships

The Trinitarian mystery is also found in intimate I-thou relationships. We are I-thou and mystery—the mystery of our presence to the world, to the universe, to ourselves. We are the mystery of our stories, our traditions, our questions. We are I, thou, and mystery, and therefore Trinity, in the closeness and allure of a profound relationship that leads us to a deeper level of intimacy, of desire to know one another, of tender sharing. For this reason, knowing one another requires not only time, patience and dialogue but a constant and challenging investment of ourselves. We are challenged to enter into a process of shared self-revelation, of unmasking ourselves, of manifesting an ever greater part of ourselves. We will find that what we reveal is drawn from those things that are known and unknown to ourselves, and therefore to others.

The Trinity in Every Person

Our own personal being is Trinitarian: it is mysteriously multiple at the same time that it is one. And most important, this extraordinary reality can be seen in the lives of all peoples; it is present in all biological functions, in all cultural and religious processes. This vision gives us a new worldview and a different anthropology, on the basis of which we see ourselves as persons who are *of* the earth and *of* the cosmos, participants in the extraordinary process of life's evolution. "The new heavens and the new earth" are always on the way: they were coming to be yesterday, they are coming to be today, and they will be on the way tomorrow. Heaven is not opposed to earth; it does not present itself as something superior or as the final aim of our efforts, the place where we will at last enter into a state of divine peace and harmony.

The Celebration of Life

By trying to understand the Trinity as a human experience, as an experience of the earth and of the cosmos, we are able to celebrate life in a new way. "In a new way" means we ourselves are celebrated as we celebrate life in the Trinity. It means, too, that we experience a broader oneness with the life processes that are beyond our own boundaries. We praise ourselves; we praise the earth; we praise all beings as we raise our voices in praise of the Trinity, using the symbolic language that is most dear to us. We include ourselves in the celebration. It is not just something apart from us; it starts with our own existential experience, in our communion with all forms of life and all the cosmic energies.

The Trinity and the Problem of Evil

The ancient problem of evil is very much with us today, above all because, as I pointed out previously, we see an increase in the destruction of persons, of groups, and of the earth itself. Our society seems ever less capable of devising formulas that permit dignified human sharing and the possibility of survival on the earth. We have the impression that our present world, despite its theories, its analyses and its designs, has turned ever more often to violence and exclusion in order to solve its problems. This in turn has brought about a growing wave of destruction, greater than at any other time in history. The wretched of the earth, the hungry, the landless, the unemployed—those who thirst for justice—feel ever more acutely the silence of God even when, hoping beyond all hope, they continue to speak of God's justice.

A Trinitarian vision of the universe and of humanity does not identify evil, destruction, and suffering as realities that are outside ourselves and need to be eliminated through violence; neither does it say they should be accepted as God's will. Rather than point to "the other" as the source of evil, it recognizes that what we call evil is in ourselves; in a certain sense evil is also our body. Evil is a relationship we ourselves construct; it leads to the destruction not only of the individual but of the entire fabric of human life.

The Trinitarian view of the universe places us at the very energy source of all that exists. At the same time it makes a distinction: on the one hand is the creative-destructive process that is inherent in the evolution of life itself; on the other is moral evil, evil defined in ethical terms. The latter refers to human evil, the evil worked by ourselves: actions that, when combined with our inherent frailty, can make us murderers of life in all its multiple expressions.

When we speak of human beings, we always speak in terms of good and evil. But when we speak of the cosmos, of the universe, we need to speak of forces that are at once creative and destructive. This constitutive reality of the universe, these positive and negative poles (we use these terms with an awareness of the limitations of our language) are inseparable in all the life processes. The birth of our solar system required the destruction of others. The appearance of a desert region may mean the death of a river. The use of fish as food may require the destruction of many of them, and so on.

The fact that we are the "consciousness" or the thinking process of the universe leads us to label things good or evil according to the way they affect us. Today we need to have another look at these reflections in the light of our contemporary historical situation and our more global and articulated sense of the life processes.

Ethical evil is evil wrought by human beings. On the one hand, it arises from the dynamics of life itself and from our human condition of frailty, dependence, and interdependence. On the other, the Christian tradition has always taught that evil actions arise out of our selfishness and the excesses of our passions.

But ethical evil is also a result of our very limited understanding of ourselves and our relationship with all other beings. We have acquired a highly developed sense of our individuality, of our superiority or inferiority, but have relatively little sense of our collective nature, of the way in which our communion with everything else assures our survival and shared happiness.

Because of our narrow affirmation of our personal, racial, religious, and even class identity, we have created systems to protect ourselves from one another—the systems based on greed or on the perceived superiority of those who regard themselves as "the strongest" or "the finest." These systems do not allow us to perceive the ephemeral nature of our individual lives and projects. Instead, we exalt the individual and regard the most powerful, wealthy, or brilliant individuals as absolutes, quasi-divinities to be protected against all the ebbs and flows of history.

From this perspective we developed the idea of a God who is above and presides over history. This in turn led us to construct an image of a just divinity outside our world—a powerful deity often fashioned in the image of the powerful of this world. This God, who is also an "individual," is always just, strong and good—the very opposite of our fragility and depravity. This is the God of theodicy, a God who is very difficult to reconcile with the tragic reality of human history. It is a God whose goodness "in itself" must always be affirmed and defended, as if in defending the goodness of a supreme being we could guarantee our escape from our own tragic iniquity.

The poor continue to bend their knees before this deity, begging for mercy, clemency, and help in satisfying their most basic needs and harboring the spark of hope in their daily lives. They act toward this God much the way they act toward the powerful of this world, hoping to be treated with consideration and left with some prospect of earning their bread with dignity. The poor are slaves of many masters and, by analogy, also of a supreme master.

To leave behind this crude and highly patriarchal, hierarchical, materialistic, individualistic, dependent, and class-biased understanding of God and of the Trinity seems to me an essential step for the present and the future. Above all this is a spiritual path, a personal and collective empowerment that opens us to a wider and freer perspective. By "spiritual path" I mean a path that transforms our inner convictions, a demanding path that goes beyond adherence to a political party's program or obedience to a code of canon law. It is a spiritual path because it is the path of the Spirit, which blows freely where it will; no one can hold back its movement. It is a spiritual path because it is the path of God in each and all of us.

We are constantly being invited to return to our roots: to communion with the earth, with all peoples and with all living things; to realize that transcendence is not a reality "out there," isolated, "in itself," superior to all that exists, but a transcendence within us, among us, in the earth, in the cosmos, everywhere. That transcendence is here and now, among those who are similar to us and different from us, among plants and animals, rivers and seas. That transcendence invites us to reach beyond the limitations of our selfishness and respond to our call to a new collective ethic centered on saving all of life. That transcendence is a canticle, a symphony unceasingly played by the infinite creativity of *Life*.

What, then, is evil in this traditional yet novel perspective? Within this perspective, what we call evil is the unbalanced situation in which we find ourselves, our millennial thirst for individual power and our millennial hunger to eat more and more while preventing others from consuming their rightful share.

The basic evil propagated by our species originates in the desire to possess life and make it our own—selfishly. It is the appropriation of goods by individuals and groups—the self-appointed proprietors of the earth—of other persons and groups, whom the dominant regard as of secondary importance. Evil is the growing dysfunctionality in both personal and social life that leads me to the narcissistic cultivation of my own individuality and my ecclesiastical, political, or business interests.

Evil is the excess or abundance that is held back and hoarded, whether it be food, land, power, knowledge, or pleasure. It remains in the hands of the owners of capital: those who, with the support of their direct and indirect accomplices, present themselves as veritable gods upon the earth.

Evil is the idolatry of the individual, of the "pure" race, of the messianic people, of the empire that dominates by insinuating itself into everything, even into people's inner being, inducing them to believe in their own inferiority. Evil is the ascendancy of one sex over another, its domination over all personal, social, political, and economic realms.

Evil is the proclamation and imposition of my gods as eternal and exclusive, capable of saving all of humanity. Evil is the claim that some people know the will of God and are commissioned to teach it as irrefutable dogma, while others are obligated to humbly recognize and accept their own ignorance.

Human evil leaves us perplexed. It poses innumerable questions, many of them unanswerable. Cosmic "evil," on the other hand, is the creation-destruction process inherent in the universe, and it only frightens us when we suffer its consequences.

Cosmic evil has two faces: it is rooted in the Trinity we are and in the humanity and divinity we participate in. This evil is the negative aspect or, to use a different term, the emptiness found everywhere in the universe, on earth, and among human persons. This emptiness opens the way for opposition, conflict, tension, and destruction; but at the same time it bears extraordinary creative possibilities for the unfolding of our sensitivities and the opening of our inner being to that which is beyond ourselves.

In some way, too, things that appear negative have an energy capable of developing within us the capacity for loving others, bending to those who have fallen in the street, taking in an abandoned child, replanting a ravaged forest, cleaning up a polluted river, or feeding animals during a time of drought. Out of the garbage we accumulate, a flower can bloom; dry bones can return to life; the horror of war can become a cradle of compassion. We ourselves and the whole universe are made up of the same energy, an energy that is both positively and negatively charged. This very energy continually creates and re-creates the earth and human existence.

Human history bears witness to the fact that great gestures of mercy and tenderness are born of dramatic, life-threatening situations. When another's pain becomes unbearable, it becomes my pain and stimulates the birth of loving gestures. The Buddha, Jesus, Mohammed, the thousand Francises, Clares and Theresas, the ever-present unnamed saints turn pain into a source of compassion, mercy, and new prospects for life.

This new vision, which is present in our reflection on the Trinity, helps us leave behind the dualistic and confining anthropocentrism that has characterized our Western Christian tradition, a dualism that not only regards the dyad God and humanity as opposites but does the same to the dyads spirit and matter, man and woman, and good and evil. Throughout the course of our history, dualism has engendered a thousand and one antitheses.

The saying attributed to Jesus of Nazareth, "Love your neighbor as yourself," should be taken up by us and understood as the way back to a Trinitarian balance. If we have excessive love for ourselves, we will fall into a sort of unlimited narcissism and the virtually implacable destruction of others. We will continue to build empires: Nazism, fascism, racism, classism, *machismo*, and all kinds of excesses that end up turning back on us, and above all, on the poor. A balance between I and thou, I and we, we and they, ourselves and the earth is the way to turn around and allow the human, as well as plants and animals and all the creative energies of the earth, to flourish anew.

This new vision calls on us to see the universe as our body, the earth as our body, the variety of human groups as our body—a body that is in evolution, in creative ecstasy, in the midst of destructive and regenerative labor, of death and resurrection. Everything is our body, our Trinitarian body: it is a continual tension and communion of multiplicity and unity, all within the ecstatic and mysterious adventure of Life.

Conclusion

In conclusion I want to express a hope-filled certainty. At the end of this millennium we are beginning to work together, as peoples from many parts of the earth, to build a new spirituality. It looks, in fact, like a new Pentecost; but it is a slow-moving Pentecost: patient, universal, at times almost imperceptible. It is an inner and outer Pentecost that bursts open our religious boundaries. It begins not only to change our understanding of the world and of ourselves, but to modify our behavior. All this is spirituality, that is, an energy that puts order in our lives, that gives meaning, that awakens in us the desire to help others to discover the "pearl of great price" hidden in our own bodies and in earth's body. We know that when people find their personal and collective "pearl," they "sell all they have" in order to obtain it. The pearl is the symbolic expression of the new spirituality that is growing in our own bodies, nourished by our human energies, by the earth, by the cosmos—in the last analysis, by the indissoluble one and multiple Trinitarian energy that is present in all that exists.

The Trinity is our primary creative reality, a constitutive reality, a reality that permeates all we do and are. A Trinity of things old and new, of stories and tales that evolve and are organized in many creative ways. The ecofeminist perspective, which is an intimate connection between feminist thought and ecology, opens us not only to the possibility of real equality between men and women of different cultures, but to a different relationship between ourselves, the earth, and the entire cosmos. This new relationship, which is still in its embryonic stages, aims at going beyond merely speculative discussions, which do not lead to a change in relationships.

We are tired of sterile religious-scientific discourse, of its powers grounded in an All-Powerful, One and Trinitarian God, distant and apart from ourselves. We are tired, to use the words of Arnaldo Jabor, of seeing the world "divided between those who bewail hell and those who live in it."[4] This refers to the hell of our society, which kills Indians, children, and entire peoples; but which can also produce individuals who designate themselves as the "conscience" of society and as critics of its ills, and who speak in the name of God but fail to recognize either the blasphemy they commit or the complicity that flaws their beliefs.

The important thing is to renew our lives daily, with tenderness, responsibility, keenness, and great passion, to experience daily our struggle to defend the extraordinary Life that is within us, in the unity in multiplicity of all things.

—Translated by David J. Molineaux

Notes

1. An abridged version of a long essay originally published in Portuguese as *Trinidade, palavra sobre coisas velhas e novas: uma perspectiva ecofeminista*. Sao Paulo: Paulinas, 1994.

2. Cited by Peter Russel in *Odespertar da terra. O cerebro global*. Sao Paulo: Ed. Cultrix, 1991.

3. Swimme, Brian, *The Universe Is a Green Dragon*. Santa Fe: Bear & Co., 1984, p. 28.

4. Jabor, Arnaldo, *"Todos temos inveja da paz dos ianomamis,"* in *Jornal do Commercio*, Recife: Aug. 25, 1993.

2

In Us Life Grows

An Ecofeminist Point of View

MERCEDES CANAS

"We are the root from which the whole people sustains itself and grows."
words of a peasant woman in a workshop on the Rights of Women,
Santa Ana, El Salvador.

In our country it is we women in particular who are conscious of the serious deterioration of the environment and its threat to "bring an end to the viability of our society and the livability of our country."[1] In this sense the contributions from the ecological groups gathered in the *Unidad Ecologia Salvadorena* are invaluable. The *Cerro Verde* Proposal, the Nutritional Food Proposal, and the Ecological Agreement, which they brought to the political parties in El Salvador, are the most important examples at the level of political theory.

We feminists, coming from different places and by different routes, are coming to the same conclusion: "The ecological problem is not an unsolvable problem. Rather, there are hopeful signs that ecological deterioration can be reversed. In order to do this it is necessary to change the focus of development from an economic one focused on financial benefits to an ecological one focused on the survival of the country and the well-being of its inhabitants. Our country has sufficient resources to satisfy the needs of all Salvadoreans, but not sufficient to satisfy the ambition of some, nor to do it in the face of the irrationality of others."[2] We are in solidarity with these struggles. They are ours also. Nevertheless we believe that feminism has contributions to make on a world level that must be integrated into a national ecological focus.

Feminism will give greater depth and breadth to the framing of the issues. We women are the majority of the population, and in us life grows. The nation, therefore, depends on the quality of our life.

Even if we dedicate efforts to save endangered animal and plant species, it is an ethical imperative to put our energies into preserving the human species and to not abandon them in a time of despair, terror, and death.

The Relation of Women and Environment

When one speaks of a parallel between women and environment, almost always the reference involves two aspects for which women are considered responsible: population growth and education in environmental protection. The one time that the proposals of the *Unidad Ecologia* refer to women, they refer specifically to this point (see the *Cerro Verde* Proposal).

Both conclusions, which we do not intend to invalidate but to make relative, can result in serious ideological, political, and ethical errors.

Environmental Degradation and Population Explosion

To locate the root of the ecological problem solely within the population growth problem does not take into account a particular form of development and how economic and political structures have brought us to these situations: (a) 80% of the natural vegetation of El Salvador has been destroyed; only 6% of the original forests remain; (b) of the 120,000 hectares of mangroves, only 30,000 remain, thanks to the uncontrolled expansion of cotton plantations and the use of pesticides; (c) the surface and subterranean waters are contaminated and constitute sources for the proliferation of diseases, which is aggravated by the drying up of water sources; for example, the aquifer level of El Salvador has dropped one meter per year; (d) 80% of the national territory shows serious signs of erosion, decreased fertility, high contamination due to agrochemicals, and loss of plant cover; (e) three species of trees, ten species of birds, and three species of mammals have become extinct in our country; (f) the loss of ecological balance each year causes more drought, more floods, more erosion, more hunger, and more deaths; 80% of the children under five years of age suffer from malnutrition, 18% of deaths are children less than one year old, and 40% of the deaths are due to parasites and infectious diseases.[3]

According to the Salvadorean Center for Appropriate Technology, El Salvador has the highest level of ecological degradation in the American continent.

In general those who connect ecological degradation and population explosion have come up with what they see as a brilliant solution, the establishment of policies of birth control under the slogan of "a small family lives better." There are those who refute this slogan.

Don't we women have the right to participate in these consultations from which decisions are made about our bodies? Who makes these decisions? Why does a woman have ten or more children? Who decides how many children we have: our husbands, the Church, fatal ignorance or luck? Who? Do they know something about this, or is it that we women just foolishly procreate? "It is inacceptable to tell women who have few other alternatives to choose to have less children so they can have a better life. For these women children are the only way they have of being valued as persons."[4]

Who are the ones responsible for the grave ecological crisis? Is it the majority population or the power elites who have imposed an economic model that makes profit the basis of decision making, no matter what the costs? "The destruction of the environment always offers advantages for growth in the short and medium run . . . so the maximization of growth tends to destroy the environment, even though the environment determines the limits of this maximization of growth in the long run."[5]

In El Salvador isn't it perhaps the large indigo growers, the large coffee growers, sugar growers, cotton growers, construction companies, etc., who have historically degraded the environment? Moreover, isn't it the majority population, and of these, the female majority, whose quality of life is affected, along with the environment, by these economic models?

Women as Educators in the Care of the Environment

This is a new job for those in the world who "do two-thirds of the total hours of work, receive only 10% of the pay and own less than 1% of the world's property."[6] It is women who are the producers of half the food grown by developing countries.[7]

This is one more job which we women are undertaking. No one can deny that the majority of women learn to protect that which they respect and recognize as vital to life: water, forests, soil, plants, animals. Women are not to blame, because the degradation of the environment doesn't come from the female majority. Those who abuse and degrade are others, not our starving children. And yet the great planners give us one more job. Who has the most responsibility for this planet? Are the children only the responsibility of the father and mother? Shouldn't the care and education of children be a social responsibility? In relegating this job to women, doesn't this perpetuate the idea that women are good only for being mothers? Why don't they invite us to participate in policy development?

A thousand questions arise and we women are ever inventing and seeking out answers, but perhaps it is time that those interested in saving the environment should also be interested in the needs of women.

The Ecofeminist Response

Different groups of feminists and women ecologists have broadened the meaning of ecology. When one defines ecology as the study of the interrelationships between the components that make up the natural world, then one must include as an object of study the relationships between human beings. Therefore, to seek to break the domination of men over women should be considered an ecological issue. This relationship of domination indicates the loss of the "balance between the two polarities (the extreme sides of a unity) which exist in all of nature. This balance has been lost in human relations, resulting in the privileging of one aspect to the detriment of the other. Feeling, intuition, and altruism are considered typically feminine and have negative connotations, while aggression, competition, the analytical, and the rational are linked to masculinity and are privileged socially. To achieve equilibrium in social and ecological relations necessitates both intuition and rationality, altruism and self-affirmation, a dynamic interaction is needed between the two elements which come together in a unity."[8]

Ecofeminists are setting forth other basic issues. "The domination and exploitation of nature and of women by Western industrial civilization are mutually reinforcing because women are considered similar to nature. The life of the earth is an interconnected web, and no privileged hierarchy of the human over nature, justifying its domination, exists. A healthy, balanced ecosystem, which includes human and non-human inhabitants, must maintain diversity. Ecofeminism promotes a global movement founded on common interests and respect for diversity, in opposition to all forms of domination and violence. The continuation of life on this planet demands a new understanding of our relation with nature, with other human beings and with our own bodies."[9]

In addition, ecofeminists recognize that the impact of the degradation of the environment affects women in a different way, because as women they are part of the same ecosystem that is dominated and exploited irrationally.

In Central America, women have great concern for achieving the means for adequate family life: among these are nutrition, health, income, and the education of children. At the same time they have gender-specific problems, such as the need for better education and training. Women struggle for equality of opportunity and against aggression and violence. Any program that involves women and their relation to the environment must involve these concerns of great urgency. . . . The incorporation of women in a process of working toward sustainable development can't avoid the restoration of an environment which, until recently, was the basis of life resources for family welfare, and which today, due to scarcity of resources, has almost doubled the hours of labor for the great majority of women in every aspect.[10]

In the rural areas, moreover, women fetch and use water for the household, and women gather the wood for heating and cooking. Women, therefore, are the most affected by the deterioration of quality water systems and tree conservation.[11]

Therefore, it has been shown that "one must see how the woman is more vulnerable than the man in respect to environmental pollutants. Numerous studies have established a link between defects in the newborn and environmental contaminants, such as lead. . . . Studies in regard to such effects on women show, moreover, that contaminated substances are even found in mother's milk. It is known, for example, that some chemical products, such as pesticides and organic fertilizers and herbicides, become concentrated in mother's milk."[12]

To conclude, ecofeminism sets forth its views in a responsible, rigorous, undogmative manner, without excess but with determination and joy in breaking the silence in which we women have been kept for centuries. It is our hope to contribute to a world that we women have succeeded in protecting from terror. Respect and love for life, the good society we seek is a society into which, for all men and women, "it is worth the trouble to have been born." We seek a society in which childhood can be a time of play and stimulation; in which youth can be a time of freedom to decide what we want to be, a time of affirmation, generosity, and creative energy; in which old age can be a time of rest, of deepening, and a time to share experiences. We seek a society where no one lacks the material necessities of life nor lacks love, solidarity, friendship, and tenderness, which keeps the soul intact.

Notes

1. *Unidad Ecologia Salvadorena*, "Propuesta del Cerro Verde," San Salvador, Junio, 1990.

2. *Ibid.*

3. Data adjusted from that in *UNES y El CESTA*, in the *Cerro Verde* Proposal and in an informational handout, respectively.

4. Marge Berer, "Hacia una Politica de Poblacion Feminista," *Palabra de Mujer*, No. 2, El Salvador, 1991.

5. Franz Hinkelamert, *Democracia y Totalitarismo*, Costa Rica: DEI, 1987, p. 55.

6. "Conferencia Mundial del Decenio de las Naciones Unidad para la Mujer," Copenhagen, July 14-30, 1980, Ministry of Culture, Madrid, 1980.

7. "La Mujer y La Problema del Media Ambiante," *Mujer/Fempress*, No. 107, Santiago, 1990, p. 25.

8. Veronica Rossato, "Feminismo y Ecologia," *Mujer/Fempress*, No. 93, Santiago, 1989, p. 6.

9. Veronica Rossato, "Una Vision Ecofeminista del Manejo de los Recuros Naturales," *Mujer/Fempress*, No. 115, Santiago, 1991, p. 6.

10. Viviene Solis and Marta Trejos, "Presentacion para el Taller Regional: Mujer y su Aporte en la Implementacion de Los Planes de Accion Forestal," mimeograph, San Salvador, January, 1991.

11. *Op. cit.*, note 7.

12. "La Contaminacion Afecta Especialmente a la Mujer," *Mujer/ Fempress*, No. 108, Santiago, 1990, p. 25.

3

Latin America's Poor Women

Inherent Guardians of Life

GLADYS PARENTELLI

Ecofeminism suggests putting aside a paradigm imposed by an androcentric vision linked to Western religions and patriarchal "civilization." In this paradigm both the earth and women,[1] as well as all powerless people, are exploited and have no recourse to their rights. Feminist ethics offers a new paradigm where the earth and all the life she nurtures is held to be as sacred as human life. Indeed, the very fullness of human life is now seen to depend on a respect for the entire web of life generated by the earth.

In 1992, Latin America was the scene of two events of global significance. First, Pope John Paul II used the occasion of the 500th anniversary of Columbus' arrival to America to "celebrate" the supposed beginning of this continent's evangelization. Second, the U.N.-sponsored Earth Summit took place in Rio de Janeiro. In both events the protagonists were powerful men, including those of the Catholic hierarchy; it goes without saying that women from Latin America's poor rural and urban communities were not invited.

In general, the vast majority of Latin Americans felt there was nothing to celebrate when it came to the so-called "evangelization" of America or to the Spanish conquest. The conquerors, *with the approval—and frequently the collaboration—of the Catholic hierarchy*, denied the validity of the cultures of America's primal peoples. The foreigners failed to understand that they had landed on a continent where a society existed that, among other factors, had evolved in an environment totally different from that of Europe. The conquerors did not take into account the beliefs or the wisdom of the indigenous peoples; they forcibly changed their ancient agricultural systems, introducing plant strains and animal species that required other ecosystems for their cultivation and continued growth. In the long run, this assault has spawned a series of ecological disasters that have become glaringly apparent in the last half of this century. Soil erosion, desertification as a result of over-grazing and monoculture, the felling of the continent's vast forests are all catastrophes that do not correspond to the natural evolution of our environment.

Nor did the conquerors respect America's native populations, the owners and mistresses of these lands. Instead, they took over everything of value they came across. They treated the primal peoples as objects. Little is said of what was done to the native women, although we can conclude that they suffered as much, if not more, than the men.

Some contemporary scholars speak of the "mixture" of the Spanish and indigenous populations as one of the positive results of the Conquest, positing that from this union a "new man" was born. But we must never forget that this "mix" was brought about through the violent rape of indigenous women by white men, men to whom it never occurred to contract marriage. White men marrying indigenous women was indeed frowned upon by the mores of the times; even more anathema was the marriage of an indigenous man to a white woman. In Mexico, for example, the derogatory term *chingada* to refer to a loose woman deeply marks that country's psyche and culture. *La chingada* is the mother who has been opened by force, violated and ridiculed. And the child of *la chingada*—the supposed "new man"—is conceived in violence, by rape and in ridicule.

At the Earth Summit, in the face of critical environmental problems, such as the greenhouse effect, ozone depletion, the rapid depletion of both biological diversity and primary resources, the participating "experts" came out in favor of "sustainable development." Two years have now passed, and although this new vision of development has not yet left the drawing boards, the Summit at least contributed to popularizing the view that the earth—the ancient *Pachamama*[2]—has rights as a living organism of which we all form a part.

Just as the Spanish conquerors represented the armed branch of the major power of their era, today's modern patriarchs are found at the pinnacle of the power pyramid[3] of every country, ignoring the rights of the great majorities. Their economic power is vast, especially in industries such as weapons manufacture, where astronomical sums of money are wasted in expenditures that have nothing to do with the common good of ordinary people.[4] Likewise, the telecommunications industry with its hi-tech grids and hard-sell publicity works with imported resources and then re-exports improved goods to countries that give security to their investments.[5]

In Latin America, the political patriarchs control and consume the bulk of the resources and financial pool of each nation, which belong to its citizens, embezzling unimaginable sums for purposes that the majorities neither understand nor approve. For example, in Venezuela from February to October, 1994, the government invested $9 billion to bail out eighteen private banks that were in danger of bankruptcy because of corrupt dealings—while at the same time insisting that there were no funds available for public hospitals, which are so short of supplies they are barely able to function. Nor was there money to pay workers' pensions, which had been frozen for thirty years by the Venezuelan Social Security Institute. Nor were there funds for schools for rural and indigenous children.

Some 80 percent of the total population of Latin American countries is made up of women, their children, and of recently arrived immigrants.[6] It is these groups that must shoulder the major burden of each country's production, yet the state systematically excludes them from their legitimate right to a job and to basic services, such as health, education and welfare.[7]

In the judgment of a growing number of women's groups throughout Latin America, poor women are the region's greatest resource. They are largely responsible for the production of their country's wealth in that they bear and raise children, their country's future; furthermore, they protect and preserve the local environment and its resources. And they do all this without any help or encouragement whatsoever from the patriarchal powers that be. Even more scandalous is the fact that these patriarchs systematically exclude them from any possibility of justice in their personal or community lives.

Thus poor women survive through their own efforts and raise their children often with no support from either the fathers of the children or the government. Nevertheless, these same governments are quick to insist that the sons of these poor women have a duty to "serve the Fatherland" and are conscripted for obligatory military service where they are paid less than a minimum wage.

The Vatican is, without a doubt, part and parcel of the same patriarchal system as its economic and political counterparts. Too frequently the Vatican speaks of defending moral or ethical standards. It has slowly dawned on us, however, that for the church's hierarchy the priority is not merely to proclaim the truth of Christ, but also to dominate. Although the hierarchy theoretically recognizes women as "subjects" with rights of their own, in practice women are considered as "objects" with assigned roles—as wives, mothers, or virgins. The roles of wife and mother are at the service of the patriarchal system in general. A nun, or consecrated virgin, is cheap labor at the service of ecclesiastical hierarchies. In each of these roles, women are controlled and expected to follow church-established norms. What patriarchal churches will never be able to accept are those rights women have to make use of their sexuality as they judge appropriate (i.e.: to make decisions about how many children to have, whether to end a pregnancy, to be a lesbian, to enjoy sex between women, or not to have children). Woman-based construction of sexual values would erode the very basis of patriarchy and, consequently, of the monotheistic churches. One manifestation of the attempt to block women's agenda was the alliance between the Vatican and Islamic fundamentalists at the 1994 U.N. Population Conference at Cairo where they united to block any move that would give women the right to freely and fully exercise their sexuality and control their fertility.

Nevertheless, women make ethical decisions as a part of life. I am referring specifically to poor women—indigenous and black women who are the victims of racism, *campesinas*, and shantytown dwellers. Women may have no honored status in patriarchal society, but they still know best how to care for life and the land and they are least likely to destroy the environment. They decide what is best for themselves personally, for their children, for their extended family—including the husbands who may have abandoned them— for their neighbors and their community.

Making ethical decisions implies having a deep respect for all that is living and for everything that directly or indirectly affects life, whether it be persons or other forms of life—animals, plants, forests, water, land—or objects that in various ways impinge upon life, such as tools, machinery, etc.

Ethics supposes an all-encompassing respect for life. It demands a continual reflection with regard to the consequences of my love or my aggression, my responsibility or my irresponsibility, my respect or lack of respect, my options, my decisions, my words, my actions, my omissions, what I consume, what I save, what I spend, what I throw away, what I preserve.

Traditionally, women have been seen as the protectors of life and lovers of peace. Generally speaking, women do not tolerate violence, nor do they provoke it. For example, when a pregnancy is in its last stages, women walk with their shoulders thrown back further than usual and thus show their pride in the pregnancy. Women who are with child are proud to bring a human being into the world; they are happy at the perspective of caring for a beautiful but defenseless being, of hugging it, of touching the baby's skin while nursing or bathing it — all those infinite number of acts that make the new infant grow up healthy. Why? Because of the tremendous love women have for their newborn. Women who live in poverty express, like no others, the joy of surviving one more day and pride in simply being alive, which they have achieved by their own initiative: of finding or receiving a seed, of putting it in the ground; of seeing it grow; of waiting until, one day, it gives fruit; of conceiving a child even if this happens as a result of a roll in the hay; to nurse the child with the hope that they will not be alone in the future.[8]

In general, women love life so much that it is very unusual for them to choose to abort it. Even when they are given the option to have an abortion, poor women make that decision only after much reflection, doubt and advice from women friends, neighbors, a religious sister, even perhaps the parish priest. The decision to abort is never, never a happy one. If poor women make such a decision, it is generally in the midst of great personal turmoil; they know full well that an abortion could cost them their own lives, given the unsanitary, clandestine conditions in which abortions—which are also usually illegal—are performed in Latin America. Women who opt to have an abortion do so only because of the precarious family situation in which they find themselves: because the men who impregnated them have disappeared and thus offer no support; because their other children or other, often elderly, family members depend on them for economic and emotional support that would be eroded with the arrival of a newborn. Furthermore, pregnant women usually have no assistance from religious, social or legal organizations which leave them to their own fate and condemn them as "irresponsible."

Poor women are administrators *par excellence* because no one makes better use of things than they do with the little they have. For that very reason, they organize alone or with their friends and neighbors who have similar needs. As such, they are generally in the front line of any struggle, joining to create and make work organizations that address their problems and those of their children. These organizations are usually more egalitarian than those run by men.

Let me offer a brief overview of how a significant number of poor women treat resources, the environment and other human beings. The practices described below are not simply quaint, isolated habits. They come from an intrinsic attitude that is both profound and global in its respect for all people and for all of life. I am convinced that women are inherent guardians of life and of the earth's resources.[9]

Women take advantage of the tiniest piece of earth, an empty can or jar to plant vegetables, spices, beans, even a fruit tree so that there are always sweet-smelling herbs and fresh, medicinal spices to give flavor to soups and salads. A garlic clove will grow into a plant from which more cloves will sprout to spruce up future meals; an onion patch, planted when she first arrives with her family to a new place, will continue to reproduce throughout her lifetime, replacing the more expensive dried onion. A banana plant that someone gives her as a gift will produce a bunch every year and every once in a while, another plant, which will give another bunch each year. From the peaches and the plums eaten in the summer she'll plant the seeds to have peach and plum trees—the fruit will be smaller for sure—but they'll bloom every summer. In tropical areas, a plant will sprout from a coffee bean that gives lovely white flowers followed by red buds which will be picked and dried in the sun, then toasted, making a rich coffee that has no additives.

In preparing food, poor women buy what is least expensive in order to get the most from their meager funds: chicken or fish rather than red meat which is more expensive and harder to digest; beans and grains rather than meat; seasonal vegetables and fruits produced in the area or in the country. In this way they support the local campesinos and avoid paying the energy costs related to transporting products from other parts of the country or from other countries.

From fruit, they use skins and pits to make juices, jams and jellies or as food for their egg-laying hen, or a rabbit or pig that will be, often enough, the only meat the family will eat during the entire year.

In preparing food they use methods that in the long run have proven to be much healthier. If food is left over, they invent ways to present it differently so that it doesn't get boring. In especially difficult circumstances, women from poor neighborhoods put together their few food resources and make soups together with onions or rice that one or another throws in. These "soup kitchens" or "common pots" were a frequent fixture in Chilean *poblaciones* during the Pinochet dictatorship (1973-89) and offered at least one nourishing meal a day to children, old people and pregnant and nursing mothers—those hardest hit by the economic austerity measures of the military regime. Likewise, women from Peru's shantytowns (euphemistically called *pueblos jovenes* or "young towns") have organized the "glass of milk a day" program to combat the chronic malnutrition affecting the vast majority of Peru's children as a result of that country's economic disintegration during the past ten years.

In countries which have four seasons, when autumn arrives women salvage the best seeds from corn, beans and peas to plant them the following spring; watermelon seeds are saved to plant in the family's garden. They do the same with seeds and bulbs from flowering plants, which are replanted so that the following year they will have flowers to adorn the house, to place on the tombs of loved ones, to sell or to give as gifts.

Women pass down their knowledge of the curative effects of herbs, which they themselves have learned by watching their mothers and grandmothers. Many have herbal gardens which replace going to the pharmacist for expensive, unknown medicines or to a physician.

Rarely would poor women throw away a coat, a dress, a pair of shoes. What belonged to an older brother or sister who has outgrown it, is now passed on to the younger children. A coat is passed down from grandparents to grandchildren. Even when a coat is faded or a pair of boots are old, they are used to avoid getting wet during the rainy season when the goat or cow has to be milked, the chickens fed or the garden pruned.

Neither do poor women throw away a piece of cloth: when a dress or suit belonging to an adult can no longer be used, the best parts of the cloth can be used to make a dress or skirt for a little girl or a pair of pants for a little boy, or for underwear. And when these wear out, old cloth can be used as stuffing or for rags. Wool socks are used to shine shoes. An old sweater, with holes in the elbows, outgrown by a little boy, is washed and pulled apart; when there is money to buy a little more yarn, she'll knit him a new one.

While the wealthy are in a hurry to buy new furniture and imported stereos, televisions, or new appliances,[10] indigenous women collect pumpkins and squashes, using the shells as gourds. If they are small, the gourds are used as cups; if large they become serving bowls, water jugs or jars for saving seeds. Indigenous women also collect and weave fibers for making hammocks or utensils for domestic use. Everyone takes good care of the chair or the bed they inherited from their mother or the beautiful wooden box the *patrona* gave as a gift. The seat of the chair that grandfather made is rewoven with new fibers every time it wears thin. Irons and other electrical appliances last for years: if a cable or a wire wears out, they know how to rewire it.

In preparing meals, only what is necessary is cooked. If they have the use of electricity or gas, poor women never use a high flame, and thus conserve energy. If they have a big oven, they only use it when they have to prepare large quantities of food; otherwise they use a small burner to heat water for coffee or tea. If they cook over a wood fire, they use dried branches that have been blown off the trees or dried cow manure or pieces of wood from boxes and cartons the rich have thrown away.

Electricity as well as kerosene or candles are only used when necessary. Daylight is taken advantage of for as long as possible to crochet, knit, sew or mend dark-colored clothing; at night, poor women will work with white or light-colored materials to avoid the need for a powerful lamp.

Water is essential to life, but it is not always available. Using rudimentary systems, women collect rain water that falls on their roofs. They know that if they wash with rain water, hair is softer; if they use rain water for washing clothes, they'll need less soap. Moreover, the water that was used for washing clothes can then be used to wash the floors or the patio; water for washing fruits and vegetables is then used to water the plants. The land around the house is terraced in such a way that rain does not cause erosion; rather it waters the trees and the garden; it is also caught in barrels or other containers for the chickens and other domestic animals. In general, these women "ecologists" avoid the use of poisons which they know from experience will harm the environment.

In the countryside or in the shantytowns that circle the cities, nothing is considered garbage. For example, vegetable and fruit skins and pits, if not re-cycled back into soups, juices or jams or to feed domestic animals, are used as fertilizers for plants, just as excrement from chickens and rabbits are used. Branches from a dry tree will make a wonderful fence or pen. A truck tire, filled with earth, becomes a flower bed or stops erosion on an unlevel part of the land; the inner tube can be patched and blown up again where it is transformed into a swing or a water raft for the kids to play with in the canal by the house or when they go swimming in the river in the summer.

Poor women collect containers that others throw away and use them as bags and boxes for the unpackaged food they buy—the pinch of salt, the cup of sugar, the two eggs, the quarter liter of cooking oil. Or they use the containers for jams and other preserves they prepare for the winter; or simply as vases for flowers or plants or herbs; or to store nails, screws or bolts that can be reused whenever necessary. A vine from a flowering plant put near the sidewalk or path will delight a passerby.

Before concluding, I think it important to emphasize that upon discovering the attitude of respect for the earth that poor women and some middle-class women here have, we must not forget that the capitalist system itself is respon-sible for today's runaway consumption. There are women who have been caught up in this consumption and whenever they are sufficiently solvent to do so, they will buy and throw away as easily as the wealthy. Also I want to emphasize that, when I speak of poor women I am not idealizing their situation. However, in this article I've given priority to describing practices that reveal a profound attitude of a significant majority of them.

It is also necessary to distinguish between poverty and misery. Women who live in a state of misery are those who do not have any love for the earth and who do not know how to take advantage of the few resources they have at their disposal. Perhaps they are in this sad state because they have not been able to learn how to benefit from the *Pachamama's* treasures. It has been my experi-ence that the very difference between women who are poor and women who live in that state of misery—and they may indeed be neighbors—is rooted in the attitudes of each in relation to the earth.

Women, not only those who define themselves as feminists because they have developed a greater awareness than other women of patriarchal oppression,[11] but particularly simple, ordinary women who suffer the injustice of being on the periphery of society, are found to be carrying out committed practices that are guided by a natural ecofeminist ethic. The practices described above are not sporadic; they reveal a response that runs very deep in women who reach out to care for and protect all manifestations of life.

Their attitude at every moment and in every place is one of fostering practical love, hard but meaningful work, democratic organization and struggle against the injustices they perceive. They work to build a society where an authoritarian, unjust and corrupt patriarchy finally gives way to a society where there is more justice for all, where every citizen has the right to exercise their freedom, their creativity, their responsibility, their intelligence and capabilities, where everyone is able to participate in the decisions that affect their personal lives, that of their families and that of all life springing from Gaia, Mother Earth.

Uncontrolled ambition for power, a mentality or culture that rests on exclusion and represents death for those who practice it, has little to do with poor women. For them, life makes them strong because they are vowed to life, from the humble herb that still blooms after a fire, to the hen to whom she throws the dregs of the soup bowl each evening, to the child who grows up bright-eyed around her table.

In a Latin America that for 500 years has been devastated again and again by wave upon wave of patriarchal powers, poor women have intuitively known how to save life from destruction and genocide. Such women who even today are considered "minors" by law, forgotten and trampled upon by the current patriarchs, are the only ones who—without help from anyone—preserve and carry out the ancient wisdom of respect and love for all life forms. May the *Pachamama, Bachué*[12] and the other feminine deities that, according to our traditions, were the creators of this continent, continue to inspire us!

Notes

1. In this article, the plural will be used in speaking of Latin American women in order to underscore the fact that there is not one type of woman but rather women who live in a variety of situations, family compositions, cultures, ethnic groups, sexual preferences, etc. The use of the word in the singular or plural is not theoretically irrelevant, in that *woman* refers to a unique feminine essence (the "eternal feminine," for example), which is ahistorical and rooted in biological as well as metaphysical concepts. In contrast, *women* conveys a diversity of situations and a historicity in which women actually find themselves (De Barbieri, 1992).

2. In the southern part of Latin America—namely, Bolivia and Peru—the earth has been traditionally called *Pachamama*, a term closely connected to the term "Gaia," used by James Lovelock to describe the earth as a living organism. See J.E. Lovelock, *Gaia: A New Look at Life on Earth*, Oxford University Press, Oxford, New York: 1979, 1987.

3. I am referring to the classical powers that control every society, as well as

transnational powers which, in today's world, brandish more power than their "national" counterparts.

4. According to a recent OAS report, the governments of Latin America and the Caribbean annually budget about US $10.8 billion on military expenditures. (Reuter News Agency, *Diario Ultimas Noticias*, Caracas: March 19, 1994, p. 70.)

5. We can also speak here of illegal businesses, such as drug trafficking. According to Raymond Kendal, Secretary General of INTERPOL, in 1992 narco-trafficking generated an estimated US $350 billion worldwide. (Reuter News Agency, *Diaro El Universal*, Caracas: April 14, 1994, p. 11, col. 1.)

6. The statistics in this article are taken from UN reports, as well as other international organizations, women's groups or NGOs that work in a variety of social sectors throughout Latin America and the Caribbean. The use of official government statistics has been avoided because in general they are manipulated to serve the purposes of the patriarchal power in control.

7. In Latin America, as in other parts of the Third World, more than 70 percent of the population lives in conditions of poverty, which include the categories of extreme poverty and misery. Basic public services, under the control of the government, function more or less adequately for wealthier neighborhoods, which usually have clean drinking water, garbage collection, electricity, sewers, etc. But these services function only minimally or not at all in poor neighborhoods or in the countryside. With regard to other basic public services, such as health or primary, secondary and technical education, even while an infrastructure exists (hospitals, schools, etc.) in general, they simply don't function. Furthermore, while the upper class has access to subsidized services, the poor who cannot afford them do not receive state subsidies. One example of this is that 98 percent of children in poor neighborhoods have cavities that go unattended by a dentist. Given the sophistication of modern society, technical competence is demanded for skills such as filling cavities: however, when it comes to getting a job that demands some skill, young people from the upper and middle classes are always the ones who are employed because of their training. Meanwhile, unemployment reaches desperate proportions among the illiterate marginal classes, who are lucky if they have a primary education. A small proportion of poor men obtain minimum-wage jobs that need no skill; others work in the informal sector where wages are higher. The great majority of women, meanwhile, cannot qualify for work in the "support services" because they do not have *buena presencia*, a term which implies that one is the right social shade, wears the right clothes, shoes, hairstyle, etc. They can only obtain the worst paying jobs, most of which revolve around domestic help (watching children, washing and ironing, cooking, etc.). Some women work in the informal market, selling food of a very limited stock of goods in their improvised street stalls. Others turn to prostitution.

8. Women constitute 60 percent of the world's population, but only receive one percent of its resources. In Venezuela, like other Latin American countries, more than 50 percent of all families are headed and supported by women. Without help from the state, women have cut fertility rates in half in the last 25 years. Some 80 percent of all children in Latin America are born to poor women; some 60 percent have not been recognized by their progenitors, who offer nothing in the way of basic necessities such as love and care, food, clothing, housing, education, etc.

9. An attitude which, many times, poor women cannot verbalize or express in writing because it is so much a part of them.

10. Purchases such as the latest model computer or the luxury car that gives more status—with the corresponding loss of dividends for the country—form part of the

transnational game which is interested only in expanding profit margins by offering every possible incentive to raise consumption levels.

11. Although there would be much to discuss concerning their activities, in this article I have not specifically addressed the action of women who define themselves as feminists or ecofeminists and are at the forefront of the organized feminist movement.

12. *Bachué* is the mother of humanity according to the mythical accounts of the Colombian indigenous people, the *muiscas*. According to the Colime tribe of Tolima, their mother god is named *Auxisue*. For the Kogi Indians, their universal mother is called *Haba*. The *guajiros* and *wayúus* of Colombia and Venezuela dedicate their children to the goddess *Igua*. The cult of Maria Lionza is practiced by thousands of Venezuelans; this ancestral cult is thought to have the largest following of any cult in Latin America.

References

Buxó i Rey, María Jesús: "Vitrinas, cristales y espejos: dos modelos de identidad en la cultura urbana de las mujeres Quiché de Quetzaltenange (Guatemala)," *Mujeres y Sociedad*, Lola G. Luna, ed., Barcelona (España), Universidad de Barcelona, 1991.

De Barbieri, Teresita: "Sobre la categoría género; Una introducción teórico metodológica," *Fin de Siglo; Género y cambio civilizatorio*, Santiago, Chile, Isis Internacional, 1992 (Ediciones de las Mujeres No. 17).

Carbonell, Nora: "La mujer en la mitología indígena colombiana," *Chichamaya, Barranquilla* (no date).

Martín Medem, José Manual: *Niños de repuesto. Tráfico y comercio de órganos*, Madrid: Editorial Complutense, 1994.

Ress, Judy: The ecofeminist paradigm (mimeo), 1993.

Rostworoswki de Diez Canseco, María: *Pachacamac y el Señor de los Milagros*, Lima: Instituto de Estudios Peruanos, 1992.

Ruether, Rosemary Radford: *Gaia and God: Ecofeminist Theology of Earth Healing*, HarperSanFrancisco, 1992. (Spanish edition: Gaia y Dios: Una teología ecofeminista para la recuperación de la tierra, Mexico: Demac, 1993.)

Todorov, Tzvetan: *La conquista de América: El problema del otro*, Mexico: Siglo XXI, 1991.

Trapasso, Rosa Dominga: *Ecología: Una visión global y transformadora*, Lima, Circulo de Feministas Cristianas Talitha Cumi (No. 24), 1993.

4

Foreigners

A Multicultural Dialogue

JANET W. MAY

Eve, Rachel, Sarah, Hagar, Ruth, Naomi and Jezebel. Besides being women of the Old Testament, what do they have in common? They are women who lived as foreigners, outside their countries of origin, struggling to preserve their identities and their faith. Eve was expelled, like the political refugees today. Rachel abandoned her family to follow her husband. Sarah accompanied her husband in his wanderings. Hagar was forced to go wherever her owners chose. Naomi abandoned her country because of famine and returned as a widow, without husband, children, almost without faith. Ruth left her country to accompany her mother-in-law, building a future for both of them in her new country. Jezebel, the object of a political marriage, struggled to maintain her ancestral religion in a country that hated her for her nationality and for her faith.

For each of these women, there is today a sister who walks in a similar path. The political refugees, those who follow their husbands, those who seek new opportunities, the victims of famine who emigrate from the rural areas to the city, the women tricked into enslaving prostitution—all of them have predecessors in the Bible. Today as yesterday they experience marginalization because of their cultural and national origins, their gender, and for their struggle to discover a spirituality that helps them to live a satisfying life. On the margins of the dominant society, they seek to build their identities within the context of their spirituality. They are marginalized women, women on the edge.

As a white, Protestant woman of the middle class, with a good education, I am a product of the culture that dominates not only the United States but the whole Occidental world. Twenty years ago, I left the U.S. in order to work as a missionary in Latin America. Even though my roots are within the privileged class, I have also experienced oppression—sexual violence, political exile and marginalization as a foreigner. These contradictory experiences of privilege and oppression have been among the principal factors that have helped me to be sensitive to the contradictions that others experience. They help me to be aware of the presence of different perspectives, and to accept differences as voices which enrich diversity. These diverse voices question dominance and clamor to be heard.

In response to these diverse voices, I drew together a group of women like myself in that they are all foreigners yet diverse in their national, cultural and religious origins. Confronting the differences of our varied experiences of spirituality, we have sought to identify the common elements of our struggle. Five women participated in this dialogue, and after our initial dialogue, each of them has read and commented on this paper in its various drafts, giving me both verbal and written suggestions.[1] All of these contributions form the backbone of this article. Therefore, the real authors of this article are:

Participant	Nationality	Culture	Religion
Elena Kelly	Nicaraguan	Afro-indigenous	Moravian
Anastasia Mejía	Guatemalan	Maya Kiché	Maya
Silvia de Lima	Brazilian	Afro-Brazilian	Catholic
Esther Camac	Peruvian	Quechua	Methodist
Janet May	US	White	Methodist

Spirituality and Marginalization

One experience which we all share is that we live in Costa Rica as foreigners; we all experience separation from our culture of origin. This is an experience which has brought each one of us to reflect deeply, even to confront a personal identity crisis. While this crisis can be risky, it also has brought the possibility of distancing ourselves from our original culture, of evaluating and measuring the impact of our culture of origin on our lives. It brings the possibility of experiencing different ways of seeing and being in the world. Even more, the experience of being a foreigner provokes in each of us a daily questioning of identity and the search for communities in which we feel accepted. This search could be identified as a cultural crisis that even affects our spirituality.

This crisis has many possible resolutions. Some foreigners try to resolve the crisis by rejecting the new culture, which may be what Jezebel did. The women who reject their new cultural setting try to recreate their home country wherever they go, justifying their rejection with a constant barrage of criticism of their new setting. In terms of spirituality, this would signify a rejection of any religious expression that does not parallel their previous experience. Their faith would solidify, without the capacity to grow or deepen. Even though this is a common reaction, none of the participants in our dialogue found this acceptable.

Another possible resolution of the cultural crisis is by submerging themselves in the new culture and trying to integrate completely. This, however, means that they renounce their culture of origin. In terms of spirituality, this would mean renouncing their religious beliefs and practices that they brought with them, and adopting the religion in the new setting, following the example of Ruth. The women who participated in this dialogue discovered that this was not an acceptable solution. As an Aymara Indian friend explained to me long ago, "An outsider can never be fully accepted as an Aymara, because their mother was not Aymara."[2]

Regardless of one's attitude toward the new culture, sooner or later, foreigners are confronted with the reality of difference. The new culture is not the same as one's own, the cultural values are different, and people who are not part of the dominant culture are seen and treated as inferior or suspect. However, it isn't necessary to be a foreigner to be treated as if you don't belong. This also happens to national minorities. Elena Kelly, a Nicaraguan who grew up in the Moravian Church tradition, has experienced marginalization in her home country because of her mixed racial and cultural heritage. Elena is black, but she has a great-grandmother who is Rama, one of the Nicaraguan coastal indigenous groups. One of her grandmothers is Garífuna, another indigenous group of the Caribbean coast. Elena recalls a time in church when one of her aunts was told that "the sins of her ancestors accuse and condemn her." For Elena, it is difficult to be indigenous since she is black, and to be black because she is also indigenous. Elena has now lived in Costa Rica for the last six years, following her husband, who came to Costa Rica to study theology. Here in Costa Rica she continues to experience marginalization: "I feel like I don't belong because I'm not Costa Rican, not rigidly traditional in my religious beliefs, and because I'm a woman."

This observation points to another common experience which all have shared: cultural marginalization is combined with gender discrimination. Twenty years ago, when Elena expressed her own desire to study theology, she was told "not to waste her time doing that." So, she studied nursing instead. Nevertheless, when she got to Costa Rica, she took advantage of the opportunity to study theology, discovering here a community where theological studies by women was not considered "a waste of time."

Esther Camac comes from the Peruvian Quechua culture. Her maternal grandmother was an indigenous spiritual leader, but she renounced her traditional practices when she converted to Christianity. Nevertheless, in Esther's community the majority of the people continued to follow traditional religious practices, which she observed closely as a little girl. She says that she experienced a sense of contradiction. She was surrounded by traditional indigenous spirituality that affirmed her cultural roots, but her family denied them. At the same time she was discriminated against in Peruvian society for being indigenous. She felt marginalized for being indigenous and also for being part of the Protestant minority. Years ago, she came to Costa Rica to study theology. She married a Costa Rican and remained here. In the shift from one culture to the other she experienced doubts about her own identity, observing "on arriving in San José, I began to search for my cultural roots."

Anastasia Mejía is a Maya-Kiché from Guatemala. She, like Esther, grew up in a context of conflict between traditional religious practices and Christian faith. Her mother was a Roman Catholic catechist and considered traditional religious practices to be like "talking to the devil." Her father renounced his role as a Maya-Kiché spiritual leader in order to marry Anastasia's mother. Nevertheless, Anastasia's grandparents continued as spiritual leaders and Anastasia had many opportunities to observe, participate and learn, asking many questions. She also came to San José to study. She reflects, "While I was at the Latin-American Biblical Seminary, a Guatemalan friend introduced me to the Maya League. When I arrived in Costa Rica, I felt confused, limited, discriminated against because I am indigenous."

Silvia de Lima also came to San José to continue her theological studies. She is a Roman Catholic from Brazil. Even as a child she felt concern for the suffering of the poor and wanted to respond as a Christian. Because of this, she entered a Franciscan convent when she was fifteen years old. As a Franciscan she taught in a Catholic school and assisted in pastoral work. These responsibilities satisfied her desires to serve, and she continued in this work for ten years. However, little by little, Silvia began to feel that these responsibilities were not adequate. She wanted to be closer to the poor, and at the same time she was growing in her awareness of herself as black and female.

This growing awareness was the catalyst to push her into contact with the *Agentes Pastorales Negros* (Black Pastoral Workers' Group), an ecumenical organization of black people who work with poor black communities. Stimulated by their support, she left the Franciscan convent. She and two other workers founded the Black Missionary Community. They are under the supervision of their bishop and take the three traditional vows of religious orders: poverty, chastity, and obedience. The community works in the Baxia Fluminense neighborhood, seeking to combine social commitment, a spirituality of hope and an affirmation of black identity.

In Brazil and in Costa Rica, Silvia has also experienced discrimination as a black and as a woman, noting that "There is a structural racism and a sexism that is expressed in small ways, in gestures, in the market, on the bus, in looks and in words that you hear on the street." She explained that these are a combination of many small details. When she goes into a store, vendors either do not wait on her or they offer her less expensive items than those she requests to see. On the bus, men harass young women, including herself, with whispered insults or with casual touches that might appear to be accidental if they were not so frequent. She notices that passengers avoid sitting next to black males, even when all other seats are full. All of these gestures are daily expressions of racism and sexism that marginalize, without distinguishing between foreigners and nationals of minority groups. Gender discrimination is compounded with racial discrimination.

The Affirmation of Our Christian Roots

A common element of our spiritual journeys is an appreciation for our Christian roots. These roots have helped us to understand traditional religions and other non-Christian expressions of spirituality as part of the sacred.

Silvia especially appreciates the incarnation of Jesus, observing,

> I always had a very strong appreciation in my spirituality for the mystery of God's incarnation in Jesus. I perceived in this form of being God/ess a constant search to come closer to humanity. God is not satisfied to be close, but decides to become flesh. God becomes flesh, assumes our own humanity and takes the place of the other. This was and continues to be a challenge to me. The dynamic of incarnation continues in the suffering faces and sacrificed bodies of our time. We are presented with the dynamic of God/ess that gives shape to creativity and always is present, insisting on participating in history.

Elena comes from a family that is deeply rooted in the Moravian Church traditions. In spite of the discrimination which she has experienced, the Moravian Church has been a place where she has experienced the meaning of community. Her Christian faith is the foundation that strengthens her social commitment to the poor and the marginalized. The affirmation of her Moravian roots is an affirmation of a part of herself that gives her strength to continue in the struggle with others.

For Esther Camac, the discovery of the changes undergone by God's people in biblical times has provided her with tools to interpret her own people's changing history in context of time and territory.

> For me, what I appreciate about my Christian roots is the recognition of how it has contributed to my self-awareness as a woman, and the strength my faith has given me in the process of reconstructing my sense of identity. As I read about the roots of the people in the Bible, I discover that I have value as a person, and that I, too, have a history and have roots. Spirituality is a process of self-recognition and valorization of our heritage, of the consciousness that we are a part of history. It is a cosmovision of relationship to each other and to Mother Nature, in a defined place and moment. Our present and our future draw strength from this heritage and from this connection.

My own Christian roots are in the United Methodist Church. Methodism has given me a rich doctrinal heritage that helps me to confront different experiences of spirituality with openness and acceptance. Methodism's traditional ecumenism helps me to understand other expressions of the Christian beliefs as part of Christian tradition. This has helped me to work among Pentecostals, Lutherans, Baptists, Catholics and others with respect for their theological, historical and cultural heritages. At the same time, the experience within Methodism of wide liturgical flexibility taught me that faith does not require any particular form of expression in order to be "correct." Even though I have my own liturgical preferences, my tradition has prepared me to accept that others may worship God in ways that are very different, but very important to them, and as equally valid as mine.

Another inheritance that I value from my Methodist roots is the doctrine of prevenient grace. This doctrine affirms that even though Jesus of Nazareth is the maximum expression of God incarnate, the Holy Spirit is present in all creation. Therefore, holiness can be manifest in non-Christian cultures and religions. This allows me to affirm the presence of the holy in all life, and not just in that very limited expression of life that is dominated by Christianity.

The Limitations of Traditional Christian Spirituality

Even though we appreciate our Christian heritages and we give them great importance in our lives and spirituality, what we have received from our churches has not been sufficient. Each one of us has experienced the sensation that something is lacking from traditional Christianity. Elena, Esther and Anastasia grew up in families where there were both Christian practices and traditional indigenous practices. For Silvia, the encounter with Afro-Brazilian religions came later, "at a time of spiritual need, accompanied by the affirmation of my identity as a black and as a woman." As a part of her work in the Baxia Fluminense slum, she began to accompany the people in the Candomblé rituals that were celebrated there.

Elena observes that the Moravian Church is very rich in its traditions, but very rigid in its doctrines, discriminating against any who ask questions, who seek to go beyond traditional answers, or who try to introduce change. Anastasia recalls that, when the time came for her to receive her first communion, she asked questions about the meaning of what she was learning and doing, and the answers were not satisfactory nor meaningful. Silvia, within the Franciscan context, sought missionary alternatives that made sense, but found that affirmation of black, female identity was lacking. For each one, the Christian rituals were not enough. Something was lacking.

Each one expresses a feeling of being accepted in the church "in spite of . . . ." This "in spite of . . ." always revealed a form of discrimination, with accompanying restrictions to full participation. As Elena discovered, for women to study theology was "a waste of time." For Anastasia and Silvia, in addition to the exclusion of women from participation in the priesthood and in decision-making, they did not find space in Catholicism capable of responding to their needs as indigenous and black.

Perhaps the greatest area of insufficiency in Christianity has been in the area of human sexuality. With the traditional teachings that "touching women" is unclean, that sexual relations are sinful, pardonable only when their purpose is for procreation, and with the promotion of chastity as holier than a sexually active life, the churches are doing great harm to both men and women, but especially to women. To this is added the silence of the churches in situations of domestic violence, the confusion, even in the Bible, between sexuality and sexualized violence, the advice to victims to pardon their aggressors, without the corresponding advice to aggressors to repent and to manifest their repentance through changes in conduct (conversion expressed through action). It is no surprise that the churches are considered to be totally lacking in moral authority in addressing sexual issues, marginalizing all who search for a voice of sensibility.

For each of the participants in the dialogue, affirmation of themselves as women has included an affirmation of their body and of their sexuality as a part of their identity. The affirmation of one's sexuality is seen as an affirmation of oneself and of one's identity as a woman. Overcoming the prejudices toward sexuality has facilitated self-affirmation, improved self-esteem and made it possible for each one to assume autonomy in the control of their sexuality. Nevertheless, this doesn't mean that each one feels pressured to assume a sexually active life, nor is it necessary to have a child in order to affirm oneself as female. Rather, it is an affirmation of their bodies and of their sexual desires as healthy, good, and normal. It is the affirmation that a sexually active life, far from being sinful, is one of the most profound expressions of pleasure and human intimacy. It affirms that we can choose to express this aspect of ourselves in appropriate ways and contexts without feelings of guilt or sinfulness. The mutual determination of sexual relationships with others, decisions about maternity and paternity and about the enjoyment of physical pleasure have been redefined as positive means of building intimacy with oneself and with one's partner.

Integrity and Traditional Religion

As women, each one has gradually become aware of the contradictions which they confront in society, but also of many which they carry inside. Each one has come to a point in which they have affirmed their non-Hispanic roots and the religious practices expressed by their cultures of origin. Also, there is a growing realization of the need to reconstruct the link between their cultural identity and their integral relationship with the environment. Esther comments that she experienced three awakenings: the importance of faith in her life, the affirmation of her identity as an indigenous person, and the affirmation of herself as a woman. When she left the Andean village in which she was born, she took up work with Quechua-speaking women in one of the shantytowns of Lima. She says that there she began to realize that she "didn't need to apologize for being indigenous." Arriving in Costa Rica, she began to explore her indigenous heritage and discovered that "I know how to pray to the God of Christianity, but I don't know the faith of my own ancestors." For Esther, the practice of traditional indigenous religion has been a way of overcoming the dualisms of Christianity, of affirming her identity as an indigenous and as a woman.

> Spirituality is related to self-discovery, rediscovering the wealth which we have been taught to deny, the wealth of daily living as an expression of cultural identity, the affirmation of the values that formed us—solidarity, respect for others, equilibrium, the relationship between humanity and the earth.
>
> Spirituality isn't something that is finished and rigid; rather, it is a creative process. Spirituality affirms the individual in the context of community. Because of this, we emphasize that identity doesn't mean just our name or place of origin. Identity means the way in which we live; it means sharing our personal and collective stories as part of the process of affirmation. It means identifying myself as an indigenous woman in a patriarchal, western culture that denies the differences between us.
>
> For us as indigenous peoples, first of all we begin by understanding our spirituality as the recuperation and reconstruction of our cultural heritage, beginning with the pain we have suffered for centuries. We remember this pain and bring it to conscious awareness in the present, to help us understand present reality, and to help us visualize renewal in the future. Spirituality in the context of cultural diversity shapes the way in which we see the world, remembering the teachings of our ancestors, and recovering the equilibrium between cosmos and humanity.
>
> This search for equilibrium, that forms a part of our indigenous identity, comes from the teachings of our ancestors, and is an integral part of our spirituality. So we say that spirituality isn't something that is finished, but rather is constantly being renewed in the search for full humanity. It includes the relationship to our environment and to human diversity, to beauty and to life.
>
> Spirituality isn't unique or exclusive to Christianity. There are individual and collective spiritualities from all cultures, and these are a treasure trove for all humanity, because spirituality is diverse and multicultural.

Anastasia decided to leave the Christian tradition because this religion did not make sense to her in her life. For her, Maya-Kiché spirituality made more sense. In the Maya-Kiché traditions she perceived an affirmation of her identity as an indigenous woman and her culture. Years ago, when she was playing the marimba in a traditional celebration, she told one of the elders that she hoped some day to become a spiritual leader. The elder told her that it was possible for a woman, but that few assumed this calling because of other responsibilities.

Later, an elder told her to take an offering to a specific place. There she encountered fifteen to twenty other men and women of all ages who were in preparation for the traditional priesthood. When the time arrived, she told her parents of her decision. Her father accepted her decision, telling her that she should continue, and not allow herself to stray as he had. Anastasia tells us about what the Maya-Kiché spirituality means:

> Today the Maya women are present in all levels of life, maintaining our spirituality, our view of the world and of life, the Maya cosmovision, that is manifest and affirmed each day. Like many women who are spiritual leaders, we are guardians of the way. I am still young, but I live the hope of my ancestors, and of my Maya grandparents who said "keep the memory of our people; share it with those who can see and live." This is my mission today, to feed the light, this calm in our hearts, the quietness and peace in our land.

Elena has only recently begun to affirm her indigenous roots. She reflects that being Afro-indigenous means that she experiences a double discrimination, which she also has internalized. On the one hand, she is discriminated against by the whites for being black, and on the other hand she is discriminated against by the blacks for being of indigenous ancestry. The internalization of these discriminations has resulted in a rejection of herself which she has had to confront. As she observes, the resources for overcoming her own attitudes are rooted in her own family: "I had a close relationship with my Garífuna great-grandmother and with the other indigenous people in my family. My mother did what she could to keep us close to our roots. . . . Now, with the years of study and reading about different perspectives, for the first time I can affirm that I am Afro-indigenous."

Silvia participates in both Christian and Afro-Brazilian celebrations as a part of her spiritual journey. Reflecting on what she finds meaningful in Afro-Brazilian religions, she tells us:

> I am in a sacred space with other men and women. I hear the voice of God/ess as both male and female. For this God/ess my desires are not sinful; they are integral and important aspects of life.
>
> Life isn't just human life; it is also nature. We depend on nature; nature feeds us, protects us and cures us. At the beginning this seemed magical to me, but later I began to understand. The problem is that humanity has become separated from the earth, from the grass, from the flowers, from the very air that we breathe. We forget that they are a part of us and that health depends on rediscovering and rebuilding this relationship, this communion with the cosmos and the created world. Nature, trees, are also part of history. The earth has a history. Its roots are very long, and they

flourish. God is present in natural history, as well as human history, waiting and caring for us.

Esther, Elena and Silvia have incorporated both Christian and non-Christian traditions into their lives. For them, the participation in their cultural traditions and in Christianity is not seen as a form of syncretism nor as a dualism. It is not syncretism because the traditional religions are not added onto their Christian practices, nor is Christianity combined into traditional faith. However, neither is it a dualism, because there is no rupture with one religion when they participate in the other, nor are they maintained compartmentalized in their lives. The two religious practices have a complementary relationship that facilitates the integration of their identities as peoples from ancient cultures who live in a world dominated by Christianity.

Spirituality and Solidarity

Here in San José, Esther and Anastasia work for the National Council of Indigenous Women, an organization that works in favor of indigenous rights in political, economic and cultural spheres. For them, the work with women of different indigenous cultural groups is an affirmation of the cultural and spiritual identity, and of their identity as women. According to Anastasia:

We are many women and men and we have the mission to care for all that surrounds us. Perhaps my own experience is different than other spiritual leaders from my culture, because I am going through my formation here in Costa Rica, rather than Guatemala. But this is a wonderful and beautiful experience.

The work which we have as women is double. However, our opportunity to give is also double. Our suffering is double as well. Our horizon is still off in the distance, but as long as we see the sun and the moon, our voices will be heard and we will make our presence known.

Elena finds her most meaningful expression of spirituality in nursing, in serving those who are in need.

Of the twelve years of practice of nursing, I spent seven serving the most needy communities. I find that I'm not just providing services as a nurse, I am sharing these people's lives, and I share their risks, riding horses, travelling in boats, sleeping in improvized huts. I recognize that this gives me great satisfaction and great spiritual meaning. So this for me is also a part of spirituality.

Now that Silvia has finished her studies in Costa Rica, she has returned to Brazil. There she continues to work at ISER (the Institute for Advanced Studies of Religion) and also in the Fluminense neighborhood. Both her teaching and her neighborhood ministry are expressions of her spirituality. For her, in addition to the affirmation of her identity as a woman and as a black, solidarity is one of the principal elements of spirituality.

My own spiritual journey as a foreigner has taken two turns. One is learning from the wealth of traditions that surround me, not to add them artificially to my Christian beliefs, but rather to appreciate them for what they are—expressions of the human encounter with holiness. The other direction that my spiritual journey has taken has been through painting. Through painting I express gender theory, social analysis, affirmation of women, solidarity with those who suffer, and the denunciation of violence against women—in short, a visual spirituality.

Conclusion

The routes toward an integral spirituality vary a great deal in their individual, specific expression, but there are some elements of consensus in the meaning of spirituality. For all of us, spirituality is a fundamental expression of our identity as women, as members of a specific cultural group, and of communities that accept one another. Integral spirituality strengthens our identification and commitment to healing the breach between our human relationship to one another and our relationship to the environment—to the community of all living things in which our human life stands—as spirituality is more than the Christian experience. And, spirituality, although it includes self-affirmation and self-discovery, is expressed most concretely in solidarity.

For Anastasia, spirituality is "sharing, respecting each other, seeking balance and harmony. It is the vertebra of all that exists." For Elena, "it isn't about being religious so much as it is about being a people." Esther defines spirituality as the "strengthening of our identity as persons with each other and reconstructing our relationship to the natural world." Silvia, in reflecting on her own experience, reflects feelings shared by all of us in our own respective journeys:

To be black and female is a discovery that I live every day as a process of encounter and construction of identity. I say process because it isn't something that is done, finished. It is dynamic. I am constantly challenged through new experiences. To be a black woman is to seek personal realization, to seek happiness, but it is also a political project of social commitment.

It is also the encounter of God/ess manifest in the poor and suffering. This has been my experience in Christian base communities and in Candomblé. . . . These two experiences bring me to recognize God/ess revealed in the history of my people. This "discovery-shock" creates in me an openness to the marvel, indignation and commitment that are constantly expressed in the faces of the poor, the faces of God/ess. I live with an attitude of permanent contemplation that expresses itself in an ethic, a commitment to the struggle of my people, a respect for the differences in people (not only religious, but also ethnic-cultural, gender, sexual orientation and other differences), and in the struggle for life and dignity of marginalized peoples.

Eve, Rachel, Sarah, Hagar, Ruth, Naomi and Jezebel. They are not the only women of the Bible to live in foreign lands. Silvia, Esther, Anastasia, Elena and I are only a few of the millions of women who live today as foreigners, among people very different from our own. Our experiences are insufficient to speak for the many others. However, they are testimonies to strengthen the struggle for self-definition, self-affirmation and the search for a spirituality that sustains our journey, creating in our midst communities of support for each other.

Notes

1. All quotes in this article, unless specifically noted, are from an initial group conversation with all of the participants, or from follow-up conversations and notes exchanged as we developed this manuscript together.

2. Unfortunately, this was told to me so many years ago that I no longer remember the circumstances, nor the specific friend who shared this observation with me. Obviously, it was in the Bolivian context, where I worked from 1973 until 1985. I believe that the source was Antonia Poma, an Aymara woman from Ancoraimes, Bolivia.

5

After Five Centuries of Mixings, Who Are We?

Walking with Our Dark Grandmother's Feet

MARY JUDITH RESS

I belong to a women's collective in Chile that for the past three years has been trying to weave a network of women throughout Latin America who are interested in feminist theology, spirituality and ecofeminism. Besides publishing a quarterly called *Con-spirando*, we also hold women's rituals where we create our own sacred time and space and share our experiences of the holy in our lives.

During a recent ritual to honor our many unknown ancestors, we were asked to "walk back" through history by imagining ourselves first walking in our mother's feet, then in our grandmother's, great-grandmother's, and so on, back through the generations. We were to see each in her own landscape, going back in time 500, 600, 700, even 1,000 years ago. I soon found myself back among poor peasant farmers in the stony hill country of Connemara in western Ireland. A Lutheran missionary saw herself wrapped in animal skins around a fire on the steppes of what is now Sweden. But all the Chilean women expressed tremendous confusion, once they got to their grandmothers, about their surroundings: were they in Spain or were they here in Chile? And even further back: were they Mapuche? Aymara? part of the extinct Ona tribe that once roamed the vast Patagonia? While they were clearer about their European roots, their indigenous lineage was foggy.

In 1992, the question of Latin American identity—always simmering beneath the surface—burst into the open as a result of the fanfare surrounding the 500th anniversary of Columbus' "discovery" of the Americas. The *Con-spirando* collective also wrestled with the question: Who are Latin American women—

after 500 years of resisting, adapting and accommodating ourselves to continual waves of foreign invasion?

A partial answer is that we are a mix—European with indigenous; and a mix of mixes—Spanish, Portuguese, German, British, Irish men (they came alone, without women from their own cultures) with Mapuche, Aymara, Quechua, Maya, Aztec women; Chinese and African male slaves with women of the first mix. Neither white nor black, nor indigenous, we are a new race, a new synthesis.

While the term "new synthesis" may sound upbeat, the almost universally violent union of European men with indigenous women has left deep scars on the Latin American psyche. As Chilean anthropologist Sonia Montecinos writes, "The very birth of the *mestizo* takes place within a ritual of sex and war. The indigenous woman, a prisoner of the definitions of her culture, is connected with the earth and nature and receives the carriers of masculinity by invasion; thus a mixed, dualistic people begins to populate a new territory modeled after Spanish dominion."[1]

Montecinos contends that if the child born of this union is male, he will never know his father as a role model; his progenitor will always be generic, never a specific man. He will never be accepted by his father's people because of his indigenous blood. Thus, his only concrete relationship will be with his mother as a son; his concept of father is one who only performs the act of helping to conceive a child. If the child is a female, she will imitate her mother, a sacrificing, hard-working woman who provides for and protects her illegitimate children, but who is also solitary and self-sufficient. Her role will be defined as "mother," reproducer and sustainer of life. The mestiza girl will learn to relate to men as a mother to her son, rather than to an adult, sexual partner.

"The most significant event of these 500 years is the birth of 500 million Latin Americans," writes Brazilian novelist Diego Ribeiro. "But to birth us, they killed thousands of people who had their own languages and cultures; they exterminated at least three great civilizations (the Inca and Aztec empires and the Amazon Basin communities)."

"We are disloyal children who, although we are rejected by our fathers because we are 'impure,' we have never identified with the race of our mothers," says Ribeiro, who even more than the Spanish Conquest laments the fact that *mestizos* have been the most feared and hated oppressors of Latin America's remaining indigenous people. "Shaped by foreign hands and wills and then reshaped by ourselves, but now with the consciences of colonized people, we were fashioned not to exist, not to appear or recognize that which we really are. This is the source of our continual search for our identity as an ambiguous people; we're no longer indigenous people, but neither are we Europeans. Yet we still cannot accept ourselves proudly as the new people we are."[2]

Acknowledging our mixtures, our *mestizaje*, "what should be my responsibility to my forebears, to my white grandmothers as well as to my dark ones?" asked Elena Aguila, a founding member of *Con-spirando*. "I am a woman of both worlds; I refuse to reject one and embrace the other. I feel the urgent need to dialogue with the voices of all my grandmothers."

Elena goes on to ask why so many Latin American women ignore the indigenous roots in the mix in favor of the white European ones. Her answer: "Because 'whiteness' is synonymous with 'power'—economic, political and cultural power. For example, power to ask theological questions and suggest answers, power to define the holy in one's own image and likeness, power to institutionalize religious practices, power to establish the myths and rituals of a culture." Indigenous, on the other hand, has meant oppression, poverty, and a life of abnegation. (There is no denying that throughout Latin America, the poorest of the poor are the still existing indigenous communities.) She challenges Latin American women to rediscover the power of our mixture, to stop denying "the plurality written on our faces," to revindicate the dark grandmother's wrinkles and scars because "who knows what hidden knowledge, powers and secrets are kept there?"[3]

We took up Elena's challenge and invited our network to reclaim our indigenous heritage. As *mestiza* women, we recognize that the cosmovisions of our Mapuche, Aymara or Maya ancestors deeply color our emerging Latin American spiritualities and theologies. At the same time, as feminists, we reject the "*indigenista* movements" that predict some sort of catastrophe that will turn the world on its head and restore the ancient regime (the time of *Pachakuti* for the Aymara; the time of *Wedawun mapu* for the Mapuche). Our research and experience lead us to conclude that, while certainly more ecologically sensitive and egalitarian than Western society, indigenous societies are certainly not "paradise lost." Some, such as the Aztec and Inca empires, had degenerated into a period of warfare, expansion and rigid hierarchy by the time of the Spaniards' arrival. While women were revered and deities were both masculine and feminine, men were still the rulers. Even more disconcerting are the origin myths of tribal peoples such as the Ona (Selk'nam) of southern Argentina and Chile, the Sherenté and Chamacoco of Brazil and the Toba of the Chaco region of Argentina, Bolivia and Paraguay. In these stories in all cases, women once ruled or were "above, in the sky" but had to be subdued by men; the female had to be sacrificed for the reproduction of the species to continue. (In the case of the Ona and the Toba, women possessed *a vagina dentata* which "ate" the male member.)[4]

No, we have no romanticized desire to "go back." But these are times of great paradigm shifts and there is need for a new synthesis, new energies, symbols and initiatives. And so we return to our dark grandmothers. What can we learn from them? What do their voices whisper to us of the holy? of our origins and our destiny? We are only beginning to decipher the secrets hidden in the wrinkles of their daughters' faces. Perhaps even a more crucial question is, how will these ancient beliefs, long suppressed as paganism by our European grandmothers' people, challenge and shape our Christianity?

Because our collective's home base is Chile, we are more familiar with the Mapuche people. However, we are also drawn to the Aymara people of northern Chile, Bolivia and Peru where our innards tell us that some of our grand-mothers once roamed.

Mapuche Roots

In Chile, there are still about one-half million Mapuches living in some 2,000 rural communities and in cities such as Temuco, Valdivia and Santiago—forming one of the largest ethnic groupings still existing in the Americas.

To the outsider (*"huinca"*—one who comes to kill and steal, one whose word has no worth), the Mapuche are a rugged, stoic and warlike people whom the Spanish could never conquer. But drawing closer to these "people (*che*) of the land (*mapu*)," it becomes apparent how closely this culture is wedded to the earth. "My whole faith rests in the land," one Mapuche woman told us during a ritual on images of the sacred. "The earth is always faithful, giving us its fruits year in and year out. It is the one constant in my life that I can rely on."

"We are the dream of the earth," says Leonel Lienlaf, a young Mapuche poet. "She dreams us, just as on other planets there will be beings who are their planet's dream—and they too will be marvelous. Indeed, the universe is a communion of dreams." Dreams are of great significance in Mapuche cosmology; they clarify, give direction and serve as a bridge between the community and the spirit world. It is through dreams that the Mapuche understand how they are to participate in the larger drama of the universe.

The *machi*, the Mapuche shamanic figure, is called to her vocation through a dream or vision. It is a call one cannot refuse, and although anyone from the community can be called, most frequently it is a woman. In the case of men, homosexuality or a physical disability frequently dispose them to be *machis*. The *machi* is the link between the local Mapuche community and the Divine; she must communicate with the spirit world and ward off the harmful forces that bring sickness and disaster to her people. She is a healer and is expected to have a wide knowledge of medicinal plants; she interprets dreams and gives advice received from the spirit world. Standing upon the *rewe*, a tree trunk which serves as an altar, and beating the *kultrún,* the Mapuche drum, the *machi* chants, dances and prays to the ancestors, the ancient ones, to bless the community. (When a Mapuche dies, he or she becomes an ancestor, an intercessor who returns periodically to give important messages through dreams. Ancestors often make themselves visible in the form of eagles, hawks, butterflies, and strikingly beautiful birds.)[5]

The high point of Mapuche religious life is the *Nguillatún*, celebrated once a year in the open plains. For three days, the entire community dances around the *rewe* to the beat of the *kultrún,* convinced that *Ngenechén* will hear what the people of the land ask. Nowhere are the Mapuche more a people than during the *Nguillatún* and the collective energy is palpable. There is a deep awareness of being part of the universe and of the interconnectedness of everything; of being a vibration that forms part of the great rhythm of life.

For the Mapuche, the Holy One, *Ngenechén,* is both Father and Mother. There is a second pair in the pantheon as well, their son and daughter. Everything is seen as paired: "Don't we have two hands for working and two feet for walking?" goes the explanation. Furthermore, all existence is marked by opposites: light and dark, matter and spirit, etc. But this polarity is complementary and tends toward equilibrium. The sacred *rewe,* the tree of life, is a vertical map of Mapuche cosmology. The *machi* climbs the seven carved niches of the trunk, representing the different zones of Mapuche underworlds and heavens, until she reaches the top, the altar, where *Ngenechén,* the Ancient of Days, lives. In this last heaven, Ancient Mother and Father, Young Man and Young Woman, are One. The One who is both old and young, male and female.[6]

Time, according to Mapuche cosmology, is cyclical. There are two great seasons: *wukan,* the time of the earth's blossoming; and *puken,* the time of the earth's rest, of dreaming. The Mapuche follow the earth's lead, working during planting and harvesting time; resting in winter, when the earth rests—a time of contemplation and dreaming. The *huinca* system doesn't understand this rhythm and dubs the Mapuche lazy. But for the "people of the land," it would be wrong to save up for the future when one has what one needs. Mapuche leaders strongly criticize the *huincas* for abandoning the law of reciprocity: "they invented money because they don't want to pay back the earth in kind," says Leonel. "If you use the wood of a tree, you must plant another tree—not pay for it with money, which is simply worthless paper."

For these "people of the land" all that happens to the earth will also happen to its people. All earthlings, past and present, will share the same destiny. That is why the Mapuche are in the forefront of the movement to save Chile's ancient old growth forest. The native rainforest of the Araucaria in southern Chile is holy ground, the matrix of the Mapuche. Each tree is an altar, an antenna linking earth and heaven; some are 50 meters tall, some more than 2,000 years old. The fact that these trees are being felled by transnational companies and turned into chips for computer paper or into paper for money is ultimately species suicide for the Mapuche: "When they've cut down the last tree and contaminated the last river, when there are no longer any fish left, only then will humans realize that you can't eat money," sighs Ernesto Mcliú of Quinquén. "We are asking that the lands of our ancestors be given back to us. You can't keep on cutting down the Araucaria—she is our mother!"[7]

Mapuche poet Leonel Lienlaf dubs a system that would kill the forest for money "self-petrification." The first time he came to Santiago and saw how the city was covered with a smoggy cloud of poisonous gases, he said that the only solution was to cover the city with a cement top of the same thickness as that which covered its streets, making the place into a huge sandwich filled with human beings. "It can serve as a monument to the dangers of progress," he said, adding that wherever they go, the people like the ones in the sandwich would pollute their environment.

Leonel also says that despite the fact that most Mapuches, if asked, will say they are baptized Catholics for the record, the two cosmovisions are incompatible. Mapuche belief is earth-based; there is no need for churches, for a personal god or for revelation other than that which comes from dreams. Jesus Christ, whom most Mapuches don't know much about other than that he died and went to heaven, is seen as an important historical figure. But next to an ancient Araucaria tree, Christ and his message seem very recent indeed.[8]

In Santiago, a growing number of young, more urbanized Mapuches are joining Pentecostal churches. "My mother was a *machi*, and when we came to the city the only place where she felt she could still exercise her calling was in our Pentecostal community," says Gloria, who is currently studying *mapudungun*, the Mapuche language, in an effort to reclaim her roots.

"We tell the priest we're Catholics, just so he leaves us alone," says Juana Calfunao, a leader of the Mapuche movement *Ad Mapu*. "They come to evangelize us—for 500 years they've been coming! When will they learn that we have our own great religious beliefs and practices, our own God, our own holy places."

Juana was attending an end-of-the year fiesta in Santiago where a group of shantytown women dramatized a Mapuche New Year's ritual. These women—most of whom said they don't know if they have Mapuche ancestors—are searching for their roots and finding much to nourish them in the process. Reverence for the earth, the Holy one as paired (male/female; old/young), the role of the *machi*, allowing women to mediate the sacred—all this is very appealing. "But doesn't this conflict with your Catholic beliefs?" I asked them. "No, not really. After all, *soy católica, pero a mi manera.*" (I'm Catholic, but in my own way.)

Aymara Roots

Some of the women in the *Con-spirando* collective come from northern Chile. Marked by the great Atacama desert and the rugged peaks of the Andes, this is copper mining country. Copper is Chile's chief export. Once home to thriving nitrate mines, this area has a proud history of labor militancy. Many Chileans have grandparents, parents, aunts and uncles who lived and worked in the mining camps. Some of these relatives had come looking for work from their Aymara villages in the Andean highlands.

Like that of other indigenous peoples, the spirituality of the Aymara is marked by their surroundings. The majestic, snow-capped mountain ranges sheltering the vast plateau of the *altiplano* are deeply imbedded in the Aymaran psyche. The distant, unknowable creator God, *Viracocha*, dwells far off in the heavens, beyond the mountains. The mountains themselves are ancestors, frozen in time. *Inti*, the Inca sun god, is paired with *Quilla*, the moon goddess.

But what interested us most was the Andean world's steadfast reverence for the *Pachamama*. Is she the ancient Mother Goddess? Is she the female principle, the earth mother, the counterpart of a father god?

"The *Pachamama* is not a person; she is life itself, the source of life," Diego Irarrazaval told us. Diego, a Chilean priest and respected liberation theologian, has lived and worked with the Aymara people since 1981. "*Pacha* refers to all living space and time; *Mama* means woman, but woman with a family. The *Pachamama*, then, contains all that exists. We are part of her and our relationship with her is all engulfing because she is as limitless as life itself, she is pure goodness and indescribable mystery. And because of her goodness, the Aymara are called to experience life as goodness. Because she nourishes them, they must also nourish her, in reciprocity; one must return what one has received, thus the Aymara traditionally give the first sip or bite to the *Pachamama*. They come from her and return to her when they die. Thus their response is one of gratitude. That is why the fiesta is so important to the Aymara; celebrations of giving thanks for life is their most profound religious experience," says Irarrazaval.

The *Pachamama* can be understood as the earth, which is both a physical, social and spiritual space. Aymara people see themselves as sojourners on earth, but also the earth's fruit. In terms of time, the *Pachamama* is the present, but is also related to the past through the ancestors who now lay to rest within her. For instance, it is very important that one's parents and grandparents are buried in one's own fields. The dead are very present as protectors who will bless the harvest if they are treated well. (On November 1 and 2, the Feasts of All Saints and All Souls, which is also the beginning of the planting season, the Aymara take the deads' favorite foods to their tombs.) There is a tremendous resistance to selling these fields because they hold a person's future; indeed, an Aymara without land loses something fundamental as a person.[9]

In our conversations with Irarrazaval and other religious workers who have spent years living in the Andes, we were told again and again that the key to understanding Aymara spirituality is the interconnectedness of all life. For instance, when someone becomes sick, the Aymara believe that somehow life's harmony has been broken and reconciliation is needed. The *curandero/a*, or healer, is in charge of the spiritual and psychological health of the community as well as its physical health. Like the Mapuche *machi*, the Aymara believe that a healer is chosen by God and given special knowledge that must be used in the service of the people. Healers often try to discover the root of a person's sickness by going into a trance induced by chewing cocoa leaves or by taking other hallucinogenic herbs. To be cured, a patient must have faith in the healer.

Women play key roles in Aymaran society. They are the midwives who receive the newborn and present them to the *Pachamama*. Women give birth in a squatting position, so that the baby falls to the earth and is received by her. Women are the marriage brokers. They accompany a family at the time of the death of a loved one. For centuries women have been village *curanderas*, counselors, local political leaders, and priestesses. Yet there is still an inequality between the sexes, Irarrazaval admitted. "I argue with other theologians about this, but even though there is much more complementarity, there are subtle manifestations that I wouldn't call *machismo* exactly, but a certain hierarchical ordering that places men first."

For Irarrazaval, indigenous people can offer modern society new forms of political organization that combine respect for authority with consensus and co-responsibility, new forms of economic organization based on reciprocity, new ways of enjoying and celebrating life.

Women who participate in *Con-spirando's* rituals and workshops incorporate ceremonies surrounding the *Pachamama* into their daily lives: Before drinking a glass of wine, a first drop is given as a libation to the *Pachamama*; organic garbage "goes back" to the *Pachamama* as compost; at solemn moments of commitment, one puts her hand on the earth and pledges her word "by the *Pachamama*."

Relativizing Christianity

What do we do with this theologically? This is much more than syncretism, of adapting elements of Mapuche or Aymara belief and practice into Christianity or vice versa. Largely ignored energies are surfacing that tap ordinary women's ability and desire to connect with the holy, to redefine ethics and spirituality according to their own experience. And it is no secret that these energies are emerging precisely at a time when indifference to Catholicism is growing and that church authority, unquestioned in Latin America for almost five centuries, is eroding in the face of greater access to information and education by even the poorest sectors of society.

Brazilian feminist theologian Ivone Gebara suggests that to remain sane, we must relativize Christianity, seeing it as "only ONE experience of how human beings explain Divine Mystery." She says that the "Jesus movement" offers a response to humankind's search for meaning, but it is only one response, not THE response. She insists that it is only one small key. "And even if we were able to bring together all the keys, all the responses, even then we would not be capable of imagining the Mystery in which we live."[10]

Our white grandmother has had the defining word about who we are for too long. It is time we listened to the dark grandmother—without rejecting our other ancestors. Here in Santiago, we at *Con-spirando* are drawn to hold our rituals outside under the trees—even in the winter when we are "sandwiched" in a cloud cover of poisonous gas. We are pulled to dance and chant to the beat of the drum as we try to pick up the rhythms in the earth—the *Pachamama*—and in our own bodies. We are attracted to the modern *machis* and *curanderas* walking the streets, old aunts and grandmothers who tell us what to do for our kids' asthma or for our own aches and pains—who seem to offer balm for the spirit as well as the body. The sense of interconnectedness present in the Mapuche and Aymara traditions, of the need to give back to the earth what we take, rings so true to us and we hunger to put it in practice. We sense that the root of our current ecological crisis is rooted in our having forgotten the reciprocity that we contemporary "people of the land" owe the *Pachamama*.

We are just beginning this process of recovering our origins, of walking in our dark grandmother's feet. An ecofeminist perspective of our indigenous past has to beware of falling into the fantasies of a Paradise Lost, of the simplistic stereotypes that tend to surround indigenous cultures. So much has been lost; how do we decipher the scant images, landscapes, artifacts that still remain? How do we sort out truth from legend in the myths passed down from second/ third hand, always patriarchal, sources? How do we respond to the twin challenge of not over-idealizing our indigenous past and not dismissing it as "savage"? How do we simply accept these ancestors as part of ourselves? Or as Elena Aguila puts it, "How to let these ancient women who inhabit us speak through our bodies, our lives?"

Women in other parts of Latin America are also engaged in recovering the wisdom of their dark grandmothers. Rebecca Scherkenbach, a religious sister who has lived in Peru for thirty years, works in the small Quechua community of Jesús in the northern Andes. While learning *callua*, an ancient form of weaving from an elderly weaver, Rosa Montenegro Chávez, Rebecca learned that what appeared in the design to be figures representing various Marian titles were really much older. The Marian titles "Mother of God," "Mirror of Justice," "Throne of Wisdom" appeared in Quechua as *ñuñuma*, or "Mother of Water," a salutation that pre-dates Christianity. "Cause of Our Joy," "Spiritual Vessel," and "Mystical Rose" was *Waita Ticca*, or "Sacred Flower." "Gate of Heaven," "Morning Star," and "Queen of Peace," was *Casca-Lucero*, or "Morning Star."[11]

In Venezuela, feminist theologian and historian Gladys Parentelli is studying the legend of María Lionza, the country's most popular cult figure revered by millions of poor people. A colossal statue of this ancient goddess astride a prehistoric lion and holding a large pelvis high above her head stops traffic on Caracas's main beltways. Who is she? What does she represent? What hold does she have on the thousands of Venezuelans who make a pilgrimage to her shrine in the mountains of Sorte every year? "She is the terrestrial power of America; she is Mother Nature and has existed since the beginnings of the American continent," writes Parentelli.[12]

Women in Guatemala are reclaiming the teachings of their sacred book, *Pop Wuj,* and showing how the ancient Mayan vision of the unity of all things can offer solutions to save our planet.[13] Women in Mexico are pondering the secrets of the recently unearthed (1978) moon goddess, *Coyolxauhqui*.[14] Others are examining the relationship between Our Lady of Guadalupe and the Aztec Creator goddess, *Tonantzin,* over whose temple the Guadalupe shrine was built.[15] And still other Mexican women are rehabilitating the figure of Malinche, the Aztec princess who supposedly betrayed her people to Hérnan Cortés by being his interpreter.[16]

And all over Latin America women are taking a new look at the region's persistent and overwhelming devotion to Mary. Is she the Mother of God or Mother Goddess? Why is she, rather than Christ, the principal source of prayer and devotion? What relationship does she have to indigenous cosmologies? Here at *Con-spirando* we are also grappling with this dear and ancient mother, who may also be a source for our oppression as well as our liberation.[17] Much to be done. But we've begun.

Notes

1. Interview with Sonia Montecinos, "El mestizo nació dentro de un rito de guerra y sexualidad," *Revista Con-spirando*, No. 2, October, 1992. Also see *Madres y Huachos: Alegorias del Mestizaje Chileno*, Sonia Montecinos, Editorial Cuarto Propio: Santiago, 1991.

2. Melinda Roper, MM, "Repentance, Conversion, Reconciliation," paper given at the U.S. Catholic Mission Association Annual Conference "1492-1992: Cultures Challenge Mission," St. Louis, MO, October, 1991.

3. Elena Aguila, "Mestiza, Champurria, Revoltijeada," *Revista Con-spirando*, No. 2, October, 1992.

4. Montecinos, "La creacion de las mujeres: Mitos de sacrificio y fecundidad," *Revista Con-spirando*, No. 6, December, 1993.

5. Bridget Cooke, "Llamada a ser nexo: la machi-chamana mapuche," *Revista Con-spirando*, No. 6.

6. Malú Serra, *Mapuche, Gente de la Tierra*, Editorial Persona: Santiago, 1992.

7. *Ibid.*

8. *Ibid.*

9. Interview with Diego Irarrazaval, "El Mundo Aymara: Un lenguaje de simbolos, danzas y colores," Mary Judith Ress and Josefina Hurtado, *Revista Con-spirando*, No. 6. See also *Cultura y Fe Latinoamericanas*, Diego Irarrazaval, Ediciones Rehue, Santiago: 1994.

10. Interview with Ivone Gebara, "Ecofeminismo holistico," *Revista Con-spirando*, No. 4, June 1993.

11. Rebecca Scherkenbach, "Las letanías de María," *Revista Con-spirando*, No. 6.

12. Gladys Parentelli, "María Lionza: La fuerza telúrica de América," *Revista Con-spirando*, No. 2.

13. Interview with Dora Vásquez, "Yo soy tu espejo como tú eres mi espejo: la cosmovision maya," *Revista Con-spirando*, No. 6.

14. Maria Anzues, *Coyolxauhqui, Nuestra Madre Cósmica*, Mexico: Consejo Nacional de la Cultura Nahuatl, Centro de Estudios Tepiteños, 1991.

15. Louise M. Burkhart, "The Cult of the Virgin of Guadalupe in Mexico," *Southern and Meso-American Native Spirituality*, Gary H. Gossen, ed. New York: Crossroad, 1993. Also see Helen Carpenter, MM, "Maria, ¿Qué pasa con la libertad de las mujeres?" *Revista Con-spirando*, No. 2.

16. Marie Moore, MM, "Hemos cruzado las fronteras de nuestras conciencias," *Revista Con-spirando*, No. 2.

17. The entire issue of the September 1994 issue of *Con-spirando* was devoted to Mary.

PART 2

ASIA

Asian women, within Asian liberation theology and struggles for social justice in the 1980s, moved quickly to interconnect the themes of feminism, ecology, and liberation from dependency and exploitation. Feminist women in Asia have taken a leading role in ecological awareness as an integral element of their critique of neo-colonial developmentalism and of patriarchy, both as it was imported from the West and within its earlier forms in their own cultures. It would be no exaggeration to say that, in Asia, the leading form of ecological awareness is social ecofeminism.

The person who has taken the lead in shaping this social ecofeminism, for Indians in particular and for Asian women generally, is Vandana Shiva, an Indian woman trained in physics. Shiva founded and leads the Research Foundation for Science, Technology and Natural Resource Policy in Dehradun, Uttar Pradesh near Delhi. Shiva's 1989 book, *Staying Alive: Women, Ecology and Development*, has become a classic for Third World ecofeminism.

In her article "Let Us Survive: Women, Ecology and Development," which appeared first in 1986 in the Indian women's magazine *Sangharash*, Shiva sounds some of the key themes which she developed in her book. She critiques Western development as a form of neo-colonialism that increases the poverty and ecological devastation that began with Western colonialism and which heightens the poverty and marginalization of women, especially rural women.

Shiva carries this critique of development as a patriarchal and neo-colonial project into a critique of Western science as the foundation of a world view of fragmentation, dualism and hierarchical domination that underlies Western patriarchal, colonial projects. For Shiva these Western mindsets and projects heighten the victimization of women, especially poor rural women, which is already present in earlier Indian forms of patriarchy.

But the woman-nature connection is more than a basis of victimization of women. Women also take hold of the positive side of this connection between their lives and the natural world to defend the means of life for nature and society against this system of destruction. Shiva sees both women and also

61

traditional Indian village society as rooted in a culture of life-giving interdependency, which traditional Hinduism called *Shaki*, or the "feminine cosmic principle." This cosmic principle is for Shiva the authentic nature of things upon which women and colonized people can stand to oppose the forces of exploitation and destruction.

Aruna Gnanadason has been a leader in the Indian feminist movement for many years who has also become a leader in the promotion of women and feminist theology within the Christian churches in India. Having been the head of the All India Council of Christian Women, Gnanadason moved in 1991 to head the women's desk in the program unit on Justice, Peace and Creation of the World Council of Churches in Geneva, Switzerland.

Gnanadason's essay, which explores the basic components of a feminist eco-theology for India, draws on the work of Vandana Shiva. Gnanadason also critiques the Western development model and its roots in Western science as both a world view and system of domination which impoverishes most Third World people and their environment. She points out the particularly harsh impact on women of this impoverishment of Indian people and their environment.

In addition, Gnanadason sketches the basis for an ecofeminist theology of resistence and renewal of life. She draws on the Hindu cosmology of the dynamic interconnection of feminine and masculine principles, not as a vision that divides men and women from each other or humans from nature but rather as a dynamic of creativity present in both women and men, uniting humans with nature.

As a Christian, Gnanadason also refers to examples in the biblical tradition in which women defended life against oppression. Gnanadason takes for granted that an Indian ecofeminist theology can and should draw on both these spiritual heritages. It does not need to set one against the other.

Gabriele Dietrich is a Catholic feminist theologian who has taught for many years at Tamil Nadu Theological Seminary in Madurai, South India. The themes of devastation of natural resources and poor people, especially women, by the modern model of development are discussed by Shiva and Gnanadason in a general way. Dietrich, however, addresses them by focusing on two specific local communities in her regions: a community of coastal fisherfolk in Tamil Nadu and Kerala and urban slum dwellers in Tamil Nadu.

Dietrich fleshes out the interconnections between women, natural resources and social processes through a fivefold lens. She looks at the work that women do in each of these communities; the way women's bodies and sexuality are constructed by their work roles and by cultural ideologies; the relation of women's work and women's bodies to the natural resources on which these communities depend; the spiritualities, both Christian and Hindu, on which women draw for survival; and the struggles to reconstruct sustaining social and ecological relationships in the wake of the devastation inflicted on these communities by "modernization."

Having given the reader a glimpse of the complexity of the interconnections between the five aspects of these two communities, Dietrich then turns to the biblical tradition for a theological vision of hope. How can culture, spirituality and society be reconstructed for life-giving relations in the wake of the current impoverishment and disintegration of traditional systems of survival? Dietrich draws on a number of biblical themes that reveal both the depths of human alienation and God's redemptive presence in recreating the world on the side of life, using the theological symbol of "the world as God's body" as her normative model for the God-creation-society interrelation.

Victoria Tauli-Corpuz, who comes from the tribal community of the Igorots in the mountainous region in northern Luzon, the Philippines, provides a critical perspective on the role of Christianity in her country. The missionaries, Catholic and then Protestant, have been the mediators of a Western colonization which has disintegrated the traditional cultures and systems of survival of her people.

Alienated from the Christianity of her upbringing by what appeared to be its other-worldly irrelevance to real life, Tauli-Corpuz was also alienated from the traditional spirituality of her animist ancestors by the Christian condemnation of it as "paganism." Christians were taught to shun these ancestral customs as both evil and ignorant, the source of the "backwardness" of their people, and to embrace Christianity and Western methods of development as salvation, both spiritual and material.

In reexamining the traditional customs, rituals and spirituality of her people, Tauli-Corpuz finds that they are filled with a wisdom that underlays community solidarity, egalitarian relationships and reverence for the natural world that sustained them. Both Christianity and modernization have brought an uprooting from these relationships and poverty, with very little to replace the traditional wisdom.

Tauli-Corpuz doesn't totally reject the possibility that Christianity might provide positive values for justice and the sustaining of life. But, in order to do so, the church must cease trying to destroy or co-opt traditional culture and be willing to approach this culture with full respect for its integrity in its own right.

The final essay in this section on Asian women comes from Sun Ai Lee-Park, a pivotal figure in Korean feminist theology. In 1980, Sun Ai Lee-Park founded the Asian Christian feminist journal, *In God's Image*, which continues to be the major vehicle for the networking of Asian Christian feminism. Asian Christian feminists from the Philippines, Indonesia, Korea, Japan, India, Australia and Malaysia serve on the board of this journal. Currently based in Korea, the journal, which now stands within the Asian Women's Resource Center for Culture and Theology, continually promotes both meetings of Asian Christian feminists and publications of the growing body of their theological and social reflections.

Lee-Park's essay takes the form of a biblical study of two key passages: Genesis 2:15-17 and Leviticus 25:8-55. Her travels in Malaysia to view the devastation of the rain forests and of the traditional way of life of those who dwelt in these forests, led Lee-Park to reflect on the symbol of the forbidden tree in Genesis 2. She suggests that God's prohibition of eating from the tree of the knowledge of good and evil represents the limits within which humans are allowed to use nature to sustain life-giving relations with God, one another and creation.

Transgressing these limits brings increasing destruction: a rapacious greed uses up the natural world for the profits of the few, while most humans are plunged into poverty, and the creation itself becomes less and less capable of sustaining life. Renewal of life, justice between humans, reconciliation with nature, demands relearning these limits within which life for all can flourish.

Leviticus 25 provides Lee-Park with the redemptive vision of creation and humanity restored. The debts that grind down the poor must be forgiven; those who have fallen into servitude must be released from their bondage. Nature, the land, the animals must be given periodic rest. Those who have lost land and houses through debt and enslavement will have the means of life restored to them. Redemption is not a once-for-all event at the end of history, but rather a continual process of restoring just balances between humans with each other and with nature.

The biblical redemptive vision is here revealed to be holistic. Salvation is not simply about the forgiveness of sins, reconciling humans with God in a way that has no effects on real life here and now. Rather this reconciliation is itself manifest through the establishment of just relations between humans and life-sustaining relation between humans and the natural world. For Lee-Park the Bible, read from the viewpoint of poor Asians and Asian women, is a vehicle for an eco-theology of liberation.

6

Let Us Survive

Women, Ecology and Development

VANDANA SHIVA

"Development" was to have been a liberating project—a project for removal of poverty and levelling of socio-economic inequalities, based on class, ethnicity and gender. While the dominant image of "development" persists as a class and gender neutral model of progress for all, the experience of "development" has been the opposite, polarizing the dichotomizing society, creating new forms of affluence for the powerful, and new forms of deprivation and dispossession for the weak.

Development as a Patriarchal Project

The U.N. Decade for Women was based on the assumption that the improvement of women's economic position would automatically flow from an expansion and diffusion of the development process. Yet, by the end of the Decade, it was becoming clear that development itself was the problem. Insufficient and inadequate "participation" in "development" was not the cause for women's increasing under-development; it was, rather, their enforced but asymmetric participation in it by which they bore the costs but were excluded from the benefits. Development exclusivity and dispossession aggravated and deepened the colonial process of ecological degradation and the loss of political control over nature's sustenance base. Economic growth was a new colonialism, draining resources away from those who need them most. The discontinuity lay in the fact that it was now new national elites, not colonial powers, who masterminded the exploitation on grounds of "national interest" and growing GNPs, and it was accomplished with more powerful technologies of appropriation and destruction.

Ester Boserup has documented how women's impoverishment increased during colonial rule; those rulers who had spent a few centuries in subjugating and crippling their own women into de-skilled, de-intellectualized appendages, disfavored the women of the colonies on matters of access to land, technology and employment.[1] The economic and political processes of colonial under-development bore the clear mark of modern Western patriarchy, and while large numbers of women and men were impoverished by these processes, women tended to lose more. The privatization of land for revenue generation displaced women more critically, eroding their traditional land use rights. The expansion of cash crops undermined food production, and women were often left with meager resources to feed and care for children, the aged and the infirm when men migrated or were conscripted into forced labor by the colonizers. As a collective document by women activists, organizers and researchers stated at the end of the U.N. Decade for Women:

> The almost uniform conclusion of the Decade's research is that, with a few exceptions, women's relative access to economic resources, incomes and employment has worsened, their burden of work has increased, and their relative and even absolute health, nutritional and educational status has declined.

The displacement of women from productive activity by the expansion of development was rooted largely in the manner in which development projects appropriated or destroyed the natural resource base for the production of suste- nance and survival. It destroyed women's productivity both by removing land, water and forests from their management and control, as well as through the ecological destruction of soil, water and vegetation systems so that nature's productivity and renewability were impaired. While gender subordination and patriarchy are the oldest of oppressions, they have taken on new and more vio- lent forms through the project of development. Patriarchal categories which understand destruction as "production" and regeneration of life as "passivity" have generated a crisis of survival. Passivity, as an assumed category of the "nature" of nature and of women, denies the activity of nature and life. Frag- mentation and uniformity as assumed categories of progress and development destroy the living forces which arise from relationships within the "web of life" and the diversity in the elements and patterns of these relationships.

We perceive development as a patriarchal project because it has emerged from centers of western capitalist patriarchy, and it reproduces these patriarchal structures within the family, in community and throughout the fabric of Third World societies. Patriarchal prejudice colors the structures of knowledge as well as the structures of production and work that shape and are in turn shaped by "development" activity. Women's knowledge and work as integrally linked to nature are marginalized or displaced, and in their place are introduced pat- terns of thought and patterns of work that devalue the worth of women's knowl- edge and women's activities. This fragments both nature and society.

Productivity, viewed from the perspective of survival, differs sharply from the dominant view of the productivity of labor as defined for processes of capital accumulation. "Man's" production of commodities by using some of nature's wealth and women's work as raw material and dispensing with the rest as waste, becomes the only legitimate category of work, wealth and production. Nature and women working to produce and reproduce life are declared "unproductive."

With Adam Smith, the wealth created by nature and women's work was made invisible. Labor, and especially male labor, became the fund which originally supplies humans with all the necessities and conveniences of life. As this assumption spread to all human communities, it introduced dualities within society, and between nature and man. No more was nature a source of wealth and sustenance; no more was women's work in sustenance "productive" work; no more were peasant and tribal societies creative and productive. They were all marginal to the framework of industrial society, except as resources and inputs. The transforming, productive power was associated only with male Western labor, and economic development became a design for remodeling the world on that assumption. The devaluation and derecognition of nature's work and productivity has led to the ecological crises; the devaluation and derecognition of women's work has created sexism and inequality between men and women. The devaluation of subsistence, or rather sustenance economies, based on harmony between nature's work and human's work has created the various forms of ethnic and cultural crises that plague our world today.

Modern Science as Patriarchy's Project

Modern science is projected as a universal, value-free system of knowledge that has displaced all other belief and knowledge systems by its universality and value neutrality, and by the logic of its method to arrive at objective claims about nature. Yet the dominant stream of modern science, the reductionist or mechanical paradigm, is a particular response of a particular group of people. It is a specific project of Western man which came into being during the fifteenth to seventeenth centuries as the much-acclaimed Scientific Revolution. During the last few years, feminist scholarship has begun to recognize that the dominant science system emerged as a liberating force, not for humanity as a whole (though it legitimized itself in terms of universal betterment of the species), but as a masculine and patriarchal project which necessarily entailed the subjugation of both nature and women. Harding has called it a "Western, bourgeois, masculine project," and according to Keller:

Science has been produced by a particular sub-set of the human race, that is, almost entirely by white, middle-class males. For the founding fathers of modern science, the reliance on the language of gender was explicit; they sought a philosophy that deserved to be called "masculine," that could be distinguished from its ineffective predecessors by its "virile" powers, its capacity to bind Nature to man's service and make her his slave.[2]

Bacon (1561-1626) was the father of modern science, the originator of the concept of the modern research institute and industrial science, and the inspiration behind the Royal Society. His contribution to modern science and its organization is critical. From the point of view of nature, women and marginal groups, however, Bacon's program was not humanly inclusive. It was a special program benefiting the middle-class European male entrepreneur through the conjunction of human knowledge and power in science.

In Bacon's experimental method, which was central to this masculine project, there was a dichotomizing between male and female, mind and matter, objective and subjective, rational and emotional, and a conjunction of masculine and scientific domination over nature, women and the non-West. His was not a "neutral," "objective," "scientific" method—it was a masculine mode of aggression against nature and domination over women. The severe testing of hypotheses through controlled manipulations, if experiments are to be repeatable, are here formulated in clearly sexist metaphors. Both nature and inquiry appear conceptualized in ways modeled on rape and torture—on man's most violent and misogynous relationships with women—and this modeling is advanced as a reason to value science. According to Bacon:

> The nature of things betrays itself more readily under the vexations of art than in its natural freedom. The discipline of scientific knowledge, and the mechanical inventions it leads to, do not merely exert a gentle guidance over nature's course; they have the power to conquer and subdue her, to shake her to her foundations.[3]

In *Tempores Partus Masculus,* or *The Masculine Birth of Time*, translated by Farrington in 1951, Bacon promised to create "a blessed race of heroes and supermen" who would dominate both nature and society. The title is interpreted by Farrington as suggesting a shift from the older science, represented as female—passive and weak—to a new masculine science of the Scientific Revolution which Bacon saw himself as heralding. In *New Atlantis*, Bacon's Bensalem was administered from Solomon's House, a scientific research institute, from which male scientists ruled over and made decisions for society and decided which secrets should be revealed and which remain the private property of the institute.[4]

Science-dominated society has evolved very much in the pattern of Bacon's Bensalem, with nature being transformed and mutilated in modern Solomon's Houses—corporate labs and the university programs they sponsor. With the new biotechnologies, Bacon's vision of controlling reproduction for the sake of production is being realized, while the green revolution and the bio-revolution have realized what in *New Atlantis* was only a utopia.

Biotechnologies project themselves as ecologically benign, but the biohazards they will unleash threaten life on this planet more than all earlier technologies. The biotechnology era is the ultimate fragmentation and control of life itself. That it does not undo the disruption of nature of the mechanical and chemical phases of industrialization was dramatized most brutally in the Bhopal disaster; rather it aggravates and accelerates the disruption of life by engineering it into a reductionist mold. Biotechnologies are reductionist, centralized, exclusive and homogenistic.

By contrast, the approach to life needed for ecological stability is holistic, decentered, participatory, and respectful of diversity. Genetic engineering as a whole is a women's issue, and not just when it directly controls women's bodies through reproductive technologies. Biotechnologies in agriculture are also a threat to the health and safety of women. But, most significantly, the underlying assumptions of genetic engineering are anti-nature and anti-women, wanting to control and engineer both on the basis of patriarchal values of "improvement" and designing the "best." As argued powerfully by Linda Bullard, this exercise is, however, inherently eugenic in that it always requires someone to decide what is a good and a bad gene. It is also inherently disruptive of ecological processes, because in trying to control nature's inner workings it creates a nature totally out of control.

Modern science was a consciously gendered, patriarchal activity. As nature came to be seen more like a woman to be raped, gender too was recreated. Science as a male venture, based on the subjugation of female nature and female sex provided support for the polarization of gender. Patriarchy as the new scientific and technological power was a political need of emerging industrial capitalism. While, on the one hand, the ideology of science sanctioned the denudation of nature, on the other it legitimized the dependency of women and the authority of men. Science and masculinity were associated in domination over nature and all that is seen as feminine; the ideologies of science and gender reinforced each other. The witch-hunting hysteria, which was aimed at annihilating women in Europe as knowers and experts, was contemporaneous with two centuries of Scientific Revolution. Witch-hunting reached its peak at the time of Galileo's *Dialogue Concerning the Two Chief World Systems* and faded during the founding of the Royal Society of London and the Paris Academy of Sciences.

Systems of knowledge on which development activity in the contemporary Third World are based are historically and intellectually rooted in the emergence of the "masculine" science of the Scientific Revolution. These knowledge systems are characterized by the fragmentation of nature into discrete, unrelated, atomistic, uniform and homogeneous parts, and dichotomize society into experts and non-experts. Women's holistic knowledge of forestry, agriculture, food processing, soil, and water systems is thus delegitimized and displaced by reductionist knowledge. The ecological destruction of nature thus goes hand in hand with the intellectual destruction of women's knowledge and expertise.

Women and Ecology Movements

To say that women and nature are intimately associated is not to say anything revolutionary. After all, it was precisely just such an assumption that allowed the domination of both women and nature. The new insight provided by rural women in the Third World is that women and nature are associated, not in passivity but in creativity and in the maintenance of life.

This analysis differs from most conventional analyses of environmentalists and feminists. Most work on women and environment in the Third World has focused on women as special victims of environmental degradation. Yet the women who participate in and lead ecology movements in countries like India are not speaking merely as victims. Their voices are the voices of liberation and transformation which provide new categories of thought in new exploratory directions. In this sense, this is a post-victimology study. It is an articulation of the challenge that women in ecology movements are creating in the Third World. The women and environment issues can be approached either from these categories of challenge that have been thrown up by women in the struggle for life, or they can be approached through an extension of conventional categories of patriarchy and reductionism. In the perspective of women engaged in survival struggles, which are simultaneously struggles for the protection of nature, women and nature are intimately related, and their domination and liberation similarly linked. The women's movement and the ecology movement are therefore one and are primarily counter-trends to patriarchal maldevelopment.

Contemporary development activity in the Third World superimposes the scientific and economic paradigms created by Western, gender-based ideology on communities in other cultures. Ecological destruction and the marginalization of women, we know now, have been the inevitable results of most development programs and projects based on such paradigms; they violate the integrity of one and destroy the productivity of the other. Women, as victims of the violence of patriarchal forms of development, have risen against it to protect nature and preserve their survival and sustenance. They have been in the forefront of ecological struggles to conserve forests, land and water. They have challenged the Western concept of nature as an object of exploitation and have protected her, the living force that supports life. They have challenged the Western concept of economics and production of profits and capital accumulation with their own concept of economics as production of sustenance and needs satisfaction.

A science that does not respect nature's needs and a development that does not respect people's needs inevitably threaten survival. In their fight to survive the onslaughts of both, women have begun a struggle that challenges the most fundamental categories of Western patriarchy—its concepts of nature and women, and of science and development. Their ecological struggles are aimed simultaneously at liberating nature from ceaseless exploitation and themselves from limitless marginalization. They are creating a feminist ideology that transcends gender and a political practice that is humanly inclusive; they are challenging patriarchy's ideological claim to universalism not with another universalizing tendency but, rather, with diversity; and they are challenging the dominant concept of power as violence with the alternative concept of non-violence as power.

It is, of course, not stated here that *all* women are ecologically rooted nor that *only* women are challenging the industrial system both on grounds of its reductionist philosophy as well as its destructive impact. Such a belief would be biologism, against which feminists have been struggling everywhere. We see the categories of "masculine" and "feminine" as socially and culturally constructed, not biologically determined, and the relationship of Third World women and nature as historically conditioned.

The violation of nature is linked with the violation and marginalization of women, especially in the Third World. Women produce and reproduce life not merely biologically, but also through their social role in providing sustenance. All ecological societies of forest dwellers and peasants, whose life is organized on the principle of sustainability and the reproduction of life in all its richness, embody the feminine principle. Historically, however, when such societies have been colonized and broken up, the men have had to migrate; the women, meanwhile, usually continue to be linked to life and nature through their role as providers of sustenance, food and water. The privileged access of women to the sustaining principle thus has a historical and cultural, not merely biological, basis.

The principle of creating and conserving life is lost to the ecologically alienated, consumerist elite women of the Third World and the over-consuming West, just as much as it is conserved in the lifestyle of the male and female forest dwellers and peasants in small pockets of the Third World. It would be inaccurate to gloss over the class and cultural differences among women, or to ignore the strands of the ecology movement which do not converge with the feminist response.

What is needed is a new concept responsive to commonality, one that roots itself in the concreteness and complexity of our multiple identities that have been subjugated, distorted and fractured in different ways by the same sources of domination.

Links between Ecological Crisis and Cultural Crisis

Since diversity characterizes nature and society in our part of the world, the attempt to homogenize nature creates social and cultural dislocations and the homogenization of nature also gets linked to the homogenization of society. Ethnic and communal conflicts, which are in part a response to cultural ho-mogenization, are further aggravated with the process of development which alienates control over resources, dispossesses people, and degrades eco-systems.

The accelerated Mahaweli Development program in Sri Lanka is an example of development policies that ignore both human and environmental factors from a long-term perspective. Building dams across Sri Lanka's longest river deforested and changed the contour of vast areas of land, at the same time displacing thousands of families, mostly peasants. These peasants were then resettled in parts of the north-central and eastern provinces. This resettlement policy led to a dramatic change in demographic patterns of the Eastern Province in particular, altering a previously balanced ethnic composition in favor of the majority Sinhalese community and thereby created a situation which influenced ethnic tensions.

The recent communalization of the Punjab problem seems to have a similar basis. The Green Revolution, a "development" strategy for linking Third World agriculture into the global markets of fertilizers, pesticides and seeds, has generated severe economic vulnerabilities for both small and large farmers in Punjab. The farming community in Punjab also happens to be Jat Sikh, and economic tension between the Centre (Delhi) and Punjab farmers, and between farmers and traders, has been ethnicized easily first by the Centre and later by the people of Punjab.

In May 1984, the farmer's agitation was at its height in Punjab. For a week, farmers surrounded the Punjab Raj Bhavan—from May 10 to 18. By conservative estimates at any time more than 15-20 thousand farmers were present in Chandigarh during the gherao. Earlier, from May 1 to 7, the farmers had decided to boycott the grain markets to register their protest against the central government procurement policy. On May 23, 1984, Harchand Singh Longowal, the Akali Dal president, announced that the next phase of the agitation would include attempts to stop the sale of food grain to the Food Corporation of India. Since Punjab provides the bulk of the reserves of grain, which are used to sustain the government distribution system and thus keep prices down, a successful grain blockade implied a serious national crisis and would have given Punjab a powerful bargaining tool for its demands for greater state autonomy. On June 3, Mrs. Gandhi called out the army in Punjab and on June 5, the Golden Temple was attached; for the Sikhs, this was an attack on the Sikh faith and Sikh dignity and honor. After Operation Blue Star the Sikhs as a farming community have been forgotten: only Sikhs as a religious community remain in national consciousness. Nothing after that could be read without the "communal" stamp on it. Thus in the resolution passed at the Sarbat Khalsa in April 1986, the Sikh extremists talked of the need to "defeat the communal Brahmin-Bania combine that controls the Delhi Darbar." This, according to the extremists, was the only way of "establishing hegemony of Sikhism in this country."

The Punjab conflicts are at another level a genuine cultural upsurge as a corrective to the commercial culture spread by the Green Revolution. The Green Revolution, and the spread of capitalist agriculture, created new inequalities, disrupted community ties, dislocated old forms of life and fractured the moral and ethical fabric that had provided social norms. Alcoholism, smoking, and drug addiction spread as more money circulated in the villages. Religious revivalism became a moral corrective to these trends. In the early phase, when Bhindranwale preached from this ground, his most ardent followers were women and children because they suffered most with a drunken or drug-addicted father/brother/husband in the family. During this phase, Bhindranwale made no anti-Hindu statements. He was popular because he was seen as transforming society into a "good" society. Even today, rural people in Punjab remember him only in his capacity as a preacher and a social and religious reformer.

What began as economic demands and a recovery of ethical order was thus transformed in Punjab into a war between two hegemonic tendencies—one of the State, the other of the extremists. What began as a recovery for diversity, a search for economic security and cultural identity, has been forced to turn into ethnic chauvinism embroiling ever larger numbers, ever larger regions into violence.

We see the spread of violence as a way of life, as the culmination of patriarchal projects which have made death-risking the paradigmatically human act in place of the reproduction of our species. Capitalist patriarchy has substituted the sacredness of life with the sacredness of science and development. Patriarchal responses to this destruction of life and liberty have been characterized by the rise of fundamentalism, terrorism and communalism, which further threaten life and peace. The feminist response to violence against women, against nature and against people in general, attempts to make the maintenance and nurturance of life the organizing principle of society and economic activity. Since violence is legitimized by both patriarchal science and patriarchal religion, Third World women are engaged simultaneously in a struggle against the patriarchal culture of both science and religion. Whether it is the technological terrorism of Union Carbide in Bhopal or the terrorism of fundamentalism and communalism in Pakistan, India and Sri Lanka, we see a culture of violence and death extinguishing a culture of the generation, protection and renewal of life. It is in reclaiming life and recovering its sanctity that women of our region search for their liberation and the liberation of their societies.[5]

Notes

1. Ester Boserup. *Women's Role in Economic Development*. London: Allen and Urwin, 1970.

2. Susan Harding. *The Science Questions in Feminism*. Ithaca, N.Y.: Cornell University Press, 1986; Evelyn F. Keller. *Reflections on Gender and Science*. New Haven, CT: Yale University Press, 1985, p. 7.

3. F. H. Anderson (ed). *Francis Bacon: The New Organon and Related Writings*. Indianapolis, IN: Bobbs-Merrill, 1960.

4. See Vandana Shiva. *Staying Alive: Women, Ecology and Development*. London: Zed, 1989, pp. 16-17.

5. Based on "Staying Alive: Women, Ecology and Survival in India," Kali for Women, 1988, as well as on conversations during the FAO/FFHC Workshop on "South Asian Feminist Theory" in Bangalore, January, 1989.

7

Toward a Feminist Eco-Theology for India

ARUNA GNANADASON

As I build this dam
I bury my life
The dawn breaks
There is no flour in the grinding stone

I collect yesterday's husk for today's meal
The sun rises
And my spirit sinks
Hiding my baby under a basket
And hiding my tears
I go to build the dam

The dam is ready
It feeds their sugarcane fields
Making the crop lush and juicy
But I walk miles through forests
In search of a drop of drinking water
I water the vegetation with drops of my sweat
As dry leaves fall and fill my parched yard.

Daya Pawar[1]

Women know what scarcity of water means. Women know what scarcity of flour on the grinding stone means. At 3 A.M. if you drive through the city of Madras you see lines of women at water taps waiting to collect one or two pots of water. The sound of hand pumps assails your ears every morning in the city as women spend their energy in collecting water for the family for the day. In

74

many parts of rural India women walk miles, even today, with pots on their heads and on their hips, in search of water. This song of Daya Pawar, sung by *Dalit* women (formerly called "Untouchables") in Maharashtra, grasps Indian women's reality succinctly. The song "captures the anti-life force of the dammed river which irrigates commodity crops like sugarcane, while women and children thirst for drinking water."[2]

Women Affirming Life

Every struggle of women, particularly women in the periphery of society—Dalit women, tribal women—is a struggle for life. When women "hug" the trees in the *Chipko Andolan*, defying the contractors to saw; or when they camp around a nuclear installation, as in the United Kingdom; or when they engage in sustainable agriculture as in Brazil; or when they participate in reforestation programs as in the Green Belt movement in Kenya; or when they struggle against invasive reproductive technologies and other medical technologies that colonize women's wombs; or when they work against the Narmada Valley project of dams—they do all these things because of women's deepest longing to affirm life.

Life is one of the most sacred of the gifts from God. Shiphrah and Puah, the two midwives in the Exodus story (Ex 1:15 ff.) with feminist subversive power, protected life in the only way open to them "because they feared God." Women who have an intimate experience of what the "birthing of new life" means by the life-cleansing blood that they shed each month have always throughout history been engaged in protecting and nurturing life. Therefore, as women participate in movements around the world for peace, for justice and for the integrity of creation—when they call a halt to war and to violence, no matter who may perpetrate it; when they demand an end to all forms of violence against themselves: domestic violence, rape, prostitution and religiously sanctioned brutality, such as *sati* (widow burning); and when they plead for an eco-centered world view—they are in fact demanding a greater sensitivity and respect for life.

The Feminist Paradigm

Out of such women's experiences of struggle against forces of death has evolved a new feminist paradigm—an eco-centered feminist spirituality. This is a world view personified by the re-emergence of the dynamic energy (*Shakti*, the life energy of the universe), which is the source and substance of all things, pervading everything. The manifestation of this primordial energy is called *Prakriti* (nature).

Nature, both animate and inanimate, is thus an expression of *Shakti*, the feminine and creative principle of the cosmos; in conjunction with the masculine principle *(Purusha)*, *Prakriti* creates the world. *Prakriti* is worshiped as *Aditi*, the primordial vastness, the inexhaustible, the source of abundance. She is worshiped as *Adi Shakti*, the primordial power. All the forms of nature and life in nature are the forms, the children of the Mother of Nature who is nature itself born of creative play of her thought.[3]

The Nature—Woman Nexus

Nature has been symbolized as the embodiment of the feminine principle, from the time of pre-Aryan thought in India, and this must form the core of an Indian feminist eco-theology. There is an oft-quoted criticism against the linking of nature with the feminine as one reality. This is because the bond between women and nature has been abused by those who would reduce women's roles to their traditional mothering-nurturing roles. It is assumed in a patriarchal mindset that since women are able to give birth to and suckle new life, and since they have traditionally been the ones most affected by the depletion of natural resources, it is their responsibility to be child carers, and to find the water and fuel needed for the family's existence. This has resulted in restrictions being placed on women, domesticating them and holding them at ransom, for the precarious survival of their families. It has also been the basis for associating women and nature with the base, the inferior, the degraded, both of them to be appropriated, used, abused and discarded. (Women, of course, can be more easily dispensed with—a bottle of kerosene and a match-stick will suffice, as the frequent practice of wife-burning in India has shown. Waste natural resources, such as nuclear wastes and toxic wastes, are not quite so easily disposed of.)

As a corollary to this, while women are the worst afflicted by resource depletion, it is also true that because of forces they can scarcely understand, still less control, they are often the agents of their own resource depletion. As the major "consumers" of water and fuel (for the family, of course), they are engaged in a ruthless destruction of the environment. In the long run it is hardly profitable and it is back-breaking work. It is estimated that in some areas of Bihar:

> Women of tribal households travel eight to ten kilometers in search of firewood (which is usually procured illegally), then catch a truck or train to the nearby town (Ranchi), spend the night at the station and return with a meager earning of Rs. five-fifty on an average, for a headload of about twenty kilograms of wood![4]

A sight which stays in my memory, though I saw it several years ago, is of a tribal woman in rural Bihar with a huge bundle of wood she had cut from the forest, which she carried on her head—perhaps to burn in her own kitchen or perhaps to sell, so as to eke out an existence.

Tribal societies which have strict customary laws regarding the cutting of trees are now engaged in an eco-cide due to their poverty and alienation from the forests they love, which is the source of their life and livelihood. And so we see women in one part of India engaged in a process of breaking the bond that they have with nature, and on the other hand, women protecting this bond with their very lives as is evidenced in the *Chipko* and *Apiko* movements.

Rejection of an Anthropocentric Hierarchical Theology

Feminists are, therefore, calling for an "ecological ethic emphasizing the interconnectedness between humanity and nature."[5] Affirming this interconnectedness and wholeness, feminist theology therefore rejects the Aristotelian dualisms of mind/body; spirit/ flesh; culture/nature; women/men, which have influenced western patriarchal theology and have been absorbed by inherited theologies in the Third World too. A hierarchical understanding of the relationship between soul and body, male and female, the spiritual realm and the world of nature is fundamental to most of western theology, as is evidenced from the writings of early church fathers, such as Augustine, who held that women were created primarily for their role of procreation. As the earth cooperates with seeds to produce plants, woman is to cooperate with the male seed to produce children so that God's command to "be fruitful and multiply, fill the earth and subdue it" (Gen 1:28) may be fulfilled.[6]

Eric Lott in his article "An Eco-theology for the Future: Resources from India's Past"[7] establishes that Christianity has been strongly influenced by this dualism of humanity and nature that legitimized the arrogant and decisive "lordship" of humankind over nature in the Christian West. It is perhaps this "Christian" philosophy that makes the Nobel Prize winner in Economics for 1987, Robert Solow of MIT, assert that "The world can, in effect, get along without natural resources, so exhaustion is just an event, not a catastrophe."[8] This attitude mirrors the extent of the alienation between humankind and the earth. Such an anthropocentric world view, legitimizing "man's" dominion over matter so that it can serve his purposes, is what is applauded in this world, what is given the world's highest award! It has also been the reason why mainstream Western theology never did strongly critique capitalism or colonialism.

Feminist theologians in the West have challenged the western theological tradition of the hierarchical chain of being and chain of command. Feminist theologians have challenged the concept of the hierarchy of the human over the "non-human nature" and the right of the human to treat the "non-human" as private property and as material wealth to be exploited. Feminist theologians in the West also question structures of social domination based on class, race and gender.[9]

Women's Vision—A Holistic Vision of Interdependence

"Our mother is dying" is a tragic reflection of the present ecological crisis— and out of this cry women have drawn strength. The fear of what is being done to the earth is giving women the urgent imperative to assert their connectedness with nature—their interdependence with nature. "When sister earth suffers, women suffer too" is a commonly used expression. This has been experienced and responded to by feminist theologians all over the world, and more specially in the Third World where the struggle for survival is the most acute. This is articulated as:

> part of a quest for wholeness and self-development and as a way of experiencing God when official institutional forms of religion excluded women and female experience. Nature has appeared to offer solace to women when human contact failed them, when institutional religion excluded their experiences, probably because of the very vulnerability and openness of women to such a source of religious experience and the willingness of women to admit and welcome the sacredness of the earth as humanity's true home. Rich and poor women alike have been open to the creativity and strengthening connectedness deriving from natural resources.[10]

Indian cosmology has always emphasized this connectedness—that person and nature (*Purusha–Prakriti*) are a duality in unity:

> They are inseparable complements of one another—in nature, in woman, in man. Every form of creation bears the sign of this dialectical unity, of diversity within a unifying principle, and this dialectical harmony between the male and female principles and between nature and man becomes the basis of ecological thought and action in India. Since ontologically there is no dualism between man and nature and because nature as *Prakriti* sustains life, nature has been treated as integral and inviolable. *Prakriti*, far from being an esoteric abstraction, is an everyday concept which organizes daily life. There is no separation here between the popular and elite imagery or between the sacred and secular traditions.[11]

There is in India an ancient image of vegetation emerging from the body of the goddess *Devi-Mahatmyah* where the *Devi* is said:

> to nourish her needy people with vegetation produced from her own body. Her body is the earth, source of plant life and all that lives. As a vegetation goddess, a vital force concerned with growth of crops, the goddess is known as *Annapurna*, Plentitude of Food, the nourishing sap of all being.
> The villagers among whom mother-goddesses and fertility goddesses arose continue to center their religious life on rituals intended to restore the force of the soil and their earth dieties are true vegetation goddesses in the ancient tradition.
> Since goddess-rituals handed down from a remote antiquity often center on the springs of growth and nourishment, many plants are used in goddess worship.[12]

Forests have been central to Indian civilization. Forests have been worshiped as *Aranyani*, the Goddess of the Forest, the primary source of life and fertility. The diversity, harmony and self-sustaining nature of the forest formed the organizational principle guiding Indian civilization. As a source of life, nature was venerated as sacred, and human evolution was measured in terms of humanity's capacity to merge with nature's rhythms and patterns, intellectually, emotionally and spiritually.[13]

It is this holistic vision based on our spiritual past from which eco-feminist theology draws its inspiration in India. This "other voice" which calls for change, growth and transformation must be heeded as we attempt to develop an authentic eco-theology in the Indian context. The feminist paradigm offers an alternative vision of hope and calls for a recovery of the feminine principle, as respect for life in nature and society seems to be the only way forward, the only hope for the world. These still muted voices are saying that there are other possible categories for structuring the world and our relationships with nature; we need only to have the political and spiritual will to work them out. It is a firm voice of caution against the way we have designed our ideological and theological assumptions thus far and our over-dependence on the western paradigm. It is a challenge coming out of women's lived experiences, not only of weeping with nature for deliverance and freedom, but out of years of organized resistance against senseless destruction.

Expressions of Resistance

In India women's expressions of resistance against the desecration of creation date back to the 1730s when in Khegadali, a Bishnoie village in Rajasthan, the women, children and men, led by a woman called *Amritha Devi*, stopped the Maharaja of Jodhpur's men from cutting the sacred trees from their village. The method they had used then was to cling to the trees, defying the sword of the Maharaja's men. The record says that some 350 people were killed as the workmen continued to cut the trees. Finally, the workmen had to desist, as they found other villagers quickly taking the place of those who had fallen. Finally the Maharaja is said to have intervened and stopped his workmen's actions and brought out a decree that no trees must be cut in that area. This community is still upheld for its protective attitude to trees and animals. The *Chipko* movement in the early 1970s reflects similar defiant actions largely led by women and children.

This song, sung by these *Garhwahl* women of the *Chipko* movement, is a homage to the protection of life and rings with theological overtones:

> A fight for truth has begun
> At Sinsyari Khala
> A fight for rights has begun
> At Malkot Thano

> Sister, it is a fight to protect
> Our mountains and forests.
> They give us life
> Embrace the life of the living trees and streams
> Clasp them to your hearts
> Resist the digging of mountains
> That brings death to our forests and streams
> A fight for life has begun
> At Sinsyaru Khala[14]
> > Chamundeyi, *Doon Valley,*
> > inspired by the *Chipko* poet
> > Ghanshayam "Shailani"

Women in the Bible did in similar ways resist death and affirm life and the truth. This is our faith heritage and from this we need to draw power and strength. It is in these women's courage and selflessness in participating in movements for change that the values of community, of caring, of nurturing and protecting creation can be restored.

Women come in close contact with creation and its nature in their everyday lives. The widow cleans and sweeps her humble home in search of the lost coin (Lk 15:8-10). Women have traditionally been associated with the cleaning of the house—keeping things in order, taking care of the little details of life. The woman's pride is in just how sparkling everything around her is—even in the poorest homes. She often does this denying herself her own needs, including her need for rest and recreation. But now this concern transcends her own little house into the *oikos*—God's household—the whole inhabited earth, as women long to cleanse the earth of all that pollutes and "dirties" the good creation. The perspective of women is simply a call for a more holistic and nurturing attitude toward the earth and all that is in it. An eco-theology for India must be inclusive of this feminist eco-vision.

Notes

1. Daya Pawar, a song sung by Dalit women in Maharashtra, quoted in Vandana Shiva in *Staying Alive: Women, Ecology and Development*, (Delhi: Kali for Women, 1988), p. 195.

2. Vandana Shiva, *Staying Alive*, p. 195.

3. Ibid., pp. 38-39.

4. Bomo Amgarwa, *Cold Hearths and Barren Slopes: The Wood Fuel Crisis in the Third World*, (New Delhi: Allied Publishers, 1986), p. 17.

5. Carolyn Merchant, *The Death of Nature*, p. xv.

6. Augustine, *De Genesi ad Litteram*, XI, III 5 quoted in "Experiencing Oneness, Caring for All," WCC (op. cit.).

7. Eric J. Lott, "An Eco-theology for the Future: Resources from India's Past," *Adventurous Faith and Transforming Vision,* ed. Arvind P. Nirmal, (Madras: Gorukul

Lutheran Theological College Research Institute, 1988), pp. 29 52.

8. Narendra Singh, "Robert Solow's Growth Hickonomics" in *Economic and Political Weekly*, Vol. XXII, No. 45, (Nov. 7, 1987), pp. 1989.

9. See particularly Rosemary Radford Ruether's *Sexism and Godtalk: Towards a Feminist Theology*, (London SCM Press, 1983).

10. Mary Grey, *Redeeming the Dream: Feminism, Redemption, and Christian Tradition*, (London: SPCK, 1989), p. 48.

11. Shiva, *Staying Alive*, pp. 55-56.

12. Ajit Mookerjee, *Kali, The Feminine Force*, (London: Thames and Hudson Ltd. 1989), p. 22.

13. Vandana Shiva, *Staying Alive*, pp. 55-56.

14. Ibid., p. 210.

8

The World as the Body of God

Feminist Perspectives on Ecology and Social Justice

GABRIELE DIETRICH

Is there anything specific to be said on ecology, social justice and biblical perspectives from an "Asian" woman's perspective? I hesitate to venture into generalization of this kind. There are deep cleavages of caste, class, religious community and culture dividing Asian women among themselves. In this article, I would like to reflect on questions of ecology and social justice in specific and limited ways, drawing on concrete experiences of two communities of women with whom I happen to have had a closer experience.

These experiences are not related to any church setting. They are rooted in the basic fact that ecology is very directly a survival issue for the poor in rural-based and poverty stricken countries. The communities are not agricultural. I will draw on the housing struggles of urban slum dwellers in Tamil Nadu, on the one hand, and on the struggles of the coastal fisherfolk in Tamil Nadu and Kerala. But though removed from agriculture, the situation is closely related to the problem of a development concept which has been heavily tilted in favor of a narrow, rich urban sector orienting itself towards Western notions of progress and modernity.

The distinctive contribution of this article will be that it deals mainly with social processes, the question of reorganization of social structures disintegrating under the impact of capitalist development. Ecology then does not come in as a striving after reconciliation with the earth, honoring cosmic forces and non-human forces of life. It comes in more with a focus on setting ourselves in relationship with one another in the day-to-day survival struggles for water, a piece of land to dwell on, a patch of beach to dry the fish on, the sea as a source of bounty. All this is mediated by women's work, both in the household and in wider production processes. Protection of the right to work and honoring invisible work contributions is part of an ecologically viable lifestyle.

An important aspect in this context is the question of control over a woman's body. The vital invisible work contribution of women—crucial for the production of life as a whole—has much of the time been extracted by physical violence or by social controls denying women their sexuality and the right to make decisions over their own lives. The fish workers' movement has intuitively connected the rape of women and the rape of the sea. This however does not answer the question of an alternative to this kind of violent exploitation.

If we raise the question of where God stands in the process of social reconstruction, the answers are by no means easy. It may not be enough to say that God's spirit is present in the good creation because the good creation is violated from the outset by different kinds of human work. The primeval human fratricide between Cain and Abel reflects the differences between agricultural and pastoral society. Human work itself is related to different ways of extracting life from scarce resources under strain and suffering. The pain in childbirth is crucially connected to this work-related alienation in a sexist division of labor. The painful dichotomy between the tree of life and the tree of knowledge of good and evil has often been seen as an obscurantist atavism of theology trying to keep human beings in immaturity and dependence.

In an age of nuclear power and biotechnology, the limitations and outright dangers of a dissecting, invasive and compartmentalized method of knowing as promoted by Western science and technology have become much more manifest.[1] We have also understood this way of knowing to be patriarchal and colonial. Striving for different ways of knowing the world, ourselves and each other is becoming a survival imperative. God then needs to be present, not only in nature and in our hearts, but also as a reconciling and healing power in the new human relationships which we are trying to build in love and agony.

This is not a private pursuit or a mere religious venture. It is intrinsically linked with organizational processes. There may be need to learn from the immense sustaining power and resilience of spirituality born in small communities of intimate interdependence. While such traditional communities have also been oppressive and exploitative towards women and weaker sections, it is the very sustaining power and perseverance of poor women, *dalits* (the oppressed), wage laborers, peasants which have been witness to the affirmation of life. Western concepts of household labor and arduous physical work as mere drudgery to be made obsolete by mechanization have not helped to appreciate the basic work of the production of life. Western concepts of privacy and individual rights have not helped to appreciate the interdependence and sustaining power of small communities. It is hard to separate sustenance from oppression. We cannot afford to romanticize traditional social structures. Yet we have to cherish that which has sustained life and respect for life, beauty and dignity, even amidst violence and grinding poverty.

In the following, I will try to give a picture of the basic issues in the lives of the fisherfolk and the urban slum dwellers of South India. I will chiefly reflect on aspects of (1) work, (2) relationship to a woman's body, (3) relationship to natural resources, (4) woman's spirituality and (5) attempts to reorganize the social structure. I will then try to reflect theologically on each of these aspects. I will also place the theological reflection into the context of rising communalism in our country and the need to resist this trend by a pluriform culture, nurtured by a strong spirituality.

The Women Fish Workers

Struggles among fisherfolk of Tamil Nadu and Kerala have been going on continuously since the mid-seventies.[2] These were mainly caused by innovations in fishing technology introduced by government and international forces (Indo-Norwegian fisheries project, Japanese trade interests, etc.). Thus, since the mid-seventies, there have been struggles against trawling to protect artisanal fisherfolk from trawler overfishing. Later, the depletion of fish resources through outboard motors on traditional craft had also to be faced. At the same time, the women of the community held massive struggles against the mechanization of net making and the use of nylon nets instead of cotton, which were depriving them of a very modest but nevertheless essential source of income.

Both struggles were based on similar factors: while trawling and mechanization replaced artisanal knowledge by mechanical power requiring high capital and energy inputs, net making by machines did away with women's skill and social relationships on the beach and saw women's work as superfluous drudgery. Both the mechanized fishing and the machine-made nets have been ecologically very harmful and have contributed to depleting the fishing resources. These issues make visible the relationship between human skill, work intensity, ecological sustainability, culture and nurture.

Women's Work

The women of the fishing community are not involved in catching fish but in the distribution and marketing of the catch. A strict sexual division of labor is enforced in which women are not allowed to enter the sea (except on Christmas day if they are Latin Catholics) because women are seen as polluted. Women are subject to multiple child-bearing, and child mortality is very high. Older women go to the beach to receive the catch and to bring it to the market. In this way, women are very interactive socially: they have to buy and sell, cook, wash and clean, look after the sick, see to the welfare of the children and manage the whole family life. It has been shown that a woman's working day has lengthened considerably due to the marketing of the fish over very long distances. Women travel for long hours, get very little sleep and are subjected to sexual harassment. With the modernization of the fishing sector, the men go for seasonal employment to their places; migration is very high. This makes women more vulnerable in two ways: they are even more alone with the burden of the family management, while their access to cash is more curtailed since they depend on the money—which may be irregular and far between—sent home by their migrating men.

Control over Women's Bodies

A woman's body itself is a material resource and it is used to separate her from other material resources. The crucial mechanism of control is her sexuality. She is seen as polluting because of menstruation and childbearing. She has a mystical relationship to the sea; the blood of a woman can pollute the sea. Sexual intercourse is seen as impure. The man has to bathe before he enters the sea. The woman's chastity is seen as the protection for the man's safety at sea. Thus, sexual control is enforced by making the man's safety at sea dependent on the woman's faithfulness. The sea, *Kandalamma*, is seen as bountiful but also treacherous. *Kandalamma* can punish the woman's unfaithfulness. While this appears like a dependence of the man on the woman, it is at the same time an effective way of keeping the woman in place.

The woman is kept economically dependent and sexually confined. The concepts of chastity and faithfulness themselves, which may be valid in their own rights if affirmed by choice, are tied up with patriarchal controls which have strong economic underpinnings. They do keep the woman in a position which is not necessarily weak, but tied to the family economy, making her directly responsible for all the day-to-day sustenance. This is also enforced by large amounts of dowry in the fishing economy, which again rests on the assumptions that a woman cannot be single and of necessity needs to be married off in order to be "protected." Of course, actual protection is not there at all as the men go out to sea and women are left to their own devices.

Relationship to Natural Resources

Sexual controls over women are used to keep them separated from the means of production, i.e., boats and fishing gear. Women's skills are also curtailed. The knowledge about fish and the sea is with the men. Yet the women exert considerable economic power, handling financial affairs, running the family economy, taking and giving loans and even making decisions or at least participating in them when it comes to the purchase of boats or gear. Still, the woman and her body are seen as "nature" to be exploited in similar ways as the sea itself is exploited by various technologies.

To the extent that the sea gets exhausted and more investment is needed to keep up the catch, women are also exploited more as they either lose control over marketing and net making and have to go long distances and face hazards. Women do not even have free access to the beach. While drying fish on the beach, young women are kept confined to the house. Women's spaces remain defined in contradictory ways. Interaction with interior villages remains their responsibility as far as it serves the maintenance of the family, e.g., buying provisions, visiting family members, etc. A common saying connects the rape of women and the rape of the sea. This suggests that both women's bodies and the sea can be dealt with violently and do not need to be looked after responsibly.

Women's Spirituality

The women of the fishing communities in coastal Tamil Nadu and Kerala are mainly Roman Catholic. Their spirituality is closely connected with the practices of the church. The virgin Mary is a strong source of spiritual inspiration and ideological control. Yet, there are underlying concepts that express the power of women which get socially curtailed in order to prevent that power from being destructive. Kalpana Ram has pointed to the Tamil concept of *ananku* which connotes the capricious, unpredictable quality of uncontrolled power.[3]

Roman Catholic religion has split up female power into the benevolent, domesticated form personified in Mother Mary and the capricious negative part personified in *Eseki*, a low caste village goddess of *Kanyakumari* pertaining to the area of the old kingdom of Travancore. However, the disorderly and unruly elements of femininity are only driven underground and surface in the form of possession. Women act as oracle and dance, possessed by the goddess. The female body becomes a battlefield between the hegemony of the church and popular religion. Ideals of chastity and benevolence are played out against the threat of autonomy and the destructiveness incorporated by popular Hindu gods and spirits.

Kandalamma, the sea goddess, is another incorporation of the ambiguity of female power. Signifying bounty and the source of all life, she can also be angry and a source of death and destruction. Sexual controls over women are used to safeguard the benevolence of the sea. Women's spirituality is thus split up between controlled benevolence and powerful autonomy which is seen as destructive. In possession, some of this ambiguity gets reconciled. But possession does not question the existing systems of control, it only acts as an outlet and a symbolic protest.

How to relate these aspects of women's spirituality to the question of ecology is unclear. The benevolent controlled image of Mother Mary appears timeless, irrespective of the degree of exploitation of the sea and of women. The unbound form of women's power which is seen as destructive is linked to the uncertainties of "control over nature." However, control over nature and over women under conditions of unbound capitalism has led to the destruction of resources and the disempowerment of women. At the same time, the concepts of *ananku*, the goddess *Eseki* or *Kandalamma* unbound, cannot be simply reclaimed for ecological conceptualizations. Any ecological spirituality would need to reflect on the social processes which go with the different expressions. Catholic liberation theology, which was influenced by Marxism in Kerala, has understood neither the complexities of controls over women's bodies nor the depth of the ecological problem.

Attempts to Reorganize the Social Structures

Much of what has been said so far about the women of the fishing community reveals how social organization is related to economic structures. Under the impact of capitalist development, social organization disintegrates. As mechanized fishing becomes prevalent, more expensive inputs are required and the money economy becomes more prevalent. Women are exposed to more hardship due to the migration of men and less access to cash. *Stridan*, the marriage gift offered to women, gets transformed into higher amounts of dowry. Women's relatively powerful position in the household economy is deteriorating. They become exposed to more violence as the burden of marketing becomes heavier.

Some of the resistance against this destructive development has taken place in the formation of a fish workers' union and of different types of women's organizations more or less closely related to the union. The significant contribution of such a reorganization is that it has opened up new spaces for women through the organization of child-care centers, savings plans, production units and a new force for participation in struggles against the overall direction of destructive development and ecological devastation. Women have also organized against violence to women. This has created a safe space for women which gives them a certain amount of autonomy and is relatively more free from fear—in relation to cultural concepts which have seen women's autonomy as havoc.

Transforming the male-dominated fish workers' union along these lines is a long-drawn process over many years. At the same time this process is crucial as it is also part of an overall social reorganization taking place in independent unions in the unorganized sector, women's movements and ecological movements. As yet it is uncertain how this can be accelerated into a true force of socio-economic transformation. More agonizingly, there are no easy ways of knowing the spiritual sustenance in processes of protracted struggle against overwhelmingly adverse economic and political forces. Even the traditional tenacity of the women's capacity to pray and trust in God's goodness cannot be disowned. The question of the interaction between new social movements and traditional faith communities needs to be worked out in daily interaction. This is all the more urgent in the face of the rapid communalization of our political life, which is trying to counteract the process of social disintegration with synthetic concepts of identity projecting Brahminic ideals of Hindutva and militant versions of Ram. The fact that women are very rapidly co-opted into these pseudo-identities makes the whole problem all the more urgent.

Women Workers in Urban Slums

While the women workers in the unorganized sector in Madurai city of Tamil Nadu live in a physically different kind of environment, there are many parallels in how they face the adverse aspects of modern development and the con-

trols over their bodies. They have organized themselves mainly to fight for
housing rights, basic amenities like water, drainage, health, rations, protection
of their right to work and control over violence. Some of the basic problems in
their lives have arisen out of programs of urban development which do not take
into account the basic needs of the mass of poor people.

More importantly, the very fact of the expansion of urban slums is rooted in
development policies, which are urban biased and neglect input in the countryside. The districts around Madurai are drought stricken, and agriculture is viable only for three to four months a year. The water table is constantly sinking.
Soil erosion is prevalent. Under the World Bank plan, urban development programs are on the anvil which intends to displace tens of thousands and deprive
them of shelter and livelihood.

Women's Work

The working day of women in urban slums is excruciatingly long. They
have to start before dawn to fetch water, sweep, cook, get the children to school
or to work, line up in front of ration shops and be ready for their normal work in
the unorganized work sector. Small vendors of flowers and vegetables have to
go to the wholesale traders in the dark hours of early morning and then roam
through the streets and from house to house in order to sell. Construction workers have to assemble in the early hours in order to be hired for daily work. They
all have to face extortion of money in the form of collection of corporation
taxes through middlemen, harassment by the police for licenses or by being
driven away from the place of work.

Domestic workers do top work in up to six houses plus their own house-
work. The combination of physical and mental exhaustion creates daily tension. Quarrels in water lines, in front of ration shops and inside the house occur
constantly. The women's work inside the house is not acknowledged as crucial
for the whole survival of the family, nor is her casual labor outside the house
acknowledged as crucial for the survival of society.

Control over Women's Bodies

Women in this situation have no sovereignty over their bodies. Inside the
house, there is no privacy, and husbands can demand sexual services at ran-
dom. If a quarrel ensues, the whole neighborhood gets involved. Police, contractors, traders, masons, all can lay their hands on a woman's body. There is a
constant threat of violence. There is not much room here for the concept of
chastity (*karpu*). It is virtually acknowledged that a poor woman's integrity
cannot be safeguarded. Nevertheless, the upper caste ideology of "protecting
the chastity of a woman" remains partly operational to enforce social contracts.

The wife is seen as the husband's property, which includes the right to beat
her, sometimes even to kill her. At the same time, women constantly have to
fend for themselves as the men go off to contract second marriages. They are

split between the factual assault on their integrity inside and outside the family, the moral demand to be "good women" in contrast to "prostitutes" or "loose women," and their own need to somehow preserve their own dignity and sovereignty.

Women and Natural Resources

In the city, there are not many "natural resources" worth the name. The source of contention is land which has become a market commodity. Water is in danger of becoming marketed as well. Even *porampokku* (community) lands are now being sold out. The lease-cum-sale scheme of the World Bank lures people with the security of tenure. The land is assessed according to market value and people have to pay a percentage in a lump sum. They then have to pay installments for 15 years. The same plan applies to housing loans. The result is long-term indebtedness, incapacity to pay and, as a result, the prospect of being driven out from the land.

Normally, no *pattah* (title deed) is issued in the name of women. Only after protracted struggles, joint *pattahs* or *pattahs* in the name of women have been issued. It is the women's movement which has raised demands against the privatization and marketing of land, suggesting that the land remain common property and that a title be issued only for the structure of the house itself. This implies that private buying and selling will be prevented. It is also the women's movement which has insisted that land should be given close to the place of work for all workers in the unorganized sector. This connects the question of the right to work with an alternative view on land and basic amenities.

The right to life and livelihood becomes the key issue around which the reorganization of the city should be envisaged. Also resources like water should be made available first for basic survival needs, not for five-star hotels, swimming pools, and city beautification. The crucial issue is the connection between the resource and the people's needs and life, rather than the marketing of resources. What is involved here is an underlying critique of the whole development concept. Economic growth has happened at the cost of the people's right to work and to control the resources.

Women's Spirituality

Women in such situations need a tremendous strength of spirit to survive and safeguard the survival of their families. Perhaps the most important factor is their commitment to life itself. One sees this in their capacity to laugh and crack jokes in the most adverse circumstances. Poor women observe the routine festivals, but even here it is a matter of providing the basics of life, like at least a decent meal, some sweets, perhaps even clothes. Caste barriers are perceived as something more specific to men than to women. Some of the women go to temples, where possession by the god/goddess is prevalent, and act as a medium. They fall into a trance, dance and prophesy. Prevailing social norms are rarely questioned at such occasions. The event appears more like an outlet of tensions.

At certain occasions, social disputes are settled by vows or curses. For example, a *panchayat* may be held at a certain temple and the assumption is that whoever lies or cheats at this occasion will suffer harm in the form of punishment by god/goddess expressed in illness, mental agony or economic misfortune. There is an underlying assumption that the god/goddess safeguards the integrity of the community and the truthfulness and responsibility towards each other. There are other occasions where seeds are sprouted for several days during a festival. These are remnants of village culture where it was the responsibility of women to test the viability of the seeds for agriculture.

There is a certain spiritual quality in the way the daily routine itself is structured. For example, the sweeping of the house and front space, sprinkling with water to keep the dust under control and putting of a *kolam* (rangoli-design with white powder based on a system of dots) has to do with ordering of the cosmos, keeping chaos under control, warding off evil. Women feel a deep interconnection with the water used for working and cleaning. Women undertake severe drudgery, lining up for water, lifting pots, washing clothes and dishes, and this is compounded if the women work as domestic laborers. Yet, water is something which cannot be taken for granted in this setting.

Likewise, women bear the brunt of the fuel crisis, collect cow dung for cow dung cakes, forage for fuel from shrubs and dustbins and keep the kitchen fires burning under pains of damage to their lungs and eyes. They are centered around the basic survival needs, the rice and the water in the pot, the fire underneath, the social disciplines of the survival of work. While it is desirable to change the a division of labor to relieve women and children from some of the household burdens, preoccupation with the sustenance of life also nurtures women's tenacity in collective struggles, the courage to face the administration and the police, and the imagination to reach out to others and to project alternatives for urban development.

Efforts to Reorganize Social Structures

The urban women's movement among slum dwellers has tried to intervene in many aspects of life. While the main preoccupation has been with housing issues and basic amenities, major policy issues of urban development have also been addressed, the emphasis being on the basic survival right of the poor and on the community control versus privatization, a streamlining of the city along the lines of a Singapore model. An important point has been to connect the right to work to the right of residence in the city itself. Issues of violence against women are also tackled and communal harmony and interreligious solidarity are a matter of day-to-day interaction.[4]

Organizationally, this means that women form area committees and take action on survival issues of the community at large. This changes their pattern of life as they move about in different areas, negotiate with the authorities and also participate in area meetings, rallies, *dharnas*, speak in public and cultivate literacy skills as well as skills in accounting. Family control over women is loosened and their standing in the community is enhanced.

As the issues faced are very serious, solidarity is built with unions in the unorganized sector, like construction workers, rickshaw pullers, cobblers, scavengers, street hawkers and also human rights organizations. While such new organizations cannot replace the traditional bonds of family, caste and religious community, they come to the rescue where traditional means of support fail, disintegrate, turn destructive or are powerless to fight for the protection of survival.

Some Theological Reflections

The stories of the fish workers and slum dwellers have raised many explicit and implicit theological questions which need to be examined. In the title of this article, the metaphor of "the world as the body of God" has been used. This metaphor occurs in feminist ecological theology (e.g., Sally McFague), as well as in the philosophy of Ramnanuja. This metaphor interconnects spirit and matter. God's spirit is not accessible to us outside the body which is the world. The world is not just nature, the good creation, but also society, the way human beings are interacting with one another and with nature. Exploitation and violence are thus a disease of the body of God, inflicted by a violation of the spirit which safeguards life in freedom and sustenance. This disease afflicts nature as well as society, often in deadly ways.

In the following, we are trying to trace the different linkages of human organization and of human interaction with nature which safeguard the flow of the spirit towards freedom and wholeness (shalom). The focus will be on work, control over a woman's body, relationship to resources, spirituality and community organization.

Women and Work: The Production of Life

Today we are not dealing with nature or creation as a web of life which we can still recover in its integrity. Nature is already transformed and wounded by human labor and exploitation. This distortion in human relations and in human interaction with the good creation has to do with the fall, which is a fall into patriarchy itself.[5] Even in the Jewish narrative of the fall of creation and its consequences, the blessing is sustained when the human being calls his wife Chawah [Eve], i.e., "The mother of all living beings" (Gn 3:20). This refers not only to human life, but to the sustenance of the whole creation. The flow of blessing is upheld even in the face of death and threat of extinction. Life embedded in nature, maintained through the cycle of death, is fundamentally different from the visions of deathless life, which are the ultimate visions of biotechnology (a different kind of "living forever").

The drudgery envisaged in Genesis 3 can be of two kinds: it can be exploitative, or it can serve the sustenance of life and of community. There is a link between the sustenance of life and women's labor, not only the labors of childbirth but also the daily work contribution. It is astonishing that despite the deeply patriarchal legal setting in which women are dealt with among the movable property,[6] the contribution of women's work is made visible in texts like Proverbs 31:10-29. While the woman in the text is defined in patriarchal relations, her work from early morning until late in the night is affirmed. She is the source of her husband's prosperity, provides food and also organizes the productive activity of the household, attending to fields and vineyards. She also does the marketing, produces garments and sells them. She opens her mouth with wisdom and teaches kindness. Her children call her blessed and her husband praises her. While this is a somewhat idealized image of woman in a patriarchal peasant culture, the life-giving aspects of women's work come across very well, while the controls over her body, the curtailment of her movements, remain invisible.

The physical vulnerability of women is also often expressed in the narratives of the Bible. Gerda Lerner, in her book *The Creation of Patriarchy*, has argued that the physical enslavement of women is at the root of slavery.[7] We see this in many variants in the Old Testament, from the slave woman Hagar (Gn 16) to the taking of Bathsheba by David (2 Sm 11) and the violation of David's daughter Tamar by her brother Amnon (2 Sm 13). Those narratives show the extent of patriarchal power and the tragedy of the victim. They do not depict women as seductive, but show men in power in a critical light. Appreciation of the contribution of women's work must be read against the backdrop of this extreme physical vulnerability.

In the biblical narratives the blessing on creation transmitted through production of life goes one step further and shows the "mothers of the Messiah" in astonishing violation of the patriarchal codes of Israelite society. We see this in the genealogy in the book of Ruth where the marriage of Ruth and Boaz is solemnized. Boaz, who redeems Ruth from her widowhood, is a descendant of Perez who was the son of a Canaanite woman by the name of Tamar. She had been married to the oldest son of Judah, one of Joseph's brothers, but that son had died. When she married the younger brother according to the law of the levirate, that son died too. She then dressed up like a whore, seduced Judah, became pregnant and bore twins, one of whom was Perez. When Judah learned what had happened, he exclaimed: "She is more righteous than I!" (Gn 38:26). That is, she had safeguarded the continuous blessing over the good creation, which goes through the genealogies, by her bold and law-breaking intervention. The continued blessing over the good creation goes through the line of women, independent of the laws of patriarchy.

Another line of liberation thought confronts economic power and state power in direct ways. Thus the name of God—revealed in Exodus 3:14 "I AM WHO I AM . . . I AM has sent me to you"—not only applies to the Exodus migration, but also the sustaining power of women who keep life going by the labor of their wombs and of their hands. We see this in the vision in Revelation 12. The woman clothed with the sun—the moon under her feet, and on her head a crown of twelve stars—is with child, crying out in her pangs of childbirth, in the anguish of delivery. She is persecuted by the great dragon. The child is carried to God's throne, but the woman is persecuted and flees to the desert where she is sustained. The dragon goes after her, but the earth comes to the rescue of the woman by swallowing the river poured out from the dragon's mouth.

The woman in this chapter stands for the people of God, the messianic community from which the Messiah is born in the birth pangs of history.[8] The dragon, representing the destructive power which inspires the tyrannical empires, tries to devour the child and to kill the woman. It is the earth which rescues the woman from the destructive power of chaos. The earth is allied with the woman and the messianic promise. The labors of women, in childbirth and in the work of their hands, will be redeemed by breaking down the patriarchal conditions of the production of life in the new community of the people of God, which will be rescued by the alliance with the earth.

Arise, My Beautiful One, and Walk by Yourself

In contrast to the legal position of women as movable property, the "Song of Songs" knows of love unbound. The lover calls the beloved to arise and walk by herself (Sg 2:10,13), to come away from the house. In the "Song of Songs," it is the blessing over the moment of love which calls the woman the rose of Sharon (Shulammite) to arise and walk by herself. The blessed moment is expressed in the repeated plea: "Stir not up nor awaken love until it pleases" (Sg 2:7; 3:5; 8:4). Love is not a question of conjugal rights, and violence is unthinkable. Yet, this love unbound has to break its path in a society full of walls, fences and guardians of the respected order of society.

The woman hears the call of her lover:

> My beloved speaks and says to me:
> "Arise, my love, my fair one,
>   and walk by yourself;
> for lo, the winter is past,
>   and the rain is over and gone.
> The flowers appear on the earth;
>   the time of singing has come,
> and the voice of the turtledove
>   is heard in our land.
> The fig tree puts forth its figs,
>   and the vines are in blossom;
>   they give forth fragrance.
> Arise, my love, my fair one,
>   and walk by yourself."
>   The Song of Solomon 2:10-13

Here, we do not only glimpse the abundance of nature in the blessed moment of love, but also the walls, the fences behind which the woman is kept. Her brothers are angry with her. The brothers are trying to make their sister's body a fortress (Sg 8:8-9); but she became like one who brings peace (8:10), asserting: "My vineyard, my very own, is for myself" (8:12). The woman seeks her beloved. She roams through the streets and squares, but she is tracked by the watchmen (3:1-4). She tries to follow the call of the beloved, but she is found by the watchmen and beaten up (5:2-7).

The watchmen are not guarding the city walls against the external enemy, but they protect the powers of patriarchy from the woman who subverts them. Protection is in the house of the mother (3:4) where she can love her beloved. Both the world of the fathers and the world of the sons—which Abraham is called to leave—have an alternative in the world of the mothers, who love in freedom and continue the blessing over the good creation in their own unorthodox ways. There is no father in the "Song of Songs." The lover himself calls his beloved to walk by herself in freedom towards the promised land.

Society as it is does not allow this kind of love to be lived. Yet the fragmented reality of this love asserts itself in blessed moments which make the patriarchal safeguards crumble. If the woman is no longer a property, the property relations at large and the appropriation of nature for gain are in question as well. Nature blossoms in the blessed moment of love. Yet this love is not at our disposal. We are reminded of Lord Krishna who calls to the dance, plays his flute with lilting tunes, loves, enchants and remains forever elusive. This too is part of the separation from the world of the fathers and of the sons.

Krishna is not only the lover but also the playful child. Radha who loves him is like an elder sister to him. Patriarchy is overcome, but she too has to walk on her own in a new freedom, separation, longing and fulfillment. We find something of this in the sustaining power of poor women who have to fend for themselves, but still love abundantly.

The watchmen and the brothers of the woman are familiar figures in our daily lives. Women are constantly suspected, beaten, subjugated. This physical subjugation is at the root of all the structures of slavery. But it is not easy to link the liberation of the poor with that of nature. The promise that justice and peace will kiss each other if truthfulness and loyalty are sustained (Psalm 85) has implications for the reorganization of society. The revolt of the women who safeguard the continued blessing over the good creation cannot stand alone.

The Earth Is the Lord's

The perception that the earth and the fullness thereof are the Lord's also includes "all those who dwell therein" (Ps 24:1). This insight is expressed in the image of the world as the body of God. It is not a question of the world being God's property, but of the world and those who dwell therein being the bodily expression of the spirit. It is in this light that neither the earth nor human beings can be owned or possessed. Women, children, slaves cannot be anyone's property, neither can the earth or the sea.

The Torah had a deep perception of this reality. While society deviated often from this rule of freedom, constant reminders were built into the observances of society. This is particularly clear in the Deuteronomic law during the Josian reform. The Sabbath, the seventh day, was given to all—human beings, including women, children and slaves, the cattle and the earth itself—as a day of rest (Dt 5:14-15). This was to remember the Exodus from slavery. Every seventh year is a year of Sabbath, when debts are forgiven and slaves released (Dt 15). In a society where indebtedness was chronic and led to bondage, this meant a radical leveling of differences. The law on tithes (Dt 14:22-29) reorganizes the tax system and gives relief to sojourners, widows and orphans, the weakest members of society. The peasants are granted a relief of two-thirds of the debt. Slaves are freed after six years; if they escape earlier they have a right to asylum.

The most far-reaching step is the redistribution of the land every fifty years in the Jubilee year (Lv 25). The land is divided equally—returning it to the families that lost it; undoing land concentration; also the land is left fallow. The class society which had developed was again radically critiqued by a communal ethos. The vulnerable spirit of freedom of the desert after the Exodus, and the vulnerable spirit of freedom of decentralized small-scale agriculture—enough for everyone's subsistence but opposed to accumulation—point to the modest utopia in which swords are beaten into plowshares. Everyone will receive a house and fig tree and the time to remember God's rest on the seventh day to contemplate the good creation. What is required is not only a radical critique of property rights, but also organized efforts to abolish debt and slavery, working towards a social structure in which the spirit of love and freedom can permeate all human relationships, as well as the relationship with nature.

This vision is diametrically opposed to the present set of policies that privatize and commercialize the land, the sea, the rivers and even the drinking water. The cycle of indebtedness imposed by World Bank loans, branding social expenditure as wasteful, drives land prices up, enhances individual indebtedness and bondage, impoverishes people by inflation, dismantles the distribution system, works toward fragmenting society and destroying nature at the same time. The sea becomes polluted and depleted of fish, the traditional skills are destroyed, the land is sold at exorbitant prices, people are deprived of shelter and livelihood. Environmental protection gets divorced from the people's survival rights and is played out against local communities.

This violent fragmentation breeds competition, recklessness and violence. Faced with this fragmentation, communal ideology projects a fictitious kind of unity, pitting religious minorities against one another in a confrontation which may end in civil war. In this situation local communities disintegrate, and women bear the brunt of destruction. In the face of this combination of destructive economic policies and impending communal warfare, in which ecological issues can hardly be mentioned, the awakening of a new spirituality is imperative. This spirituality needs to be integrated into the building of the new communities through the struggles of social movements.

Spirituality and New Community

Spirituality is a crucial factor in sustaining traditional and new communities. We find this vision expressed in Hebrews 10 and 11, in the confession of hope without wavering, stirring one another to love and to do good works. Faith is the assurance of things hoped for and the conviction of things not seen. The spirituality of Hebrews 11 is very much related to the Exodus, the constant move from the unseen to that which is being made visible. Hebrews 11:3 also relates this faith to the creation itself. Here we find the connection between the blessing over the good creation and the spirituality of the Exodus. This connection is also visible in the vision of the New Covenant which is promised in Jeremiah 31, in the rich imagery of verses 15-22, where the return from the second exile is led by women and the "new thing on earth" is that "a woman protects a man."[9]

In the new era, the weary soul will be renewed and destruction will be ended. Children will no longer suffer for their fathers' sins. This is a most stunning promise in our age of potential nuclear holocaust and bio-technical intervention, where generations are made to pay for the sins of their forefathers over tens of thousands of years. There is a profound ecological meaning in this vision. Patriarchal images of militancy become redundant. A similar vision is found in Psalm 85, where steadfast love and faithfulness meet. Justice and peace kiss each other and the land will yield its increase. Both peace and equity are crucial for the survival of nature itself.

Yet working towards such a vision requires intense power struggles. The tension between the time of community building and the revolutionary kairos is also reflected in the Pauline letters. The ambiguity of the situation is enormous. The coming of the end of time seems to be at hand; the powers that be are seen in this light, while remaining very powerful. The new community stands between society as it is and the dismantling of all former social relationships. Meanwhile, a new faith community also needs to be built and sustained on a day-to-day level.

The crucial event of intervention has been the cross itself. In Colossians, Paul talks of the reconciliation of all things on earth and in heaven, of peace, by the blood of his cross (Col 1:20). It is through the cross that the principalities and powers have been disarmed and made a public example (Col 2:15).

We are also reminded of the death of Rajani Rajasingham who took on all the principalities and powers in Sri Lanka by being the driving force to document human rights violations not only of the IPKF and of the Sri Lankan Army, but also of the militants. When she paid for this with her life, the caption on her commemorative poster read: "You have not been buried, you have been sown."

In Romans 8, this spirit of the cross and resurrection is related to the groaning of the whole creation in travail. The promise of blessing over the good creation is upheld here as the promise of the resurrection for the earth subjugated in bondage. The crucial hope is that nothing can separate us from the love of God which is lived in the love for one another. Neither tribulation, distress, persecution, famine, nakedness, peril, sword, nor death nor life, nor principalities nor powers can separate us from this love.

This love itself also critiques the ideologies, visions and actions of revolutionary movements. This love keeps hope awake in order to carry on. Love for one another and for the growing creation as a whole becomes the criterion for the viability of all that we are to do. What we love cannot be possessed or exploited. In love, we have to allow future generations to live.

The World as God's Body

The metaphor of the world as the body of God underlies the whole of this article. The spirit is embodied in matter. Matter is present in nature in animated and non-animated form, but the spirit permeates all of it. The spirit embodied is also found in the human community, in the physical existence of human beings, in the safeguarding of life on earth in organized ways.

Sally McFague has developed her theology in a nuclear age around the image of the world as the body of God, God as a mother, God as lover and God as friend.[10] In the light of the situation which we have reflected upon in this essay, these images take on a richer life. We can see the world in the dialectic between organization of society, human community and nature, as a web of life which needs to sustain and be sustained by a loving community. The body is the whole, human beings cannot subjugate nature, but neither can the human community be subsumed under nature. There is a constant struggle going on about how to keep a balance.

Motherhood, as we have seen, is connected with the production of life and subsistence production, with the labor of women and workers in the unorganized sector of society. But motherhood cannot be kept in subjugation by patriarchy. The sexual division of labor between patriarchal technological, political and economic structures, and the privatized pursuits of mothering and nurturing, lies at the root of the ongoing ecological destruction. If we recognize God as a mother, then motherhood and nurture must also be the guiding principle for the reorganization of economic and political structures. Motherhood, the continued blessing over the good creation, follows its own unorthodox ways. It is not tied to the confines of patriarchal society. Yet it will be fully unbound only if the shackles are broken.

Love unbound frees us for love as a way of life. This way of life is expressed in the image of God as friend. Friendship is not tied to blood relationships. It preserves the spark of love in loyalty and truthfulness. It transcends the sacred moment of fulfillment in love and surmounts barriers of caste, family, political affiliation, cultural identity. It sustains life in the most enduring ways.

In Emmaus, the risen Christ met his disciples as a friend. He broke the bread for them and their eyes were opened. They were afraid because they remembered the hardship of the persecution and the cross. When he enters their fearful community, he asks for something to eat. They share fish with him, reminding us of the feeding of the 5,000, the great meal of sharing. The promise of his presence as a friend holds the ecological vision of an economy of sharing in which life on earth can be sustained in solidarity. The image of this promise lives daily in the communities of sharing which we build up. This work of community building sustains our vision and protects life itself.

Notes

1. See Vandana Shiva: *Staying Alive: Women Ecology and Survival in India*, (New Delhi: Kali for Women, 1988).

2. For a brief summary, see Nalini Nayak: "The Kerala Fish Worker's Struggle," Ilina Sen (ed.): *A Space Within the Struggle. Women's Participation in People's Movements*, (New Delhi: Kali for Women, 1990); Nalini Nayak: *A Struggle Within the Struggle*, (P.C.O. Center, Trivandrum, without year, around 1983).

3. Kalpana Ram: *Mukkuvar Women. Gender Hegemony and Capitalist Transformation in a South Indian Fishing Community*, (New Delhi: Kali for Women, 1992).

4. For the background of this section, see my own earlier articles on "Women and Housing Struggles," (EPW, October 17-24, 1987); Nanditha Shah and Nanditha Gandhi's "The Sky for a Roof. The Essential Houselessness of Women," (Conference paper of NCHR at Thambaram, August, 1987).

5. See Phyllis Trible: *God and the Rhetoric of Sexuality* (Fortress Press, Philadelphia, 1979), pp. 72-143.

Gabriele Dietrich: "Perspectives of a feminist theology: towards the full humanhood of women and men." In: Peter Fernando/Francis Yasas (Eds): *Woman's Image Making and Shaping* (June, 1985). This article was published in International Inter-communications *I.I.* 26, June 1983, pp. 17-22; and Nr. 27, September, 1983, pp. 15-23.

6. See my writing on legal background in above-mentioned article.

7. Gerda Lerner: *The Creation of Patriarchy* (OUP, 1986).

8. Bastiaan Wielenga: *Revelation to John. A Brief Commentary*. (TTS Publication, 1989), p. 47.

9. I have worked this out in more detail in my article "On Doing Feminist Theology in South Asia," in: *Kristu Jyoti Journal*, Vol. 6, Nr. 2, June 1990, pp. 26-65. Also published in *I.I.*, see note 5 above.

10. Sally McFague: *Models of God. Theology for an Ecological Nuclear Age* (Fortress Press, 1986).

9

Reclaiming Earth-based Spirituality

Indigenous Women in the Cordillera

VICTORIA TAULI-CORPUZ

Spirituality is a concept that has been alienated from us by religion, the church, Western education, science and technology. When I was asked to write an article on the spirituality of Igorot women, I was hesitant to accept the task. I felt I was not competent to write on spirituality. Moreover, I didn't like the word *spirituality*.

Spirituality to me has always been associated with religiosity, the church, life after death, self-righteous people, and, worst of all, with die-hard fundamentalists who speak of nothing else but "personal relationship with Jesus, Lord and Savior." Spirituality has been something which is not of this world and which is not the concern of those who are struggling for justice and peace, something which is detached from earthly concerns and which has perpetuated or justified the idea that human suffering on earth is inevitable.

While I know that indigenous peoples are a very spiritual people, I was raised with the idea that their spirituality was nothing but paganism. I was told this was a major factor why indigenous peoples were "backward" and needed to be Christianized. My father, a retired Igorot Anglican priest, belongs to the first generation of Igorots who were educated by American missionaries. It was his mission to Christianize his people and his family. Somehow, this first generation of Igorot priests found it impossible to reconcile the indigenous people's spirituality with Christian spirituality. This was and still is a major source of tension between my father and his animist relatives.

I had to acquire and read books and articles on spirituality written from a more radical perspective. I also entered into discussions with a few people to whom spirituality is important. Only then did I understand that my view of spirituality had been very limited. I learned that everybody in this world has his or her own spirituality. I also understood that it is important for oppressed and marginalized peoples to own and articulate their spirituality.

I realized that I had been victimized by the dualism prevailing in Western religion and education, the dichotomization between spirit and nature or spirit and matter. Such dualism actually underpins the domination of man over woman, the rich over the poor, technology over humanity, and so-called "spiritual leaders" (the priests, bishops, and so on) over the common *tao* or ordinary person. With my newly found awareness of what spirituality is, there have been many new realizations for me. I can say that my journey towards creating a new consciousness for myself and for the women and men I have been organizing is in itself a spiritual experience.

This article is part of the whole process of re-educating myself on spirituality. It is part of the process of looking at and articulating spirituality from the eyes of indigenous women. Finally, it is part of a process of reclaiming our indigenous spirituality from which we have been alienated.

Spirituality and Nature as Integral

The spirituality of Igorot women is reflective of their roles in production and reproduction. The majority are peasants engaged in subsistence agriculture. As such, they work very closely with nature and any aberrations in nature will directly affect their productive and reproductive capacities.

Nature to the indigenous women and men is thought of in spiritual terms. In spite of the aggressive Christianization drive among the Igorots, the majority are still animist in orientation and practice. Nature spirits are revered, respected and feared. Rituals are done to thank or appease nature spirits and ancestors. Practice of these rituals, however, is paganism from the perspective of Christian missionaries who insist that only one God should be worshiped and revered.

Rituals coincide with agricultural cycles and the life-cycles. So before planting and harvesting rice, during births, weddings and deaths and at other such times, different indigenous rituals are done. Among my people, the Kankana-eys, such celebrations are generically referred to as the "*begnas*." Before anyone starts to plant rice, a *begnas* is done. An *ubaya* (indigenous holiday) is declared and nobody is allowed to go out or come into the community. The elders converse or say prayers to the ancestors and nature spirits, some parts of butchered pigs or chickens are offered, then everybody dances to the beat of gongs and drums.

Every major activity undertaken by the people is actually done in a sacred manner or it is a ritual in itself. Each major event, like the birth of a child or the death of a person, has its own ritual. Before a new rice paddy is made, rituals are also done. When a calamity strikes, rituals are done to appease the spirits. There is also a ritual to ask for the rains to come.

The Ifugaos have the *bulol*, the rice god or goddess. Each household used to have two *bulols*, a male and a female, located outside the house or the rice granary to ensure good harvests. When the missionaries—both Catholic and Protestant—came, they demanded that these *bulols* be burned. At present many houses don't have them anymore. They are now commercially produced as wood carvings sold to tourists.

Each family among the Kankana-eys of the Mountain Province used to have their *takba* or sacred basket. I first saw one in the hut of my paternal grandmother. She brings it to the place where the celebrations take place during the *begnas*. She said that in the earlier days this contained the jaws of the heads hunted. However, since headhunting stopped, it now contained remnants of the animals which were offered as sacrifices in the rituals. Thus the story of each family can be found in their own *takba*. Unfortunately, today many of these *takbas* are gone, again, because of the insistence of the Catholic priests.

Among the Ifugaos, when harvest time comes, the rituals are done right beside the fields to be harvested. However, it is only the men who perform the rituals, while the women harvest. The men take time out from the ritual to carry the harvest to the rice granaries. Rice wine and native chickens and pigs are always part of these rituals.

Generally, it is still the men who are in charge of the rituals. However, the Kalingas and Ifugaos have priestesses who are referred to as *manchawak* (Kalinga) or *menbaki* (Ifugao). The *menbaki* can be a male or female, but the majority are males.

Harmony with Nature and with the Community

The basic belief of the Igorots is that nature or the earth is a living thing and it has a spirit, just like all the living things in it. The rivers, mountains, trees, rice fields, and so on, each has its own spirits. This is why it is important to live in harmony with nature. This is also why we cannot own the lands, the forests or the rivers. As Macli-ing Dulag, the famous Kalinga leader said, "How can you own something which will outlive you?" We take care of the land and the earth also takes care of us. So for Igorot women, there is interdependence between women and nature, between women and the rest of the *umili* (village folk).

A ritual must be done when the earth's natural state is altered by people. So when a rice paddy is carved out from the mountainside, or a *swidden* (field) is made, those responsible should do a ritual to ask the permission and blessing of the spirits of the land. When a house is put up over a piece of land, similar rituals are required.

The ancestral land or domain is even made more valuable because lives are sacrificed in its defense and our ancestors are also found here. For the women, who are the main food producers, the land should be nurtured and defended because this is their partner in ensuring the survival of the clan or tribe. When a woman gives birth, the placenta, the source of life of the baby inside the womb, has to be buried in a carefully chosen place. This makes the land more valuable.

The spiritual link between the women and the ancestral land is very well established, so it is not so easy to let go of the land. It is not any wonder, then, that the women are very actively involved in the struggles to defend the ancestral domain. The old saying, "land is life" is still very valid, as far as indigenous women are concerned. The land also defines the people's identity. I am "i-Payep" which literally means "of Payeo." My father and mother come from the village called Payeo, so while my ethno-linguistic group is Kankana-ey, my identity is "i-Payeo."

The basic values of unity, sharing and interdependence, democracy and consensual decision-making, collectivity and integrity undergird Igorot women's spirituality. Unity is crucial to the survival of indigenous peoples. When rituals are performed the spirits are asked to help in heightening the unity of the community. In fact, a major regret of the old people as far as education is concerned is that those who are educated in schools are the very ones causing disunity in the village.

Even our indigenous dances and songs and myths are a reflection of our spiritual linkage with the land. The beating of the gongs and drums and dancing to their rhythm has a reinvigorating effect on us. Even if one feels tired after a harvest or after planting or even after a tribal war, participating in a *pattong* or a *balangbang* or a *tadek* (variations of indigenous dances), one comes out feeling energized.

Interdependence and Collectivity

Sharing and interdependence are both very important. The motto of St. Mary's School in Sagada which, translated into English, is "We should not have a monopoly of what is good," aptly captures the spirit of sharing. Anthropologists say that, in spite of what is said about the backwardness of celebrating numerous rituals, such events are actually leveling-off or distributive mechanisms. Those who have more, share more in terms of rice, pigs, and other foods to be eaten by the whole village. This is why there isn't an enormous gap between the richer members of the village and the rest, because the richer ones become poorer after every *begnas* or *canao*. The essence of communion is more real with this practice.

The usufruct system in *swidden* farming is also a form of sharing. Although one may have improved a field, if one is not farming it any longer, then anyone else can take over the field and make it productive. Water distribution for the rice paddies is shared in a very organized manner.

Child-rearing in many traditional communities is not just the responsibility of the mother but of the clan or even of the whole community. Thus the phenomenon of wet-mothers is very common among indigenous women. If a nursing mother has to go to the fields, she can leave her nursing baby with another nursing mother. It is common to hear women say, "Oh, you are the child of this person. I breastfed you when you were small." My mother can enumerate the babies besides her own whom she breastfed.

Interdependence and sharing are further manifested in collective actions or collective decision-making. There are indigenous terms for mutual labor exchanges, a very common practice among the women. Harvesting or planting rice is a community activity. The women pool themselves together and harvest the rice of one of them. Then they move on to the next woman's field and harvest it, and so on. At the end of the day they would have finished harvesting rice from fields owned by as many as four women. This practice makes such productive activities rituals in themselves. The unity and camaraderie among the women become stronger after each major agricultural activity.

In all this, it can be seen that indigenous spirituality is in tune with the day-to-day requirements of living. One should be good and relate well with everybody because this is the essence of community. This is so different from what has been preached to us in the church, that we should be good so we will go to heaven after we die.

There is one indigenous practice done during funeral wakes which I think is more down to earth than what is done in modern societies. During a wake, the village people are very much part of the whole process. Those who know the dead person can come up and sing a *baya-o* addressed to the dead. The *baya-o* is similar to a tribute, but in this case, one can speak of both the good and bad traits of the dead person. If one wants to know the history of a person, listening to the *baya-o* will provide this. So if the dead person happened to be corrupt or a womanizer, all this will be sung during the person's wake.

Among the Igorots, this practice is an added pressure to do good while they are alive. One who has been a bad person will be the cause of family shame when one dies. But this has been changed today among the "educated or civilized" Filipinos. For them the custom is only to say praises for the dead.

Courtship and Marriage

Courtship in the olden days was done in the *ulog*. The prevailing misconception about the *ulog* is that these are centers which encouraged promiscuity among the women. The truth is that these are houses where young women sleep. A typical Igorot home would only have a cooking place, a sleeping corner for mother and father and a small space for eating. Thus when the children have reached puberty, the girls go to the *ulog* to sleep with other young girls, while the boys go to sleep with their peers at the *dapay*.

In the *ulog* an elderly woman keeps watch over the young girls. She can be a widow or someone who did not marry. Socialization and informal education on sexuality is done here. If a young man would like to court one of the girls, he can go to the *ulog* and socialize with the girls. The men who are serious in their intentions will have to declare themselves to be so. It is not easy for them to fool around because the social pressure from the others sleeping in the *ulog* will not allow it. My aunt, who belongs to the last generation of women who experienced the *ulog*, says that, in those days, there were very rare cases of unwanted teenage pregnancies.

Violence against Women as a Community Issue

Violence against women in traditional communities is considered a community issue, not a private concern. Tribal justice has very heavy sanctions against those who commit violence against women. The few rape cases which happened were settled with the rapist banished out of the village or fined very heavily. Besides rape, hitting a woman is taboo, as far as very traditional communities are concerned. Heavy fines are exacted from men who are proven to have hit women. In urban centers, which are usually inhabited by mixed populations, the extent and form of domestic violence is a far cry from that in the traditional village.

Tensions between Modernization and Tradition

While there are still remnants of the positive aspects of the indigenous culture and tradition for women, development within the last three decades has caused great changes. There are positive and negative effects. Changes have also occurred, as far as indigenous women's spirituality is concerned.

While in the past violence against women rarely happened, now according to our women, the incidence has increased, and they attribute this to increasing alcoholism. In communities where the influence of Western education and values and of Christianity is strong, violence against women is now treated as a private or domestic issue.

The spiritual link of women with nature is deteriorating because of the creation of new needs by a whole development paradigm which contradicts indigenous models. The integration of indigenous productive systems into the cash or market economy is crucial in destroying this relationship. While formerly the fallow system used to be implemented in *swiddening*, the need to generate cash has resulted in expanding the areas for cash crop cultivation. Letting the land rest in order to let it regain its fertility is sacrificed in exchange for more cash. Conversion of forest lands into commercial gardens has increased, causing environmental problems.

Weaving cloth and baskets by Igorot women to express their art, while producing what they need, is no longer regarded in the old way. There is no longer the same sense of artistic self-expression. Now one weaves in order to sell. Enterprising persons now hire women weavers on a seasonal basis to produce woven goods which are commercially sold. Most of these women are underpaid.

Unity within the clan, tribe or village, which is very much valued, is also disintegrating for a lot of reasons. One key factor is the present intensification of militarization and developmental aggression. The recruitment of CAFGUs (Citizens Armed Forces Geographical Units) within the villages has led to divisions within communities, families, clans and tribes. The imposition of maldevelopment projects like dams, mining ventures and the like means paying off individuals or groups within the community to push for the implementation of these projects. Conflicts between those who are for and those who are against such projects naturally arise.

The introduction of high-yielding varieties of rice seeds (HYV) has disturbed the celebrations for thanking the spirits, goddesses, and gods. The women can no longer plant or harvest at the same time because those who opt to use the HYVs have a totally different agricultural cycle. It becomes difficult to schedule a *begnas* wherein everybody participates. Even the respect of the *ubaya* (indigenous holidays) is destroyed.

Militarization has added to worsening the situation. The planting and harvesting seasons do not follow a common pattern anymore because the military impose limitations on the mobility of the people. Or else, the women are scared to work in the fields because they can be hit by stray bullets or bombs dropped from military helicopters.

Relocation or migration to another setting outside the village is devastating to the indigenous peasant woman. This is virtually uprooting her from an environment with which she has established a spiritual relationship. Such dislocations are caused by forcible evacuations done by the military or by their husband's need to look for "greener pastures" or by a project in the area which forces people to relocate.

Coping Mechanisms

Those who have left the village make it a point to come back even just to do the specific rituals or to attend communal ceremonies. I mentioned earlier the conflicts between the Christian religion and animist spirituality. The Igorots cope with this tension in various ways. The most common way is to practice both. For example, people get married in church, but they also celebrate in the indigenous way. The children are brought to church to be baptized, but indigenous rituals for the newborn are also done. When someone dies, if there is an available priest, he will be asked to give the blessing. But the traditionally required processes to send off the dead are done more thoroughly after the priest leaves.

Presently among the progressive clergy, there are efforts to contextualize Christianity. The prevailing focus, however, is more on form rather than on content. For example, they use wooden containers instead of a silver chalice or translate hymns into the local dialect and conduct Mass in the vernacular. In fact, the thrust is more to Christianize the indigenous practices, rather than to work on integrating or synthesizing the best in each of them. If the latter could be done, the strains existing in the relationships between animists and Christians could be diminished.

Conclusions

The spirituality of indigenous women in the Cordillera[1] is still basically earth-based. It starts with the belief that the universe is a living thing, and that it has a spirit. Everything in it has its own spirit. They believe that their capacity to produce and reproduce is directly proportional to the earth's capacity to renew itself.

Thus, the relationship between women and the earth is a reciprocal relationship. The women take care of the earth, while the earth in return provides for the needs of the women. When the earth is in pain, so is the woman. When the woman is in pain, so the earth feels the hurt. This earth-based spirituality is manifested in the day-to-day life and concerns of the Igorot women and men.

The struggle for the defense of the ancestral domain, which is participated in by whole communities, is in itself a defense of this earth-based spirituality. It is a defense of the whole philosophy, religion and lifestyle which is sustainable and viable. It is a defense of the indigenous people's spiritual relationship or partnership with the land.

With the changes brought about by colonization and continuing foreign domination, however, spirituality has become dichotomized from nature. Spirituality has assumed an other-worldly perspective which is so abstract and divorced from earthly concerns. The integral relationship of nature and spirit has been dichotomized and the insistence on such a relationship regarded as pagan, heathen or backward. A rupture has been created between the partnership of the indigenous women with the earth.

The effort of oppressed and marginalized peoples to sustain their struggles to transform an increasingly dehumanized society is pushing us to reclaim this earth-based spirituality. The global environmental crisis is also a factor in the effort to recapture what is good in indigenous religions and practices.

We should persist in developing anew our partnership tradition with the earth. The dominator model of society which is facilitated by the dichotomization of nature and spirit should be transformed. We should reclaim and reaffirm our spiritual relationship with Mother Earth.

Notes

1. The Cordillera is the most mountainous region in the Philippines. Located in northern Luzon, it is the home of one million indigenous people.

10

The Forbidden Tree and the Year of the Lord

SUN AI LEE-PARK

The Forbidden Tree—Genesis 2:15-17

The LORD God took the man and put him in the garden of Eden to till it and keep it. And the LORD God commanded the man, saying, "You may freely eat of every tree of the garden, but of the tree of the knowledge of good and evil you shall not eat, for in the day that you eat of it you shall die."

I was in Sarawak in Malaysia in March 1991 to learn about the consequences of logging in the rain forests of the region. I wished to let the people back home know about the situation in Sarawak and gather support to save the forest and the indigenous people whose life depends completely on the forests. The program was sponsored by the Urban-Rural Mission of the Christian Conference of Asia. Many ecological issues were raised in the course of this program.

We were going to the upper part of the River Renjan by canoe to reach a spot where barricades had been set up by the Kenyan people for some time. I was fascinated by the never-ending deep, dense green of the forest belts, freely spread on both shores of the river. From time to time we noticed the barracks of logging companies on the shores, from where they dispatch workers and machines to travel farther inland for operation and also send the lumber in rafts along the downstream current.

The mysterious silence which had accompanied the life cycle of the rain forest for hundreds of thousands of years, undisturbed by human invasion motivated by sheer greed, broke into my mind as a revelation. The Forbidden Tree! The forbidden tree in the Garden of Eden was being reenacted in front of my eyes. I decided to use the theme for my Bible study here.[1]

God the Creator took *ha-'adam* to the Garden of Eden for *ha-'adam* to till and keep. Phyllis Trible's reinterpretation of the creation story in Genesis 2 and of the fall in Genesis 3 asserts that Adam with a definite article is not a proper noun. It is human being with no gender specification. Adam became his name after Eve was created and named.[2] God commanded them saying, "You may freely eat of every tree of the Garden, but of the tree of the knowledge of good and evil you shall not eat, for in the day that you eat of it you shall die."

The Garden of Eden is a semi-mythical place representing luxuriant fertility, especially in the symbolism of its trees. God gave them freedom to eat all the fruits of every tree, except the tree of knowledge of good and evil. The consequence of disobedience would be death. Earlier in Genesis 2, two trees were described as being planted in the midst of the garden, the tree of the knowledge of good and evil and the tree of life (v. 9).

Scholars argue about the possible involvement of more than one writer in this version of the creation story. Whatever may be the case, a clear message of this story is the conflict between freedom and restriction which human beings face and have to deal with in life. According to the story of the temptation, the ultimate boundary that human beings were forbidden to cross is to become like God (Gn 3:5).

The concept of the absolute and exclusive sovereignty of God in the creation, especially in creating Eve, presupposes the idea of the equality of all human beings. No one can take the place of God and dominate other human beings. Yet such patterns of domination have arisen in human history.

In modern terms we can refer to relations between men and women, managers and workers, rulers and people, powerful nations and small nations, races and others. In all these relations we see the pattern of domination and subjugation. Domination is present because the forbidden trees were trespassed and the situation of sinfulness was created.

In the rain forest of Sarawak the native peoples of the land are making their living unaffected by the market economy system. They draw everything they need from the forest. Literally, the rain forest has been the source of life for them. Among them there is no hint of desire for excessive material acquisition or political and military domination of others. This reflects the primitive people's value system of peace with nature and with each other in a community where no inflated mechanics of domination and exploitation are at work. They are happy in drawing what is necessary in life from nature. They have the wisdom to be in harmony with the rhythms of nature, while the land for them is something to be revered, and not commodicized. They never think of buying or selling the land which is the sacred residence of their ancestors' souls. The Iban tribe regards the rice they cultivate in the same manner. It is so precious that they cannot make it a commercial item. I think this has to do with the idea of reverence for life. The source of life and what sustains it has an absolute value which cannot be measured in any worldly system.

However, in today's world the lumber business brings so much money that whoever gets the concession cuts down the trees mercilessly, destroying the source of the forest-people's lives. This not only involves the local economic power but also the rich nations' technology and capital that desire to consume the wood in sophisticated ways. In this hierarchical mode of exploitation the powerless natives become the immediate victims. The ecological damage caused by the merciless logging of the rain forests affects all living beings in the world. "Then his evil desire conceives and gives birth to sin; and sin, when it is full-grown, gives birth to death" (Js 1:15). The evil desire of a few reaches out to the countless many as the power of death.

Parallel phenomena are seen in other industries. Export-oriented industrial models recommended by the First World and carried out by most Third World countries in Asia and the Pacific region produced four tigers (Singapore, Hong Kong, Taiwan, and South Korea) as success cases. All the others struggle fiercely in the midst of harsh competition to obtain markets. For that matter, even the successful ones also face problems, especially when the buying nations are going through a depression, e.g., the United States, or are putting harsh conditions on imports while their exports do not meet much restriction. For example, Korea's trade deficit with Japan in 1991 was $8 billion.[3]

Export-oriented industry necessitates cheap labor. To keep labor cheap, the prices of agricultural products are kept low. The end result is the devastation of the farming industry and the importation of foreign agricultural products. In 1963, Korea's food self-sufficiency was 93.6 percent, but in 1983 it fell to 50.2 percent. Finding it difficult to make ends meet, numerous farmers went through an exodus to urban areas. The rural population in Korea until the beginning of the sixties was 70 percent, but presently it is only 20 percent. The farming industry, which is going through feminization and impoverishment, faces another problem. In 1986 the meeting of the General Agreement in Trade and Tariff (GATT) was held in Uruguay. There, United States's representatives proposed the opening up of the markets of all countries. Two outstanding items were mandated as free-trade imports, namely, agricultural products (including rice) and services. Farmers in Korea believe that the enactment of the Uruguay Round will bring catastrophe to their lives, which are already suffering greatly.

The more serious issue, however, is the dependence of Korea on the major powers who control Korea's export industry by lending capital or technology and demanding a market for their products. When Korea is pressured to import items, such as cigarettes, in exchange for an export market, she becomes utterly vulnerable. The farmers in their powerless position continue to be victimized.

The service industry, according to the Korean Christian Farmers Association, comprises 68 percent of the United States's national economy, and employment in this area is 72 percent of the total workers of the nation. This makes up for the absence of the consumer goods industry, which is being met by the Third World countries providing cheap labor. Coleen Roach, who is a champion of the New World Information and Communication Order, says: "U.S. sales of television programming to foreign broadcasters in 1988 was $1.3 billion, up by 30 percent from 1987. This figure is expected to reach $2.3 billion by 1990."⁴ American film companies are making increasing profits from foreign sales. It was $800 million in 1985, $1.05 billion in 1987, and $1.13 billion in 1988. Two-thirds of the profits came from EEC (European Economic Community).⁵

The Third World is also affected by this monopoly. A video on cultural colonialism, produced by the United Church of Christ-USA in cooperation with National Council of Churches-USA, talks about television programming in one of the Caribbean islands. The TV programming is American through and through for twenty-four hours on all channels. The concerned church leaders of the island are appealing for help with this case of cultural imperialism which must be resolved to maintain their national identity as a people. In all these cases the forbidden trees are violated again and again.

At the World Council of Churches Vancouver Assembly, a woman from the Marshall Islands spoke about the suffering of her people resulting from the nuclear testing in their waters done by the powerful nations. Jelly babies (those born without adequate bone structure) are born and people are dying of cancer. A Pacific Islander told me her story. Her brother who used to work in the nuclear waste yard died of cancer. Her sister is seriously affected also, and she herself carries the symptoms.

One of the big issues in Korea is pollution. Industrial waste smears the land, flows through the rivers, and goes into human bodies. Despite the alarming talk, not much is being done to clean it up. The air which was given to us by nature was fresh and clean, but not any longer.

In such a tiny country as Korea, eight nuclear power plants are in operation and two more are under construction. Korea's ambition is to have fifty plants by the year 2000. The given excuse is that the nation needs so much energy to run all the industries it has launched. However, one has to remember that this super-ambitious plan was made after the Three Mile Island incident which led the people of the First World to move against nuclear power plants in their own land.

These phenomena are the products of a lopsided development program in the present era which is western-oriented and not geared to the improvement of the practical life of the people. Those who indeed benefit are the multinational corporations, international money lenders, those who control technology, and those who collaborate with the powerful nations. The national authorities of these corporations justify their interests as national interests, while their own poor, let alone the Third-World poor, are increasing in number and degree of wretchedness and impoverishment.

The tenth commandment clearly states, "You shall not covet your neighbor's house; you shall not covet your neighbor's wife, or his manservant, or his maidservant, or his ox, or his ass, or anything that is the neighbor's property." Here the wife is treated in the same category as property. Feminists have pointed this out as being an expression of androcentrism in the Bible. But the Bible also forbids expropriation of the property of one's neighbors.

The violations of the forbidden tree are manifest in the concrete relationship between God and humans, and between humans and humans. The relationship can be individual or collective. In the prophetic writings, God judges the injustices committed by the rich and powerful against the weak and powerless. The prophets discern that God uses neighboring nations to punish the sins of the political and religious elite of Israel, because they were trespassing the boundary that God had set. The powerful were abusing their power by exploitative measures to satisfy their greed and to further oppress and impoverish the already poor.

The prophet Amos says,

> Thus says the LORD:
> For three transgressions of Judah,
>   and for four, I will not revoke the punishment;
> because they have rejected the law of the LORD
>   and have not kept his statutes,
> but their lies have led them astray by the same lies,
>   after which their fathers walked.
> So I will send a fire upon Judah,
>   and it shall devour the strongholds of Jerusalem.
> Thus says the LORD:
> For three transgressions of Israel
>   and for four, I will not revoke the punishment;
> because they sell the righteous for silver,
>   and the needy for a pair of shoes . . .
> they lay themselves down beside every altar
>   upon garments taken in pledge;
> and in the house of their God they drink
>   wine bought with fines they imposed (Am 2:4-6, 8).

Judah distributed the traditional family farms to the political merit-makers and turned the land into cash crop plantations for export. The farmers lost their land and had to work as hired hands for low wages in the grape or olive plantations. They could not make ends meet and many sold themselves and their sons and daughters as slaves. With the wealth they acquired in this way, the rich led extravagant and immoral lives. They even bought war instruments with the money they made from exporting wine and olive oil. As they acquired wealth they needed armaments to protect themselves, for they became the objects of envy by their neighbors.

In our meetings in Manila we shared our own stories. The stories were woven around big powers bullying small powers and the innocent suffering of people from small nations in international power politics. The stories of the suffering people caused by the greedy appetites of the lumber business people echo the stories of the suffering of the Korean people caused by the division of the country due to the military interest of the superpowers. The pain of battered wives, of people who are discriminated against due to racial or ethnic differences, and the anguish of all the poor and alienated people are all caused by the violation of the forbidden tree.

The fruits of the forbidden tree in today's world are numerous. They are the big powerful nations exploiting and dominating the small nations and the domestic political and economic powers controlling their own people. This and other kinds of abuse and misuse of power are rooted in the desire to be like God, the most powerful and authoritative being. In their dominant theology God is a dominating, self-centered being with unlimited power which is used in whatever way God may desire. For them the restrictions upon the forbidden tree which must be observed out of respect for others and for life itself is mere foolishness. Yet, the Christian gospel looks at worldly foolishness in a different manner. St. Paul says:

> . . . by means of the so-called "foolish" message we preach, God decided to save those who believe. Jews want miracles for proof, and Greeks look for wisdom. As for us, we proclaim the crucified Christ, a message that is offensive to the Jews and nonsense to the Gentiles; but for those whom God has called, both Jews and Greeks, this message is Christ, who is the power of God and wisdom of God. For what seems to be God's foolishness is wiser than human wisdom, and what seems to be God's weakness is stronger than human strength (1 Cor 1:21-25).

Grace of God Revealed in the Spirit of the Year of Jubilee— Leviticus 25:8-55

Freedom and restriction are entangled in human situations throughout history and in all cultures. The manifestations differ and how we tackle the situations also varies. We have seen the cause of sin as trespassing the boundaries of restrictions God has put in our relation to God and to other human beings. The desire to be like God, the desire to exploit and dominate others for individual as well as for collective self-interest is the origin of sin.

Because of sin the offended and victimized suffer. God does not desire them to be in the situation of unjust suffering. God's grace is revealed in the spirit of the Jubilee law. The year of Jubilee is mentioned in different places in the Old Testament. Leviticus 25:8-55, Isaiah 61:1-3, Isaiah 58:5-7 all talk about the year or the day of rejoicing of Yahweh, when the oppressed and exploited are freed from their bondage.

Leviticus 25:8-55 is the most detailed description of Jubilee. The year following seven sabbatical years, that is, the fiftieth year, is the year of Jubilee when all debts are forgiven and the land and houses that were lost are restored to the indebted to start a new life. To announce the good news all over Israel, the horn of a lamb was to be blown. The horn was called JOBEL so the Jubilee was also called the year of JOBEL.

The sound of the horn signified the great forgiveness, the liberation from oppression and suffering, the joy of recovering the original conditions through a respite. Therefore the time when the sound of the horn was heard was called in various ways, such as the "Year of Jobel," the "Year of Grace," and others.[6]

The main points in the Jubilee law are forbidding the permanent purchase and sale of land and houses, the demand for rest for the land and nature, just distribution of the produce of the land, lending money with no interest, and the liberation of servants and slaves.

The Israelites' concept of land is that land is the possession of Yahweh, and they are guests living on God's land. This attitude removed the notion of possession of land and made it possible to forbid the permanent sale and purchase of the land. The land from whence the source of life is drawn for the whole clan must be handed down to the clan for their survival. Everybody has the fundamental right to live because all lives are given and sustained by the Creator Godself.

In other words, the spirit of Jubilee was thanksgiving for the source of life and a proper response to the God of history who leads the whole humanity in justice and love. Freedom and restrictions on conduct between oneself and others are in a dialectical relation.

It is said that the law of Jubilee was never really implemented. But we see many embodiments of its spirit in various forms throughout history. The ministry of Jesus of Nazareth is the archetype of the actualization of the Jubilee. In the Gospel of Luke 4:18-19 we find the mission statement of Jesus:

> The Spirit of the Lord is upon me,
>   because he has anointed me to preach good news to the poor.
> He has sent me to proclaim release to the captives
>   and recovery of sight to the blind,
>   to set at liberty those who are oppressed,
> to proclaim the acceptable year of the Lord.

The year of the Lord is the Jubilee year when all those who had sold their land and houses because of financial crisis, thereby cutting off their means of livelihood, are restored to their source of life. It is indeed a new life for the poor, the captives, the blind and the oppressed.

In the biblical vision, the acceptable year of the Lord is when God's rule is established and the source of life is open to everybody. Then there will be no poor, no hungry, no physically and spiritually deformed, no captives in prison, and none who are oppressed, for whatever reason, in the nation and in the world. Then real peace in the world can be a reality.

This sounds too good to be true. But if more and more people are convinced and try to implement the acceptable year of the Lord through wise visions and policies that will allow people and nature to survive, the God of life will be on the side of the movement for life to bless and increase its force. This is our confession of faith. The women's movement and all other renewal movements focus on the supremacy of life. I believe this is the work of the Holy Spirit.

The year of the Jubilee will require the grateful acceptance on the part of the victimized and repentance on the part of the aggressors. Repentance in Greek is *metanoia* which means "to turn back." It is a concrete action of straightening up all the unjust relations and making them right.[7] And it must bear fruit. John the Baptist said to the multitudes that came out to be baptized by him,

> You brood of vipers! Who warned you to flee from the wrath to come? Bear fruit that befits repentance and do not begin to say to yourselves, "We have Abraham as our father," for I tell you, God is able from these stones to raise up children to Abraham. Even now the axe is laid to the root of the trees; every tree therefore that does not bear good fruit is cut down and thrown into the fire (Lk 3:7-9).

Jürgen Moltmann writes in *Theology of Hope* that there are sins of offense and sins of despair. If we plunge ourselves into the state of despair, overwhelmed by the reality of sinfulness, we are also committing the sin of despair.[8] In fact, all of us have to go through repentance vis-à-vis the vision of the prophetic tradition of the Old Testament in hope for the reign of God that Jesus Christ announced in his proclamation and concretized in his ministries of restoration to life. Jesus lived the hope in his life and death that led him to be the first fruits of the resurrection.

John rebuked all those who came out for baptism. Among them must have been some Pharisees who were afterwards the active opponents of Jesus' ministry. However, most of them must have been the *Oklos*, the exploited and oppressed masses of the day. Then why such a terrible rebuke? Perhaps John was angered by their condition of despair and use of the rhetoric of faith as an excuse for noninvolvement in the coming reign of God.

And what about the Christian church today? The church can be an instrument for maintaining the status quo, if it is happy just to jump on the bandwagon. Or the church can sink into the mentality of despair, using the rhetoric of faith in its faithlessness. Or it can be the instrument to fulfill the spirit of Jubilee in our own reality, if we sincerely repent of both sides of the one coin named "sin."

Real repentance must bear concrete fruits. The church has the advantage of working with a large constituency. One of the church's functions is education. What we teach and how we teach are important considerations. One example we can mention is the Vietnam war. It would not have ended at the stage it did if the American people had kept quiet. Of course, the best alternative would have been no war at all, and a peaceful solution which the nation could have chosen with a higher level of consciousness in the people, if that had been the reality then. What needs to be emphasized here is the importance of the church's role in influencing opinion and action.

When the church talks about action for change we mean both short-term and long-term actions. Both of them stem from the spirit of justice and the Jubilee. The spirit of justice is the moving force both for short-term and long-term actions of renewal. It provides the historical continuity for the various manifestations of the claims of justice which a particular historical period and culture stand for. And the spirit of Jubilee provides visions for actions of justice. Now is the time to anticipate a new vision. In the beginning, in the midst of darkness and confusion, the God of creation gave birth to light, life, and the sustaining order for creation. Thus the vision of the Creator became reality. Now is the time for the visions of human creatures to be realized in the spirit of the year of Jubilee.

Conclusion

Many fruits of the forbidden tree have been violated in today's world, and the powers of death hover in the polluted air of the whole universe. However, we also hear the horn of the Jubilee blowing loud among us as we experience the Christ event happening even today. Let us turn the forces that have restricted us from being active channels of love to our neighbors into regenerative forces for holistic freedom for the poor, deprived, alienated, and discriminated against to enjoy the God-given rights to life. Every individual and every group of human beings, whatever his/her identity in terms of nation, race, sex, religion, must participate in the stewardship of God's creation as mature and authentic partners of God and of each other. Then nature and all creation shall be liberated and placed under the reign of the Creator God, so that they will be able to function as lifegivers, and not as the agents of deathgiving forces acting in revenge against the irresponsible and unjust exploitation of their stewards. In short, the Spirit of the year of Jubilee means the liberation of all creatures from their victimization by the dominating powers of death.

With the coming of the year of Jubilee our eyes shall look upon the fruits of the forbidden tree with adoration and thanksgiving for their beautiful presence which enriches our understanding about what it really means to respect and love different kinds of human beings and creatures in the natural world. Then the forbidden tree will neither be a temptation, nor a curse and source of death.

Notes

1. This Bible study was presented to the conference "U.S. Involvement in the Pacific Rim," sponsored jointly by the Presbyterian Church in the U.S.A. and the United Church of Christ in the Philippines, May 1991, in Manila, Philippines.

2. Phyllis Trible, *God and the Rhetoric of Sexuality* (Philadelphia: Fortress Press, 1978), pp. 17-18.

3. *Chosun Daily*, December 12, 1991.

4. *New World Information and Communication Order*, p. 292.

5. Ibid.

6. *Women Preparing the Year of Joy: Women and Year of Jubilee 1995, Year of Reunification of the Country*, ed., Women's Commission of the National Council of Churches in Korea (Seoul, Korea, 1991), p. 17.

7. Ibid., p. 32.

8. Jürgen Moltmann, *Theology of Hope* (New York: Harper & Row, 1967), pp. 19-25.

PART 3

AFRICA

The essays on ecofeminism in Africa bring together several religious and cultural perspectives, both from white Christian and Muslim viewpoints in South Africa and from Black African perspectives that focus on indigenous religious world views and practices.

Denise Ackermann is a Christian feminist theologian and a professor of practical theology at the University of the Western Cape in Bellville, South Africa. Tahira Joyner is a Muslim feminist who is completing a second Master's degree in the area of Religious Studies and works as a psychiatric nurse in Capetown, South Africa. Writing from white middle-class Christian and Muslim contexts, Ackermann and Joyner note the ways in which both Christianity and Islam enshrine a patriarchal world view in which the domination of God over creation models the social hierarchies of male over female, white over black, rich over poor and ultimately the right of the ruling class white male elite to rule over and exploit nature.

Christianity is the majority religion in South Africa and includes all classes and races. Thus it is a basic grassroots organization that could be a major actor for environmental justice.

Although some South African churches played a key role in the struggle against apartheid, environmental destruction and its intimate link with poverty and racial discrimination is yet to be recognized adequately. The churches in South Africa have yet to assume leadership on this issue and to acknowledge either their own complicity in environmental degradation or their potential power in teaching for environmental healing.

Some individual women have taken leadership in the struggle for environmental protection, such as Tsepho Khumbane in reforestation and water resources in the Transvaal, and Nan Rice in protection of dolphins and other sea mammals in the Cape coast area. The most important mobilization of the churches for environmental protection in South Africa has taken place in Zimbabwe, where M. L. Daneel, a Christian scholar of the African Indigenous Churches, founded ZIRRCON (Zimbabwean Institute of Religious Research and Ecological Conservation) and helped develop the Association of African Earthkeeping

Churches (AAEC). There is the beginning of extending this work of environmental protection by African Indigenous Churches to South Africa.

The AAEC is a fascinating example of the symbiosis of Christian and indigenous African cosmology applied to practical restoration of the environment.
Using the New Testament vision of creation as the Body of Christ through
whom "all things hold together" (Col 1:17), as well as Shona beliefs that the
ancestors become spirits of the land, protecting it and causing drought when
their laws are violated, the AAEC in Zimbabwe has developed earth-planting
eucharists. In these eucharistic services communities confess their sins of over-
exploiting the land; they follow the reception of forgiveness and communion
with tree-planting. Preservation of water supplies and sustainable agriculture
are also promoted by these church communities.[1]

Tahira Joyner sees positive resources in Islam for both a gender-inclusive
view of God and an egalitarian view of male-female relations. Islam also contains much the same understanding of the human as given usufruct and not
ownership of the earth, commanded to be steward and protector of nature, but
not exploiter, that Jewish and Christian environmental theologians have noted
in the Hebrew Scriptures. Yet, like Judaism and Christianity, Islam has failed to
incorporate these insights into its own practice, although some young South
African Muslims, such as the Call of Islam, have taken the lead in advocating
Islamic principles for gender equality and environmental action. Thus both
Christianity and Islam in South Africa await a deeper renewal of their traditions
to take seriously the challenge of feminism and ecojustice.

Sara Mvududu is a sociologist who works in environmental protection and
gender issues with the Women and Law in Southern Africa Research Project in
Harare, Zimbabwe. In her essay on traditional woodlands management and gender she combines several perspectives. From the perspective of feminist sociol-
ogy she details how the disabilities of gender found in traditional Shona patriarchal culture combined with the racial patriarchal views brought by the British
colonialists to put rural Zimbabwe women in a difficult position. Yet Shona
customs that are still very much alive in the countryside enshrine patterns of
women's leadership as spiritual mediums in environmental protection. These
are being revived and utilized today to plant trees and protect water resources.

Environmentalists tend to look at such rural women in Africa through three
lenses: as victims, villains and fixers. African women are seen as the most victimized sector of the exploited rural society, but also those who through their
childbearing, wood and water gathering and agriculture contribute to over-population, soil erosion, deforestation and drought. Projects of environmental education aimed at rural African women often see them as no more than free or
cheap labor for protecting material resources or as "problems" whose fertility
and tree cutting should be curbed.

Mvududu argues for a deeper respect for rural women's knowledge of the
environment. She advocates a fuller empowerment of rural women, through a
combination of renewed traditional culture and modern rights to have access to
land, education, legal rights and agricultural credit, that can allow them to be

proactive agents in environmental sustainability.

Tumani Nyajeka is an ordained Methodist elder and is completing her doctoral studies in issues of women, religion and ecology in Zimbabwe in the Joint Program in Religious and Theological Studies of Garrett-Evangelical Theological Seminary and Northwestern University in Evanston, Illinois. She is teaching in religious and African studies at Berea College in Berea, Kentucky.

Her essay on Shona women and the *Mutupo* principle reveals the cosmology that stands behind the mobilization of spirit mediums for environmental protection found in the African Earth-Keeping Churches and discussed in Sara Mvududu's essay.

Nyajeka shows that traditional Shona cosmology carefully balanced aquatic and terrestrial powers in its world view and social practices, such as intermarriage. It taught a covenantal interdependence between humans and the animal world, each of which relies on the other for health and protection. As Tumani describes it, the Shona world view is earth-centered, and even animal-centered, rather than anthropocentric, as in Western culture and religions. Patterns of sacrality and taboos preserved fragile and vulnerable elements in the human and natural communities.

In Shona cosmology, not only are God and humans, male and female, human and animals, the living, the dead and the yet-to-be born interconnected, but there is a fluid interchange between them that prevents complementarity from falling into dualism. This cosmology can be a fertile source for the development of a renewed ecological cosmology to respond to the current environmental and social challenges created by western colonialism.

Isabel Apawo Phiri is a lecturer in the Department of Theology at Chancellor College in Zomba, Malawi. Her essay on women and the Chisumphi cult in Malawi adds a concrete case study of a particular territorial rain-making and earth-keeping cult to the insights found in Mvududu and Nyajeka concerning the potential role of indigenous spirituality and practices for environmental protection. The Chisumphi cult is traditionally led by women who are seen as "spirit-wives" of the deity. As keepers of the shrine they lead the village in rain-making and first-fruit thanksgiving ceremonies. They also are charged with protecting the sacred groves and pools in the area of the shrine.

However, both traditional discrimination against women which limits their activities through pollution taboos and the cultural disruption and exploitation brought by colonialism prevent these traditional practices from becoming adequately effective in meeting current threats to the land, forests and waters. Phiri suggests that these traditional cults can be more fully useful for environmental protection when the traditional patterns of discrimination against women are lessened, and when the implicit environmental ethic in the cult is redeveloped to respond to the new situation.

Teresia Hinga was a senior lecturer in the Department of Religious Studies of Kenyatta University in Nairobi, Kenya. She is currently lecturing in religious studies at De Paul University in Chicago, Illinois. Her essay focuses on land and landlessness in Africa, using Kenya as a case study. Hinga shows how disregard for the traditional environmental ethics by the colonialists and the substitution of a colonial ethic of domination led to massive landlessness for Kenyan people, as well as impoverishment of the quality of land available to them. Because of this double form of landlessness, many other problems have developed, such as ethnic clashes and internal refugees. She particularly focuses on the implications of land loss and land impoverishment for women.

Hinga concludes by pointing toward a reconstructed theology and ethic of land from the Kenyan Gikuyu tradition. There is a need to recover some of the lost values and ideas about the relationship between human beings and nature if Kenyan people in particular, and all people in and beyond Africa, are to come to grips adequately with the contemporary environmental crisis. Thus, like Mvududu, Nyajeka and Phiri in the African section, as well as several authors in the Asian and Latin American sections of this volume, a recovery of indigenous spirituality is seen as key to recreating a holistic ecojustice world view and practice.

Notes

1. M. L. Daneel, "African Independent Churches Face the Challenge of Environmental Ethics," in David Hallman, ed., *Ecotheology: Voices from South and North* (Maryknoll, NY: Orbis Books and Geneva: World Council of Churches, 1994), pp. 248-263.

11

Earth-Healing in South Africa

Challenges to Church and Mosque

DENISE ACKERMANN and TAHIRA JOYNER

South African history has been characterized by patterns of domination—white over black, rich over poor, men over women and human beings over nature. The legacy of the apartheid years confronts us with enormous divides, paradoxes and tensions. The disparate realms of ghetto and green belt[1] epitomize the fundamental inequities that exist side by side within our social fabric. In its juxtaposition of first- and third-world environmental problems and its ingrained patriarchal attitudes, South Africa is a microcosm of the environmental time bomb threatening our planet.

We are a society critically in need of healing in every aspect of our relationships: with ourselves, with one another, with God, and most urgently, with the earth. The majority of South Africans are familiar with the unrelenting relationship between social injustice and poverty. Alarmingly few, however, understand the link between the abuse of the environment and our history of social injustice. South Africa has no mass-based environmental movement. This is the challenge facing our fledgling democracy,[2] but it is one we dare not leave solely in the hands of politicians.

Against this background, we write as white, middle-class feminists, one a Christian theologian and the other a Muslim. We acknowledge our positions of privilege among the voices from the South. We share a passion for the preservation of our natural environment, one which is particularly blessed with great beauty and awesome variety,[3] yet also one which is bloodied by the systematic oppression of people and permeated with patriarchal values and structures.

The Legacies of Patriarchal Apartheid

In South Africa, sociologist and environmental activist Jacklyn Cock points out, environmental issues are deeply and fundamentally political.[4] The abuse of the environment and the imbalance of the distribution of male-dominated political power over centuries are intimately connected. The reactionary and authoritarian conservation policies of the apartheid era, epitomized in the establishment of numbers of game reserves for the privileged minority, often at the expense of dislocation for local people, have left a legacy of hostility and suspicion among many South Africans.

Deliberate policies of social engineering have had disastrous ecological consequences in our land. The "homeland" policies based on the ideology of "separate development" crammed millions of black South Africans either into impoverished, remote, barren reserves which were dependent on the Republic for economic survival, or into township ghettos. In addition, capital-intensive agriculture has resulted in mass eviction of farm dwellers from their land and homes. In the rural areas, the ever present specter of drought combined with overgrazing has produced erosion.[5] Trees have disappeared as poor people sought fuel.[6] In the informal settlements around the major cities, overcrowding, lack of basic facilities,[7] inadequate housing and air pollution cause further ecological hazards.[8]

Despite a developed mining, industrial, agricultural and commercial infrastructure, poverty is the greatest social reality in our country. Income distribution is racially distorted and notorious for being one of the most unequal in the world.[9] As Albie Sachs comments, addressing poverty requires more than simply increasing the disposable income of the poor. It involves the extension of utilities to all South Africans. The right to water, heat, light, waste disposal and communication facilities is basic to any environmental program, not simply because it saves streams, or reduces disease, but because people have a human right to enjoy such services.[10]

Poverty and rapid population growth are seen as going hand in hand. Injunctions by white government officials to the mothers of the "white" nation to breed, while launching programs for birth control for underprivileged women, have left a legacy of deep suspicion among the black population. Furthermore, ecologically inspired pronouncements on population control are often viewed with suspicion in Africa. Africans know that it is not the babies of underdeveloped peoples who threaten the world's ecology, but rather those born to well-off first-world parents. As Harald Coward points out, it is the first-world child the world can least afford. "The first-world child will, due to excessive consumption, have thirty times the environmental impact of a third-world child."[11] Ironically, while the apartheid-driven Population Development Programme aimed to decrease population growth, apartheid promoted high fertility by fragmenting families through policies of influx control which undermined the social values that limited children out of wedlock.

The under-regulated activities of local and transnational corporations have severely degraded environmental resources and resulted in hazardous pollution[12] and toxic waste[13] in our country. The misuse of fertilizers and pesticides,[14] dangerous mining practices[15] and inadequate monitoring of substances have claimed the lives of numerous workers and placed many others at risk.[16]

South Africa's "destabilization" of frontline states cost one and one-half million lives and sixty billion dollars between 1980 and 1990.[17] Military operations decimated large tracts of the environment,[18] while rogue elements in the military slaughtered elephants and set up conduits for the illegal sale of ivory.

According to the Worldwatch Institute, white South Africans are the world's worst greenhouse offenders. The point made is that if energy consumption patterns reflect income distribution, then the white population's per capita carbon emission stands at more than nine tons in 1987 while the world average was one ton.[19] Ultimately, the lesson of apartheid's ecological toll is that inequitable social institutions are incompatible with environmental sustainability.[20]

In the past, conservation projects have often negated human rights and dignity, thus alienating many South Africans. A dangerous parallel between environmental and women's issues developed and they were both frequently dismissed as bourgeois and divisive.[21] Yet, as we have seen, environmental and feminist issues are profoundly political, embedded in a mass of other issues relating to the distribution of power and resources in South Africa. As Farieda Khan observes, the most challenging task facing environmental nongovernmental organizations is the widening of their support base in order to make these issues meaningful to all South Africans.[22]

Section twenty-nine of our new constitution reads: "Every person shall have the right to an environment which is not detrimental to his or her health or well-being."[23] Such a constitutional stipulation is to be welcomed. It has also been argued that two strengths of the African National Congress in regard to environmental policy are its "ready grassroots connection and a well-developed sense of what is environmentally correct, based on its strong international diplomatic structures."[24] The government's Reconstruction and Development Programme promises to develop strategies which will respect the environment. Despite this commitment, however, the sheer size of the project and its daunting demands on resources, "casts a deep shadow over the proposal that all developments should be preceded by environmental impact assessments."[25]

For the South African environmental movement to succeed, the growth of a strong nongovernmental sector is both essential and urgent. The pressing challenge is for nongovernmental organizations (NGOs) to come together and build a constructive and supportive relationship between themselves, labor movements and the State. Yet it is imperative that environmental NGOs and religious communities continually challenge the government to implement its high ideals and ensure that environmental legislation achieves its objectives.

The impact of environmental deterioration on women's lives is profound. It is, therefore, not strange that women should be the first to protest against environmental destruction. For such protests to be translated into a country-wide movement in which women, irrespective of class, race or ethnicity, come together, we need to articulate and respect our differences and find our common need to resuscitate and nurture all living things. Finding common ground is not easy. An ecofeminist perspective which speaks of connectedness and the wholeness of theory and practice should offer women in South Africa common ground. But the very term "ecofeminism" is relatively unknown or misunderstood. An ecofeminist perspective which expresses the need to conserve the fundamental necessities of life, and which is "rooted in the everyday subsistence production of most of the world's women"[26] is about survival. It has a better chance of addressing our present environmental crisis than one which is divorced from the material.

As feminist women concerned with earth-healing, it is clear to us that patriarchal dominance bolstered by classist and racist attitudes is not compatible with caring for and about creation. In the light of the above remarks, we ask: To what extent are our faith traditions part of the problem and do they have the potential of sustaining an ecofeminist perspective?

Green Christians?

Over seventy percent of South Africans claim to be Christians.[27] Jacklyn Cock believes[28] that the church in South Africa "has an organized space at grassroots level which could promote environmental literacy . . . and be an important source for the 'new ethic' that some environmentalists are calling for."[29]

Can we pin our hopes for earth-healing on the church? At first glance this seems highly improbable. The male leadership of Christian institutions in South Africa has, thus far, not attempted to raise awareness among church members of the World Council of Churches' concern in regard to the relationship between "justice, peace and the integrity of creation." Cock's probing analysis of church documents and resolutions reveals a deafening silence on environmental issues.[30] Unfortunately this lack of interest has its roots deep in the Christian tradition itself, a pathology we share with Christianity worldwide.

As many feminist theologians have pointed out, hierarchical views of creation in which man is God's agent, minding the earth which was created for the well-being of himself and his dependents, has afforded ruling-class men unbridled license to exercise their "dominion" over all human and nonhuman forms of life. This chain of command from God to man, to animals to inanimate objects, is replicated in human relations, men over women, rich over poor, white over black, able-bodied over disabled, heterosexual over homosexual, and so on. In such a hierarchical and dualistic world view, difference is not seen as a gift but as a threat. The interdependence of all living things is simply not understood and injustice and rapaciousness continue.

Does this mean that the church should be abandoned as a player in the compelling and critical task of earth-healing? I think not. Cock is correct. As long as the majority of South Africans are in some way or other church-related, the church remains an important source for ecological reform. The church is part of what Cock calls "the rainbow coalition" of green politics. Together with the trade unions, community organizations, environmental groups and state agencies, the church is an agent in fostering the mass environmental awareness so desperately needed in South Africa. How can an ecofeminist practical theological approach challenge the church to revise its doctrines and its practices in order to be an effective member of this rainbow alliance?

Practical theology has been understood as the area of theology which deals with the active "doing" dimensions of faith. The acts of celebrating, teaching, preaching, ministering, counseling and praying traditionally constitute its field of study. Feminist practical theology focuses on women's actions, what these actions communicate, what theories underlie these actions, what impediments are placed in the way of women acting and how these actions reflect justice, wholeness and freedom. An ecofeminist practical theology in South Africa is thus concerned with the actions of women who seek healing, liberation and well-being for themselves, their families and their communities in restored environments.

The critical emphasis here is on women's participation in earth-healing praxis. Earth-healing praxis is directed at restoring relationships between ourselves and all created life, and is infused by a spirituality which reverences the sacredness of all of creation.

Earth-healing praxis requires an understanding of the interconnectedness of the different manifestations of violence. The violences of poverty, of racism, sexism and classism, of social dislocation, of militarism, of battering and rape are not unrelated to the violence against the environment. They are all rooted in the abuse of power as domination over and exploitation of "the other." Women have been particularly vulnerable in this context of violence. They have, however, discovered ways of resistance as strategies for personal and political survival and solidarity. The stories of women's resistance to the desecration of the earth, the subjective knowledge of women who have practiced survival for decades, become the starting point for earth-healing praxis.

In the South African context there are many stories of women's environmental activism.[31] There is the moving tale of Tsepho Khumbane. In the drought-stricken northern Transvaal she coordinated women from thirty-one scattered villages in a tree-planting exercise over a period of five years. Sadly, due to lack of water, few trees survived. Undeterred, Khumbane has turned to tackling the water problem because she knows that tree-planting is a priority if soil erosion is to be controlled and if people are to have fuel. This will require a great deal of cooperation between local communities. "But I don't think it's so hopeless nothing can be done. We only want the chief to say yes. With permission we will mobilize the whole community. And once we have that water, there will be a green carpet."[32]

Then there is the story of the indomitable Nan Rice. Through her Dolphin Action and Protection Group she has for over twenty years been involved in education about and protection and conservation of whales, dolphins and porpoises. Her experience many years ago of witnessing 200 dolphins being hauled out of surf nets near her home on the Cape coast changed her life. Today Rice is an accepted authority on pirate whaling and has submitted reports to the International Whaling Commission and the United States Senate Enquiry.

Her campaign against the atrocious use of gill nets has had unexpected results. When she focused on Taiwanese tuna fishermen who were robbing South African waters, the appalling working conditions of their South African crews were exposed. As a result, Rice has become a consultant to the Food and Allied Workers Union, who, in turn, have become allies in the battle against gill-netting. "There are ways and means. You must have the aims and objectives sorted out before you campaign and if you stick to them it's very easy . . . . When I look back over twenty-one years, I can see that I've achieved an enormous amount with the group. We have credibility all over the world—the word has definitely spread."[33]

Stories such as these (and there are many stories of courageous and persevering efforts of women and men for environmental concerns) show how the awareness of certain women gave birth to different kinds of earth-healing praxis. An ecofeminist practical theological approach draws on such stories in shaping liturgies, in preaching and in ministering. Teaching children the gospel stories, for instance, takes on a new guise and a new urgency when they are told in the context of the sacredness of all creation and the need to respect and preserve it. Our songs, prayers, rituals and symbols can become vehicles for affirming the sacredness of all creation. Ecological awareness and earth-healing praxis must become so commonplace that they become integral to all our acts of private and public worship, as well as focal to our acts of justice and charity.

A further story illustrates how the church can be a vehicle for "spreading the word" that the earth is critically in need of healing and that people of faith are called to be agents in transforming destructive patterns into sustainable ones.

This is M. L. Daneel's story of how an indigenous environmental revolution is taking place in which women are playing a major role. The understanding that subsistence is the key to survival and that subsistence means covering the earth with trees, trees for fodder, trees for rain, trees to shade the earth, trees for fruit and trees for fuel, lies at the heart of this story.[34]

The traditional deep affinity for the earth in Africa, based on an essentially religious understanding of the universe, is vividly illustrated by the African Initiated Churches' (AICs) program of tree planting in Zimbabwe.[35] Here the AICs are not producing environmental literature.

They are proclaiming a widening message of salvation which encompasses all of creation and they are dancing out a new rhythm in their services of worship which, in the footwork, spells hope for the ravaged earth. They have not worked out a new ethic on paper but they are "clothing the earth" (*kufukidza nyika*) with new trees to cover its human-induced nakedness. In so doing they have introduced a new ministry of compassion; they live an earthkeeper's ethic. In declaring the so-called "war of the trees" an ecumenical platform was created in order to unite the churches in a green army and to launch environmental reform in terms of creation's liberation. In the new struggle ecclesiastical structures are changing, new perceptions of ecological responsibility are emerging and innovative liturgical procedures to integrate the environmental ethic with the heartbeat of church praxis, are being introduced.[36]

The AAEC (Association of African Earthkeeping Churches) formed in 1991 promotes afforestation, the conservation of wildlife, and the protection of water resources.[37] The founders have all agreed that these objectives are undergirded by a divine mandate which has resulted in the celebration of tree-planting eucharists.[38]

The AICs express a predominantly peasant ecumenism which rests on a common commitment to the healing of the earth. Popularly they have been seen as healing, liberative institutions, with their history of prophetic healers and their support of the struggle for liberation (*chimurenga*). Now the focus has shifted to their role in the healing of suffering creation. Prophets are turning their healing colonies into "environmental hospitals" in which the patient is the denuded earth, the "dispensary" is the nursery where the correct medicine is being prepared, and the community is the healing agent.[39]

The African Indigenous Churches of South Africa, which include about 6,000 movements, have a combined membership of some fifty percent of the black population and are geographically widespread, spanning virtually the entire country. Recent initiatives indicate that a start has been made to mobilize AICs in the cause of the environment in South Africa.[40] Can African traditions of reverence for the earth offer a starting point for what Daneel calls "a massive green movement . . . [which could] have a decisive impact on the environmental future of this country"?[41]

Most Christians in South Africa, whether they are members of the AICs or of the "mainline" churches,[42] live in circumstances which are ecologically hazardous. For a mass-based environmental consciousness to emerge from large sections of the Christian church, a change of consciousness on the part of Christians is required. Stories have the power to change people's awareness and produce an earth-healing praxis.

Christians can become green once we understand and believe that the earth is God's and that we, as part of this fragile interdependent chain of life, have the potential to destroy it irrevocably or to help it survive and even flourish. We believe that God so loved the world that the drama of Jesus' life and death took place. We believe that the good news offers us a vision of healing and wholeness. Sadly, we have understood our faith in such a human-centered way that we have lost sight of the holistic vision of creation and salvation.

Ecofeminist practical theology finds the key in the interdependent nature of our relationships. Jesus taught us that we must love God with all our "heart, mind and strength" and our neighbor as ourselves (Mk 12). We have not understood that to love God implies treating God's creation with loving care. Love of neighbor has everything to do with lifestyle. An unjust economic order based on greed and indifference is hardly an expression of neighborly love. Justice and love are inseparable dimensions of our relationships, which rest on an understanding of the interdependent nature of all of creation. An ethic of interdependence requires a transformation of consciousness among people who live in the developed world that leads to giving up excessive consumption with its accompanying effects of domination and exploitation.

The legacies of our corrupt and divided past are realities we live with every day. Apartheid has violated our environment. We also live with the memory of our peaceful transition to democracy. For a short but precious period we experienced peacemaking praxis. Then we understood our interdependence in our diversity. The church played a significant role in this miracle. Having survived the important first round, the challenge now is to survive the ultimate challenge, to rescue our land from environmental destruction for ourselves and our children.

Green Christians can contribute in great measure to this task. Our survival is inescapably dependent on our cooperation across all former and present barriers for the saving of the earth. Ecofeminist practical theology points the way to developing awareness through the stories of earth-healing praxis expressed through the many actions of people in their communities of faith.

Green Muslims?

Whenever Muslims begin anything, we seek Allah's blessing thus: "*Bies'miel'laahier Rah'maanier Rahiem*" or "I begin with the name of Allah, Who is Most Compassionate, Most Merciful." The nouns *compassion* and *mercy* are derived from the word *rahim*, a feminine root noun meaning womb. It is, therefore, ironic that Allah is always referred to and revered as a male force. The primary metaphor for Allah is accordingly maternal. Implicit is the analogy between womb and macrocosm so that severing oneself from Nature is tantamount to cutting oneself off from Allah.[43] Despite this fundamental identification of Allah with the feminine, and the obvious fact that Allah transcends the splitting of being into male and female and is essentially beyond gender, the culture and faith of Islam have always imaged Allah as a male force.

The use of exclusively male-defined imagery and pronouns, as well as the role misogynistic symbols and stories play in perpetuating the institutionalized sexism in Islam, remain primarily uncritiqued. Almost all Muslims argue passionately that the language used is generic, that the terms "men" and "brethren" include women. However, streams of contemporary feminist theory have proved that language is a subtle, insidious and highly effective vehicle for socio-cultural and religious ideology.[44] In many circles it is now understood that the way women have been living, the way we have been led to imagine ourselves and the way our language has trapped us, are all consequences of the fact that the very act of naming has been a male prerogative.[45]

The historical exclusion of women from the priesthood and the domination of women by men within the family are the inevitable consequences of a religion in which maleness is seen as the only adequate symbol for Divinity and all spiritual authority rests with men. This explicit devaluing of female spiritual potential reflects how, despite a liberating motif within the original Qur'anic spirit, centuries of Muslim women have been taught a markedly inferior and often profoundly self-hating self-understanding by the very leaders and teachers that our religion demands us to respect. These cultural gender-based power imbalances are reinforced regularly in the language, rhetoric and teachings of the weekly sermons, prayers and festival occasions.

Herstory was made on August 12, 1994 when a mosque in Cape Town invited Amina Wadud-Muhsin, an Islamic theologian at Virginia University and author of *Qur'an and Woman*,[46] to deliver the sermon before the *juma'ah* prayers. The broader Muslim community responded venomously. The Muslim Judicial Council decried the precedent in the severest terms, people picketed and protested in the streets and the imam received a number of death threats.

The tragedy is that the mosques are potentially an extremely powerful tool for promoting sensitivity to issues of gender and ecology. A group of dynamic young Muslims have worked in an interfaith context in Ecoprogram, a subgrouping of both the "Call of Islam" and the "World Conference for Religion and Peace." They have produced a number of well-researched and clearly laid out Eco-Fact Sheets which have been distributed at mosques in Cape Town. Yet only a handful of imams across the land are challenging the community about the Qur'anic injunctions that the status of humanity is that of the *khalifah*, Allah's vice-regent on earth (Surah 2:30). As Merryl Davies points out, since all men and women are *khalifah* there should be a basic equality in their rights of access to, responsibility for and enjoyment of the bounties of earthly existence.[47]

Furthermore, the substance of humanity's vice-regency over the earth is primarily that of trust. A strong Qur'anic trajectory provides the following motif: "Verily, we did offer the trust (of reason and volition) to the heavens and the earth, and the mountains: but they refused to hear it because they were afraid of it. Yet man took it up—for, verily, he has always been prone to be most wicked, most foolish" (Surah 33:72).

Davies discusses how the import of this verse demands an integrated understanding of the repeated Qur'anic injunction that humanity must reflect on how neglect of spiritual truths is a recurrent human characteristic.[48] Clearly the well-being of all life on earth has intrinsic value, and it seems therefore that the trust, *ammanah*, that Allah invested in humanity was to sustain this richness and diversity, honoring our part within the wholeness of life and taking from it only in order to satisfy essential needs.

As the scholar Al-Hafiz Masri points out, early Muslims regarded all elements of nature such as land, air, water, fire, sunlight, forests as the common property of all creatures.[49] Abu al-Faraj, an early Muslim legal scholar, argues: "People do not in fact own things, for the real owner is their Creator: they only enjoy the usufruct of things, subject to the Divine Law."[50] Indeed, Surah 7:31 clearly teaches how these resources should be used: "Eat and drink, but waste not by indulging in excesses; surely, Allah does not approve of the intemperate."

The Qur'an clearly indicates that the term *khalifah* is relational and thus a vital ecofeminist task is to examine and critique how these relations are defined. The Qur'an repeatedly insists that the trust implied is a privilege balanced by duties, and not an absolute right of ownership, usage and disposal of the physical environment and all it contains. Davies argues that *khalifah* is the definition of a usufruct, a stewardship which operates at two levels. The first is between each human, regardless of caste, class, color, creed or sex, as steward, and Allah, the omniscient and omnipotent. The second is at the generational level, with crucial responsibilities within and between each generation.[51]

Despite the quality of this vision, a blatantly misogynistic theological anthropology undercuts it dramatically. It is highly arguable that dehumanizing theological anthropologies have legitimized a gross insensitivity to the essential relatedness of all forms of life. Significantly, the ground-breaking work of Carol Gilligan clearly exposes how, as the traditional caretakers, women easily identify with others, value people's feelings, and tend to base moral codes on the good of the entire group.[52] Given the primacy attributed to interconnectedness, a common motif within ecofeminist theory is that the innate understanding of the workings of the community within essentially female values offers the best means for achieving the transformation of consciousness necessary for the survival of the planet.

The imaging within the Islamic faith tradition of men as the kingpin of creation and the assumption that it is their right to dominate all flies in the face of the challenge which Allah has posed humanity to honor with integrity our role as earth stewards. Surah 14:32-3 reads: "It is Allah who . . . has made the rivers subservient to you; and has made the sun and the moon, both of them constant upon their courses subservient to you; and has made the night and the day subservient to you."

Moreover, the Qur'an not only states that women are inferior to men but endorses violence against us. Surah 4:34 reads: "Men shall take full care of women with the bounties which Allah has bestowed more abundantly on the former than the latter . . . and as for those women whose ill-will you have reason to fear, admonish them (first); then leave them alone in bed; then beat them; and if thereupon they pay you heed, do not seek to harm them."

The realization that the absence of respect for women's lives and for the fragile and pristine beauty of creation is written into the heart of male theological doctrine, into the structure of the patriarchal family, and into the very language of patriarchal ethics, has not yet dawned within South African Muslim women's awareness. According to Harrison, the most plausible explanation for this is that language functions "either to reproduce and reinforce existing social relations, thereby teaching us the legitimacy of what is given, or to enable imaginative reappropriation or transcendence of the given."[53] Language either reproduces or reshapes our social reality.

Within the tradition of Islamic faith the value and meaning of our God-given opportunity to be the caretakers of the earth has somehow been poisoned and undercut by a misogynistic ideological framework of dominance and control: "Your wives are your farms; go, then, unto your farm as you may desire, but first provide something for your souls" (Surah 2:223).

The prevalent popular belief is that the value of women resides almost solely in an ability to procreate and this within the tightly structured institution of marriage where the oldest male is head of the household and extended family. Consider, for example, this teaching from the Mujlisul-Ulama of Port Elizabeth, South Africa: "Some husbands believe that by marriage they have gained a free servant—in fact a slave . . . . A great cause for the breakdown of husband/wife relationship and the moral ruin of the children is to take the wife out of her natural home-keeping role . . . it is beyond her natural physical and mental capabilities to act out the role of both man and woman . . . . By subjecting the wife to this unjust and unlawful imposition, the home is neglected and the Divine Law of Hijab is flagrantly violated. The Wrath of Allah Ta'ala overtakes the home."[54]

This sex-role stereotyped socio-cultural straitjacket renders Islam a religion equally responsible for the imposition of unsustainable development on the planet and for perpetuating from generation to generation a grotesque imbalance between men and women. Ours is a culture of tremendous violence against women—mentally, emotionally, physically and sexually.

Inspired by Christine Downing, I am arguing that when the divine is imaged exclusively as male, women are denied the full dignity and possibility of human potential that sacred symbols represent for men. In her words: "To be fed only male images of the divine is to be badly malnourished. We are starved for images which recognize the sacredness of the feminine and the complexity, richness, and nurturing power of female energy."[55]

The planet is groaning under the strain of anthropocentric attitudes which seriously devalue women and nature. The urgency of our spiritual responsibility to assume our role as *khalifah* is denied at our peril. As custodians of contemporary culture we need to develop images which identify as authentically feminine—courage, creativity, self-confidence, resilience, loyalty, the capacity for passion, clear insight and solitude.[56] The simultaneous paradigm shift in the imaging of the sacred can prove revolutionary if subservient, self-punitive approaches to the Divine are replaced by authentic celebration of both the life process and the challenges posed by one's part in it.

Interdependent Diversity as a Power for Healing

South Africa is a country in which diversity and difference have been acknowledged only in order to separate. Differences of race, gender, ethnicity, and religion have been accentuated both by law as well as by culture and tradition. As Christian and Muslim women our differences are clearly visible in our different approaches to our common concern with earth-healing. They speak of our diversity, a diversity unlike the one so familiar to all South Africans. It is a diversity which acknowledges our interdependence as women of different faiths.

Women know that diversity and gender are related. Vandana Shiva writes "The patriarchal world view sees man as the measure of all value, with no space for diversity, only for hierarchy. Woman, being different, is treated as unequal and inferior. Nature's diversity is seen as not intrinsically valuable in itself, its value is conferred only through economic exploitation for commercial gain. . . . The marginalization of women and the destruction of biodiversity go hand in hand."

We find our commonality in our passionate concern for the healing of our land. The acceptance of diversity as a power for healing entails recognizing and embracing it in the richness and abundance of creation and the variety of women's experiences. Diversity is above all an affirmation of the exuberance, the extravagant profusion of the Creator, not something to be feared or controlled. Shiva writes that when women and biodiversity meet in fields and forest, in arid regions and wetlands, then politics of gender (and race) difference and eco-politics affirming nature's variety and difference meet. When the subjugated knowledges of women, rural women, women in informal settlements around our major cities, women in the work place, white women, black women, young and old make their voices heard in their communities of faith, the church and the mosque can become agents for earth-healing.

Women crossing male-instituted barriers in our religious communities, women preaching the truth about relationships and our sacred symbols, women planting trees and saving dolphins are all involved in earth-healing praxis. *De profundis* it is a yearning for the healing of ourselves and our world. *Mayibuye Afrika* (Come back Africa) means that the land must be returned to the people, but it also implies a healed and restored land, one that is greened and healed. The earth can be healed when we celebrate our diversity and understand our total interdependence with one another and every aspect of creation.

Notes

1. See Lesley Lawson, "The Ghetto and the Greenbelt: The Environmental Crisis in the Urban Areas" in Jacklyn Cock and Eddie Koch (eds.), *Going Green: People, Politics and the Environment in South Africa* (Cape Town: Oxford University Press, 1991), pp. 46-63.

2. South Africa elected its first democratic government in April, 1994.

3. South Africa has over 240 species of mammals, 887 different species of birds and over 20,000 flowering plants. See Jacklyn Cock, "Going Green at Grassroots" in Cock and Koch, *Going Green*, p. 5.

4. Ibid., p. 4.

5. See Henk Coetzee and David Cooper, "Wasting Water: Squandering a Precious Resource" in Cock and Koch, *Going Green*, pp. 129-130.

6. Francis Wilson and Mamphela Ramphele, *Uprooting Poverty: The South African Challenge* (Cape Town: David Philip, 1989), p.44. See also Mark Gandar, "The Imbalance of Power" in Cock and Koch, *Going Green*, p. 96, who writes: "Firewood [which] provides domestic heat and warmth to over 10 million South Africans and occupies a staggering amount of human time and effort in its collection—two and a half times the total amount of work employed in the country's entire coal mining industry."

7. See Eddie Koch, Dave Cooper and Henk Coetzee, *Water, Waste and Wild Life: The Politics of Ecology in South Africa* (London: Penguin Books, 1990), pp. 39-40, on the problems of water in Africa.

8. Medical investigations reveal that Soweto's children suffer from more asthma and chest colds and take longer to recover from respiratory diseases than do children elsewhere in the country (see Jacklyn Cock, "Green Politics in the South African Context," ASSA Conference paper, July 1990), p. 4.

9. Wilson and Ramphele, *Uprooting Poverty*, pp. 23-25.

10. Albie Sachs, *Protecting Human Rights in a New South Africa* (Cape Town: Oxford University Press, 1990), p. 141.

11. Harold Coward, "Is Population Excess Destroying the Environment? Points of Consensus and Divergence in the Response of World Religions." Paper given at the International and Interfaith Consultation on "Religion, Population and Public Policy," (Genval, Belgium, May 4-7, 1994), p. 26.

12. See James Clarke, "The Insane Experiment: Tampering with the Atmosphere" in Cock and Koch, *Going Green*, pp. 144-149.

13. See Koch, Cooper and Coetzee, *Water, Waste and Wildlife*, pp. 43-55, and Peter Lukey, Chris Albertyn and Henk Coetzee, "Wasting Away: South Africa and the Global Waste Problem" in Cock and Koch, *Going Green*, pp. 162-173. On the problem of nuclear waste, Henk Coetzee, in an interview with *The Weekly Mail* (4 May 1990), remarked that nuclear waste from South Africa's nuclear reactor at Koeberg amounted to 200 kilograms of plutonium a year.

14. See Eddie Koch, "Rainbow Alliances: Community Struggles around Ecological Problems" in Cock and Koch, *Going Green*, p. 26, for an account of the damage wrought by herbicides in Tala Valley near Pietermaritzburg. See also Koch, Cooper and Coetzee, *Water, Waste and Wildlife*, p. 37, on the contamination of water by pesticides.

15. The appalling story of asbestos pollution in the Mafefe community of the northeastern Transvaal is recounted by Marianne Felix, "Risking Their Lives in Ignorance; The Story of an Asbestos-polluted Community" in Cock and Koch, *Going Green*, pp. 33-43.

16. Thor Chemicals, a British multinational company with subsidiaries in a host of countries, including West Germany, France, Australia, the United States and Britain, has recently been involved in a mercury-poisoning trial at which three directors were accused of responsibility for the deaths of two former employees. It is also alleged that Thor Chemicals supplied incorrect figures to the governmental agencies in their monthly reports. See *Sunday Times*, March 13, 1994, and *Cape Times*, May 10, 1994.

17. A. Durning, "Apartheid's Environmental Toll," *Worldwatch Paper 95*, 1990. See also Wilson and Ramphele, *Uprooting Poverty*, pp. 227-229.

18. Durning, "Apartheid's Environmental Toll," p. 47.

19. Durning, "Apartheid's Environmental Toll," p. 25.

20. Ibid., p. 7.

21. Cock, "Green Politics," p. 2.

22. Farieda Khan, "Involvement of the Masses in Environmental Politics," Veld and Flora, vol.76 (2), p. 36.

23. Constitution of the Republic of South Africa, 1993.

24. See Victor Munnik, "Green Wings for a New Government," in *New Ground—* Autumn '94, Vol. 1, No. 15, p. 19.

25. Ibid.

26. Maria Mies and Vandana Shiva, *Ecofeminism* (London: Zed Books, 1993), p. 19.

27. According to the 1980 census figures.

28. Jacklyn Cock, "Christian Witness and Ecology," *International Review of Mis-*

sion, Vol LXXXIII (328), 1994, pp. 89-92, and "Towards the Greening of the Church in South Africa: Some Problems and Possibilities," *Missionalia*, 20 (3), 1992, pp. 174-185.

29. Cock, "Towards the Greening," pp. 174-175.

30. Ibid., pp. 175-179.

31. For the following and other stories, see Cock and Koch, *Going Green*, to whom I am indebted.

32. Cock and Koch, *Going Green*, p. 45.

33. Ibid., p. 209.

34. Kofi Asare Opoku, "The Traditional Foundations of Development," paper given at 40th Annual New Year School, Institute of Education, University of Ghana, December 27, 1988- January 4, 1989, p. 11.

35. M. L. Daneel, "African Independent Churches Face the Challenge of Environmental Ethics," *Missionalia*, 21 (3), 1993, pp. 311-332.

36. Ibid., p. 312.

37. Ibid., pp. 313-314.

38. Ibid., p. 314.

39. Ibid., p. 319.

40. In a recent conversation M. L. Daneel reported that the Nature Foundation and green bodies are making contact with the AICs locally to initiate dialogue on environmental matters.

41. Daneel, "African Independent Churches," p. 332.

42. "Mainline" refers to the churches traditionally established by the missionaries, e.g., those churches which are members of the South African Council of Churches (Anglican, Presbyterian, Methodist, Congregationalist) as well as the Roman Catholic Church.

43. Sachiko Murata, *The Tao of Islam: A Sourcebook on Gender Relationships in Islamic Thought* (New York: State University of New York Press, 1992), pp. 203-222.

44. See Beverly Harrison, *Making the Connections* (Boston: Beacon Press, 1985), p. 24 and Dale Spender, *Man Made Language* (London: Routledge & Kegan, 1981), p. 58, and L. Vygotsky, *Thought and Language* (Cambridge, MA: MIT Press, 1962), pp. 51, 125-153.

45. See Adrienne Rich, *On Lies, Secrets and Silence* (London: Virago, 1980).

46. Amina Wadud-Muhsin, *Qur'an and Woman* (Kuala Lumpur: Penerbit Fajar Bakti Sdn. Bhd., 1992).

47. Merryl Wyn Davies, *Knowing One Another: Shaping an Islamic Anthropology* (New York: Mansell Publishing Limited, 1988), pp. 92-93.

48. Ibid., p. 93.

49. Al-Hafiz B.A. Masri, "Islam and Ecology," in F. Khalid and J. O'Brien (eds.), *Islam and Ecology* (London: Cassell, 1992), p. 6.

50. Ibid., p. 7.

51. See Davies, *Knowing One Another*, pp. 93-94.

52. See Carol Gilligan, *In a Different Voice: Psychological Theory and Women's Development* (Cambridge, MA: Harvard University Press, 1982).

53. Harrison, *Making the Connections*, p. 24.

54. See Mujlisul-Ulama of South Africa (Port Elizabeth), *Az-Zaujus Salih: The Pious Husband* (Benoni: Young Men's Muslim Association, 1993), p. 26.

55. Christine Downing, *The Goddess: Mythological Images of the Feminine* (New York: The Crossroad Publishing Company, 1987), p. 4.

56. Ibid., p. 5.

12

Shona Women and the *Mutupo* Principle

TUMANI MUTASA NYAJEKA

In 1890 the British entered into the territory of present-day Zimbabwe, an area in which the Shona and Ndebele shared a common worldview centered around the *Mwari* cult at Matopos. Sources reveal that in this religious worldview women were prominent participants who were viewed as equals in all matters concerned with shaping the future destiny of their people.[1] Through this religious cosmology Shona women exercised power and authority which permeated all aspects of the life of their communities. During this period women were not just prominent priests at the shrines, but they also held key political positions within the family, community and clan.

Shona cosmology was bifocal in expression. First, through the belief in *Mwari*, the Supreme Deity, shrines were constructed to symbolize the cooperative spirit of all of existence. Second, the *Mutupo* (totem) myth of creation was elaborately constructed with the purpose of affirming the uniqueness and individuality of entities, such as species, genders, clans, and races, and to affirm the relationality of all this diversity within existence.

During this period gender relations among the Shona, for the larger part, seem to have been quite amicable and egalitarian. For example, in the nineteenth century, it was a woman who acted as *Mwari's* oracle at Matopos. In this capacity the oracle was consulted on all matters of state and culture by the political systems throughout the region. Emissaries were sent annually from the various regions to petition for rain as well as to seek counsel from the oracle on matters of polity and government. Second, young girls (*mbongas*) were trained along with boys (*hosanas*) to be the messengers of *Mwari* and both would eventually marry into the various clans in which they assumed the role of *mhondoro* (Clan/*Mwari* Spirit) among the people. The power and authority of these female figures was evidenced in 1896-97 in which Tekela wa Ponga and Nehanda

Nyakasikana helped Mkwati and Kaguvi plan, organize and execute the first *Chimurenga* (war of resistence) against British colonialism.[2]

Portuguese and British authorities also encountered and had to deal with women governors who were prominent features all over the Shona territories. Chikanga and her five sisters of the Mutasa dynasty in Manyikaland were such an example. Throughout the colonial period the British would deliberately undermine the power and authority of these women by annexing their land or ignoring them, despite the fact that their people continued to consult and recognize their political legitimacy.[3]

Such power and authority were not wielded only by women from royalty or priestly circles. Through the *Mutupo* principle a majority of ordinary women were trained to be comfortable with exercising power and authority at all levels of their society. In precolonial Zimbabwe, Shona and Ndebele women not only had access to land, power and property, but a rubric of formal and informal rules protected their rights and interests as mothers, wives, sisters or daughters. An analysis of oral Shona sources such as folklore, myths, and legends conveys a hunter/gathering and pastoral and agricultural society in which gender formations are fluid and not rigid or biased against women. These findings support Walter Rodney's argument that women in most precolonial societies enjoyed fundamental rights and privileges which were either abruptly lost or slowly eroded by colonialism and the colonial state.[4] It is within colonial and missionary sources that one finds a depiction of precolonial Shona polities as having been rigid patriarchies in which women were chattel slaves who remained legal minors subordinate to men in all matters of life.[5]

Through the analysis of Shona philosophy, from oral as well as written sources, this essay seeks to show a Shona worldview in which women were nurtured to be comfortable with the pursuit of power, authority and rights in their communities. In these polities women were featured sages, hunters, politicians, counselors, artists, dancers, musicians, farmers, miners, business people, as well as mothers in the community. Female children grew up showered with *Mutupo* praise poetry and the names of legendary female figures of their family or clan. Gender relations in Shona culture were cohesive but complex. Within that complexity lay a culture which seemed to understand that its survival depended on safeguarding the rights of the weak and most vulnerable.

The *Mutupo* Worldview

At the turn of the nineteenth century Shona and possibly the Ndebele societies were organized around the *Mutupo* principle. The *Mutupo* principle is an undergirding religious philosophy or myth around which the Shona understood their lives in relationship to each other and the rest of the world. From this myth and the belief in a deity, their societies drew out a science, as well as a moral code, which reflected their understanding of relationships in existence. In turn, the science and moral code served to protect and perpetuate the people's worldview. The *Mutupo* principle is the story out of which they not only define their place and identity in the universe vis-à-vis other entities, but it is also the medium through which they experience and express the meaning of existence.

Mutupo cosmology is the Shona myth of creation. It is a cohesive but complex story which the Shona constructed, believed in and perceived as the blueprint or primary source to their understanding of life and existence. There are three dimensions to this story. First, there is the belief in *Mwari* (God) as the creator of nature and the universe; second, there is the belief in the aquatic origins of some animals and humans; and, third, the belief in the terrestrial origins of other animals and humans.

Chigwedere reconstructs an ethnographical migrationist theory among the *Mutupo* groups of the Bantu who settled in the area of present-day Zimbabwe. He argues that the Bantu groups which settled into the area held different stories as to their mythic origin. The first Bantu group to arrive in Zimbabwe was the *Karanga* around the eighth century in land which was occupied by the *Tonga* and had belonged to the *San*. Around the twelfth century they were followed by a second distinctive group, the *Mbire*.[6]

The *Karanga* myth of creation traces the origin of life and existence to the Great Pool (*Dzivaguru*) concept. In this myth the Great Pool is believed to have been the place of origin for all of nature. Aquatic life is perceived as the beginnings of the *Karanga* people. Each clan, therefore, adopts an aquatic species as its progenitor or *Mutupo* (totem-animal). For example, a clan may claim its primogenitor-*Mutupo* as the *Mvuu* (hippo). Other clans may claim as their *mutupos Hove* (fish); *Mheta* (water-python); *Garwe* (crocodile); *Dziva* (Great Pool); *Hungwe* (fish-eagle); *Mbiti* (otter), etc. According to Chigwedere the uniting symbol for the *Karanga* clans is *Hungwe*, the fish-eagle.

The *Mbire* myth of creation claims its beginnings in the terrestrial region. Their myth centers around the Great Monkey (*Soko*) concept. Here the clans derive their *Mutupo*/primogenitors from terrestrial species. Examples of *Mbire* clan *Mutupos* are *Shava* (antelope); *Beta* (termites); *Humba* (pig); *Nzou* (elephant); *Shumba* (lion); *Tsivo* (human female organ) and *Nyati* (buffalo). The monkey (*Soko*) is the uniting symbol of the *Mbire* group's understanding of the universe. The two groups developed a pattern of intermarriage, thus balancing the aquatic and terrestrial clans.

Shona Worldview

Around the turn of the century the Shona viewed and experienced the world through the *Mutupo* principle. The foundational basis for the *Mutupo* principle is the relationality of all of existence. The *Mutupo* principle focuses on fostering the primary relationships between animals and humans, animals and the deity, humans and humans, nature and humans, deity and humans, the dead and the living. The *Mutupo* principle attempts to enumerate or approximate the ideal mode of life which assures a sustainable future for all of existence. An analysis of the fundamental elements of the *Mutupo* principle reveals that it is a principle which seeks to create a cosmology that takes the existence of non-human entities seriously. In this myth a cosmology is created which is non-anthropocentric, but at the same time celebrates as unique the experience of being human in the universe.

In the *Mutupo* myth a human clan adopts another species and covenants that "its people shall be our people." A solemn commitment to protect one another's survival is established with the assumption that the non-human will understand. The identity and destiny of the clan and the *Mutupo* are perceived as congruous, meaning whatever happens to one directly affects the other. This relationship between the clan and its *Mutupo* is axiomatic to *Karanga* worldview. The relationship is understood as the vantage point from which one experiences and comes to know the universe. This relationship is also understood as the base upon which all relationships are defined. The relationship between the clan and its *Mutupo* is a sacred covenant. In this covenant the two parties understand themselves as agreeing to be faithful, loyal, and committed to affirming one another's life and existence. To the Shona, the mention of one's *Mutupo* evokes sacral meaning. It resonates with every dimension of human experience, such as worship, security, justice, love, community life, romance, praise, dance, death, motherhood, beauty, the living, the dead and the yet-to-be-born.

There are three fundamental principles of the *Mutupo* myth. Out of these three fundamentals, a Shona moral code is constructed which attempts to grant and protect freedom for all of creation. First, there is a belief in the unity or oneness of all of nature and existence. Second, the *Mutupo* myth communicates a cosmology in which every entity in existence is perceived as inherently endowed with freedom and some rights-to-be. And finally, God (*Mwari*) is given as the source and sustainer of all of life and existence.

The *Mutupo* principle points to an intrinsic oneness or unity which translates into a status of egalitarianism of all forms of nature. All of nature is perceived as imbued with an energy force which manifests itself in diversified forms as reality or nature. The *Mutupo* concept seeks to communicate this principle. It begins by establishing that humans, the deity, nature, time and space are of the same essence. The nature of reality and existence is perceived as defying hierarchical forms. Instead the nature of reality is perceived as an intricately bonded web of relationality in which the circle as a shape can be said to accurately symbolize the nature of this dynamic phenomenon. The circle defies a search for a beginning or an end, as well as hierarchic structures. Space and time, fire and ice, humans and animals, women and men, young and old, deity and creation are understood as reciprocally interrelated. This belief is communicated by such common sayings as "*Mambo wanhu*" (chieftaincy is the people).

The Shona worldview also sees nature, reality and existence as a paradoxical mystery of interrelationality, rather than a bipolar struggle of competing opposites. The task of existence is viewed as seeking to understand the nature of this interrelationality between, for example, earth and sky, women and men, young and old, fire and ice, deity and creation, day and night. In the words of ecological theologian, Jay McDaniel, "The web of life is best conceived as a collective 'we' in which, ontologically speaking, there are no 'theys.' "[7] The *Mutupo* principle denotes that all in creation is free to be because it exists. Each and every entity in existence is understood as inherently endowed with a right and freedom to be. This continuance of existence and the survival of species is entrusted to the custodial care of all of nature as creation. The Shona have prayed to the forest to be "kind and merciful" and return the children when they have wandered and disappeared in its thickets. Entities are viewed as intrinsic values in and for themselves, even as they are of instrumental importance to others. It is at this point that one can note that the *Mutupo* principle does not take an anthropocentric view of nature and existence. Human beings are perceived as in community with all of creation and not as the focus for which the universe exists. One's totem animal continuously allows a human being to experience and look at the universe from a non-human perspective. From early childhood Shona children are initiated into this human-transcending mode through folktales in which animals and nature are portrayed as the center of the universe.

Shona folklore and idioms encapsulate the history and nature of this dynamic way of relationality. It is in African folklore that every bush, rock, river and animal has character and a voice. Humans never occupy center stage in Shona folklore, nor are they the smartest characters in the story. Instead, they always have to learn from nature and animals. In these folktales animal wisdom often saves human characters. One may argue that Shona cosmology is "animal-centric" because in the folktales humans are depicted as extensions or even caricatures of animals or nature. Shona children identify with a myriad of animal characters before they can even look around for human role models.

This world of animals is in Shona philosophy a utopian blueprint. It is a genre of literature that initiates young children into the principles of democracy, freedom, peace and justice. The law of this land is always known as a consensual democracy in which meetings are called for and everyone's voice is expected to be heard before an agreement is reached. At an early age, the children are initiated into a consciousness of the ethical and moral dilemmas of life and existence. In the animal stories lie the existential dilemmas of choice between the community's agenda vis-à-vis an individual's. In these stories a child learns lessons on friendship, love, hate, the warmth of neighbors, courage, war, kith and kin, anger, greed, commerce and frustration. It is also in these stories that a Shona child is taught to be merciful and kind.

Most Shona animal folktales are set in a context of a severe drought for two reasons. First, through these stories valuable scientific knowledge is transmitted to the human child, conditioning them to constantly remember that in Shonaland they dwell in a delicate ecosystem of cyclical droughts that perpetually threaten all of life and existence. Second, a drought setting may metaphorically represent the nature of existence and the human condition in which survival is not a personal matter but a matter requiring the mind of a community. A child is taught that "*Munhu Wanhu*" (to be is community).

In Shona cosmology one's *Mutupo* or totem animal becomes a symbol for the covenantal relationship with all things. *Mutupo* is a sacred covenant in which the human pledges to protect and always seek to enhance the life and survival of their "sibling" other species. Shona poetry, art, dance, music, folklore and philosophy express this worldview. From childhood children are showered with praise poetry and teased with gestures that imitate the totem animal so as to imprint this identity in them early. These praise names, poetry and terms of endearment actually serve to teach two fundamental aspects of the Shona cosmology to the child. First, that through its *Mutupo*, it belongs to a community larger than the human community, and second, that it can with pride claim its place in the universe because there were people before it who had made its birth possible. It is now its turn to live wisely as well.

Such daily praise poetry does not end with childhood, but is evident in the ordinary ways of Shona people. For example, Shona daily greetings of one another serve as a constant reminder of the belief in the "trans-species" relationality of existence within the *Mutupo* principle. When someone, whether male or female, whose totem animal is *svosve* (monkey) is being greeted, that person is addressed as *Mhukahuru* (powerful animal), *Chirombowe* (the powerful, awesome one), or directly by their totem animal: *Mangwanani Chirombowe, Mhukahuru, Soko*! Good morning, Awesome one, Monkey!

This greeting conveys two aspects of Shona thought. First, taken literally it is a praise poem to the existence of both a human person and their totem animal. The greeting celebrates the mystery of existence by mutually assuring one another that each has a place in the universe. Second, this salute is an affirmation to the nature of this mystical relationality of nature. The idea poignantly communicated in this salute is that of the paradox of being human, in which human beings would like to view themselves as the most awesome of all creation (*Mhukahuru*), with the capacity to think freely and manipulate the environment, but they share a common destiny with their totem animal as fellow creatures whose survival or extinction is dependent on the community of species.

The universe is not viewed as having been created for human exploitation but for sustaining all of creation. The Shona know that when the baboon baby runs out of milk, the human baby will soon face the same predicament. Shona thought acknowledges that "*Kakara kununa kudya kamwe*" (the health of one creature lies on feeding upon the other) in a way that mournfully accepts realities, such as death, but also in a way which triumphantly celebrates the mystery of an interrelational nature of existence. Everything in the universe is perceived as belonging to a community in which ultimately all entities exist for one another, entwined in a web of relationality. The challenge for humans is to affirm this interrelationality in a way that sustains a peaceable community. This peaceable commmunity is thematic in Shona folklore, music and folktales in which it is constantly emphasized that, in order to ensure survival for all, justice and freedom should prevail for all creatures.

Out of this search for a peaceable community proceeds the whole system of taboos in Shona cosmology. A critical analysis of taboos (*zvinoda*) in Shona cosmology does show that they are rules and regulations mostly designed to create a peaceable community in which the weak and the vulnerable are protected and justice is done. In Shona the word taboo (*zvinoera/zvinoda*) translates as *sacred* or *unapproachable*. It does not have the connotation of uncleanliness. An act, object or word is taboo when it is perceived to be in a liminal stage, temporarily or permanently. The weak and vulnerable, such as babies, post-partum mothers, boys or girls at puberty, the sick or the dead, rare plants and animals are taboo—holy or unapproachable. Leaders such as priests, chiefs, healers and warriors are also taboo. The tabooing of one's totem animal saved almost all species of fauna and flora from extinction in Shona society. In the *Mutupo* principle a human community enters into a pact for mutual survival between humans and animals.

The *Mutupo* myth is a religious philosophy because a Creator-Being (*Mwari*) is perceived as the author and ultimate enforcer of the principles of life and existence. The *Mutupo* principle mediates a deity who created and continues to create. All of creation, including humans, is understood as agents of the ongoing process of creation. All of creation in relation to the Creator is of equal status or worth.

Mutupo points to a deity who is deeply mysterious, never to be comprehended by the human mind. This mystery of deity is chanted in Shona music, poetry, prayer and ritual. *Mwari* is commonly referred to as, *Chibwe chitedza chinokwirwa newatanu* (the large slippery rock which only the healthiest can climb). At the same time God is known to be the one who participates and intervenes in the affairs of the universe because God's being is manifest in all of creation. *Mwari* is remembered as having fed *sadza* (meal) to the regional emissaries come to petition *Mwari* for rain at *Mutiusinazita* (the nameless tree) during the years of severe drought. *Mwari* is known as the protector and vindicator of all the afflicted, oppressed and downtrodden. *Mwari* at times is referred to as *Pfuyanherera* (the one who nurtures the orphaned).

Since all of nature is understood as of divine creation, it is perceived as endowed with the mystery and energy of the Creator. This belief explains the Shona veneration of all of creation. Within this modality rivers, pools, mountains, forests and hills are revered and are subjects of poetry. In this worldview nothing is ordinary; all in nature to its smallest detail is viewed with awe and wonder. Images of the ant which killed an elephant are imprinted in a child's mind as a way of communicating the nature of egalitarianism in all of existence. At another time the story of the ant who offered the elephant shelter from the storm communicates the nature of symbiotic existence for survival of all of nature.

Shona metaphysics also views nature and existence in terms of symbiotic and egalitarian relationality, rather than oppositional, hierarchic and exclusive bipolarity. For example, women are not perceived as the opposite of men; the two are viewed as intrinsically and permanently related. The same perception applies to God and creation; spirit and physical; the living and the dead; young and old; space and time. It is at this point of relationality of oppositional entities that the Shona believe beings can transcend their nature-specificity and dynamically become the other. God is not only understood as an exclusive being but is said to become the Great Monkey for the Soko *Mutupo* people or Lion for the Shumba people. Humans are also known as capable of transcending gender, physicality, even space and time. Furthermore all of nature is regarded as of equal worth because all is understood as of divine creation.

Studies of both gender and environment in traditional Shona culture need to understand this governing principle behind its cosmology. The *Mutupo* principle was a blueprint upon which Shona relationships were based. As typical of any community or civilization, the egalitarian ideal of the *Mutupo* principle did not always translate totally into reality. But it provided an ideal map which sought to keep members of the human community and the natural world in balance with each other. These are also principles which can be reclaimed for today, after the harsh distortions of colonialism and capitalist exploitation of the Zimbabwean people and environment, to rebuild a more sustainable and just society and relation to the environment.

Notes

1. M. Gelfand, *Medicine and Magic of the Mashona* (Capetown, South Africa: Juta and Company, 1956), p. 22.

2. M. L. Daneel, *The God of the Matopo Hills* (Paris, France: Mouton and Company, 1970), p. 32.

3. Interview, Chief Mutasa, September 28, 1993.

4. W. Rodney, *How Europe Underdeveloped Africa* (Nairobi: Heinemann, 1972), p. 248; J. Gunther, *Inside Africa* (New York: Harper and Row, 1953), p. 295.

5. *The Heathen Woman's Friend* (1899), vol. XI, No. 1; also C. Walker, editor, *Women and Gender in Southern Africa* (Capetown, South Africa: Philip and James Curry, 1990).

6. M. I. Chigwedere, *From Mutapa to Rhodes* (London: Macmillan, 1980).

7. Jay McDaniel, *Earth, Sky, Gods and Mortals* (Mystic, CT: Twenty-Third Publications, 1990).

13

Revisiting Traditional Management of Indigenous Woodlands

SARA C. MVUDUDU

This paper argues that there is a need to go beyond simple gender distinctions and look at additional stratifiers, such as an individual rural woman's access to natural resources, including use rights and control over a particular resource, in designing woodland management interventions and assessing policy and program impacts. It will also look at traditional Shona culture as a factor in forest management.

Gender differentiation cannot be easily separated from other factors in the socio-economic systems. It is linked directly and indirectly to scarce natural resources, like fertile land. Gender differentiations, as formulated by historical, cultural, religious, social, economic and educational parameters, are factored into the system that generates constraints and opportunities at household, national and international levels. Such factors and systems must form a key element in any effective conceptual framework for gender analysis in woodland management.

Why Gender in Woodland Management?

Van den Hambergh (1993:18) shows that three strongly interrelated factors are important to explain why gender, environment and development are so closely connected. These are the sexual division of labor, the feminization of poverty and gender ideology. The sexual division of labor makes women, especially poor rural women, important contributors to agriculture and often makes them solely responsible for the collection of firewood, fodder and water. The sexual division of labor means women and men have different domains of knowledge and different interests toward the use and management of natural resources.

The key links between woodland management and gender issues are deforestation and household energy needs; water availability and household needs;
and soil degradation and household food supply (Clones 1992:1). Gender is
important in three fundamental ways: social equity; effectiveness of resource
management and development; and broadening forestry to encompass the total
range of human use of forest resource.

The term gender, as it is used here, refers to culturally and historically specific concepts of femininity and masculinity, and the power relations between
men and women. Gender is also fundamental in understanding human interaction with the environment and with respect to natural resources. Gender shapes
the sexual division of labor, knowledge, responsibility and control.

Women's knowledge of the environment is often more comprehensive because
of the diversity of their tasks. The main responsibility for sustaining the family is
usually assigned to the women, increasingly so because of male migration away
from degraded rural areas. This makes women's knowledge an important issue in
environmental management and rehabilitation. Because of the sexual division of
labor and the feminization of poverty, it is often the women who bear the heaviest
burden of environmental degradation. The decline in soil fertility and in food, fodder and firewood supplies makes women's workloads grow heavier and heavier. It
affects their health and eventually that of society at large.

Gender in relation to natural resources and to the economic, political and
cultural environment is probably most evident as a dimension of power, besides class, age, ethnicity and religion. Changing the existing power dimensions is crucial for attaining sustainable development, for ethical and humani-
tarian reasons, but also because both luxury (waste of resources) and poverty
(overexploitation of the leftovers) contribute largely to environmental degradation. The connection between environmental degradation, population explosion and gender distortion, while beginning to penetrate the thinking of national and international donors, has not yet coalesced; therefore these inter-
relations continue to be treated mostly at a rhetorical level. Substantial action
has yet to follow.

There is need for us to understand the operation of woodlands ecosystems
and the interrelationships of all species that live in or use woodland resources.
To examine only how males in a given society make use of the forest fruits,
nuts, leaves, medicinal plants or fibers and dyes is to obtain only a partial view
of the forest. All these uses are interconnected, and all affect the forest and the
users of the forest. Foresters working with small-scale farmers need to know
their clients' wants; what their objectives and goals are; how and why they use
trees; how they make a living, to develop what Rocheleau (1987b) calls a "user
perspective."

Many recent studies have suggested that the so-called "minor forest products" or "non-wood forest produce" are in many areas significant forest uses,
and significant sources of income for rural people. Often women are major
users of these resources. The value of woodland products can be seen to be
sizable in terms of annual cash income, which is well under US $250 per house-

hold. Thus, by understanding women's knowledge of woodland resources we can enlarge our general understanding of forestry. Women use forest resources for fuel, human food, animal fodder, construction materials, tools, artisan crafts, traditional medicines, purifying water and a wide diversity of other purposes (Williams 1992).

Perspectives and Approaches

The application of Development Crisis and Alternative Visions: Third World Women's Perspectives (DAWN) in the analysis is very useful because it aims to be holistic, linking social, economic, cultural, political, and environmental factors. It is grounded in an alternative paradigm of social change; it is political, feminist, and attempts to link household-level experiences of poor women to macro-economic politics. DAWN promotes a "people centered" approach, sharing suitable development based on cooperative resistance to hierarchies, sharing accountability and commitment to peace, broadening and deepening the debate on gender and development.

Piers Blaikie and Harold Brookfield (1987) use a regional political ecology appoach for their explanation of land degradation, with a primary emphasis on social and economic causes. For example, on population and land degradation, they state that high population pressure is not a cause of environmental deterioration in itself, although it may create stress. It is rather the economic and political marginalizing of people, combined with the marginalization of their natural environment in a downward spiral.

Merchant (1992:10) argues that the problems of depletion of natural resources have specific roots in each country's internal history, its place in the global order and the current trajectory of its internal development. Each environmental problem therefore needs to be examined in the context of its own specific history as well as its linkages to global political economies. Environmental problems in developing countries are rooted in poverty and hunger, population pressure on marginal lands and unbalanced land distribution.

In this context gender relations need to be recognized. According to Merchant (1992:183) ecofeminism emerged in the 1970s with an increasing consciousness of the connections between women and nature. Women are also taking the lead in movements to protect nature. Common examples often quoted are from Kenya and India. In Kenya women of the Green Belt Movement come together to plant millions of trees in arid degraded lands. In India women joined the *Chipko* (tree-hugging) movement to prevent loggers from felling trees for timber.

Merchant (1992:185) quotes Warren as a philosopher who conceptualizes an ecofeminist ethic as

> both a critique of male domination of women and nature and an attempt to frame an ethic free of male-gender bias about women and nature. It not

only recognizes the multiple voices of women located by race, class, age (and) ethnic considerations, it centralizes those voices. Ecofeminism builds on the multiple perspectives of those whose views are typically omitted or undervalued in dominant discourses, for example, the *Chipko* movement, in developing a global perspective on the role of male domination in the exploitation of women and nature. An ecofeminist perspective is therefore ... structurally pluralistic, inclusive, and contextual, emphasizing through concrete example the crucial role context plays in understanding existing practices.

Third World women have borne the brunt of the environmental crisis resulting from colonial marginalization and ecologically unstable development projects. Women have organized movements, institutes and businesses to transform maldevelopment into sustainable development. Some consciously consider themselves feminists, and a few embrace ecofeminism, but most are mainly concerned with maintaining conditions for survival.

Karen Warren (1987) claims that ecofeminism is based on the premise that the solutions to ecological problems must include a feminist perspective. These principles become clearer as one determines the basic feature of the historical connection between the oppression of both women and nature. Maria Mies (1988) states that it is critical to understand why this division became asymmetrical, hierarchical and exploitative. Inspired by Marxism, she links gender and environment with class struggles, arguing that women's bodies and nature were "colonized" by patriarchy and capitalism in combination (Mies 1986).

Susan George (1992) has found strong positive correlations between high levels of indebtedness and environmental degradation, especially deforestation, and states that structural adjustment creates further stress on already fragile eco-systems. The "export-led growth model on which the IMF and the World Bank insist is purely extractive, involving the mining rather than the management of resources, let alone their conservation." Literature that combines the effects of structural adjustment on women and the environment is scarce.

Population growth is often labelled an "environmental problem," but it has been shown that it is not so much the number of people, but what they consume, what part of the "ecoscope" they use, that is crucial. Significant is the issue of northern overconsumption. Furthermore, environment problems in the South that seem local, like erosion, can often be traced back to northern economic use that is increasingly penetrating the South. Poverty and environmental degradation are linked by dominant economic structures.

Thus a more important factor to consider when population pressure and environment are linked is the overexploitation of resources to satisfy the greed of the North, as Ruth Bamlda Engo-Jeda said in her testimony on the World Women's Congress in 1992. Depletion of natural resources and increasing environmental toxicity are the by-products of societal excess; i.e., the lifestyle of affluent societies toward land and control over resources so that more and more people have to cope with less and less fertile land and other resources. Thus both poverty and excessive wealth are detrimental to the environment.

Shona Traditions and Management of Woodland Resources

The traditional role played by women in the management of indigenous resources has not been adequately recorded. If one looks back at our Zimbabwean history the crucial role that the *Svikiro* (Spirit Medium) Mbuya Nehanda played in spearheading the first war of liberation (*Chimurenga*) in Zimbabwe is legendary. This section will focus on how the career of the spirit medium and the healing and protective powers associated with the spirit became inextricably fused at the political, environment, religious and economic levels.

The Nehanda, a female spirit medium, is believed to have two separate equally legitimate traditions, one in the Mazoe region and the other one in Dande. The Mazoe Nehanda, a woman named Charwe, was a major leader of the 1896 rebellion against the new colonial state. Together with another leader of the rebellion, the medium of Kagubi, she was sentenced to death and hanged. A powerful and prolific oral tradition grew up around her name, her part in the rebellion and especially the last moments of her life after she was condemned: her refusal to accept conversion to Christianity, her defiance on the scaffold and her prophecy that "my bones will rise to win back freedom from the Europeans"(Lan 1985:3). This prophecy was fulfilled during the second *Chimurenga* war that finally liberated Zimbabwe in 1980. After the failure of the rebellion of 1896 the victorious white government set about full-scale reorganization of Shona society, intending to squeeze out the last remaining drops of resistance.

Midzimu and *Mhondoro:* The Shona Beliefs

According to the Shona people, their ancestors take the form of *mweya* (breath or air). Ancestors have no material form and so can be in all places at the same time. They continue to have emotions and desires, but they are never frivolous or mean. Their descendants are their sole concern. There is only one reason why they might make a descendant ill. This is to give a sign that they wish to possess her or him, to speak through her or his mouth to all their descendants to warn that some disaster is about to strike or to complain that they have been forgotten and to ask that beer be brewed or a child named in their memory.

A chief during his life should look after all his followers. He should provide them with grain from a common store in time of drought and maintain the peace by enforcing the law through his court. When a chief dies he is transformed into a *mhondoro* and becomes the source of the fertility of the land itself. He/She provides rain for fields and protects the crops as they grow. Rain will only be withheld if the *mhondoro's* laws are disobeyed. If incest, murder or witchcraft takes place, there will be drought, but if the descendants of the *mhondoro* obey his laws and perform his ceremonies, in due time, they will live in peace and plenty.

The royal ancestors, the *mhondoro*, may be referred to as *midzimu*, or ancestors, for they too are the "remnants" of dead people transformed and enhanced by their death. As the *midzimu* takes care of the lineage that has lost its human protector, so the *mhondoro* cares for the *nyika*, the country, that he ruled over when alive. The word *mhondoro* means lion; when a chief dies, his spirit makes its way into the bush where it enters the body of a lion.

The Shona people have always seen the relation between their past and their present as mediated by their ancestors. In the *Chimurenga*, the young fighters had to enter into a dialogue with these ancestors to justify and explain their actions and to seek ancestral help. This was dramatically represented when spirit mediums spoke the words of the ancestors while the guerrillas spoke the words of the living.

When the Zanla guerrillas entered Zimbabwe, they realized that if they were to be successful, they would have to be seen as liberators by the people whom they had come to free. It was not in terms of the political analyses of socialist theoreticians that their actions would appear legitimate, but in terms of the political ideas and interpretations of history of the peasants of Zimbabwe themselves. These folk ideas had been forged by both remote and recent events and by the people's continual struggle to make sense of their history and environment.

Lan (1985:5) aptly sums up all this in his Dande case study in which he describes an ex-freedom fighter's first contact within Zimbabwe (1971) in the Zambezi Valley. The guerillas were led into a densely wooded scrubland to the village of an ancient female spirit medium. The name of the spirit medium was Nehanda. The medium helped them by giving them directions in the forest, and telling them what type of food to eat and what part of the forest they were not allowed to stay in or sleep in, and where they were not allowed to fight.

Peasants led the guerrillas to the spirit mediums because the mediums had taken the place once held by the political leaders within the Dande. The cycle of ritual exchange which had for so long bound chief, ancestors and the living together in an unequal but flexible relationship finally broke apart. As the population living on the lands claimed by whites was cleared and resettled, so chieftaincies were broken up and their members scattered. The best known account of *mhondoro* mediums wielding political and social control is Terence Ranger's history of the 1986 rebellion *Revolt in Southern Rhodesia*. This book was the first major attempt to work out the consequences of sharing politico-religious authority between chiefs and mediums as the unique characteristic of the Shona people.

The history of the Shona people abounds with instances of resistance to changes by the white colonial settlers, including the setting up of infrastructures in sacred areas. For example, the practices of the *mhondoro* performing the rituals that protect the land from mediums expressed a powerful hostility to the economic innovations introduced by whites throughout this century in new techniques of agricultural production, especially the use of fertilizer, claiming that their spirits dislike the smell it gives their earth.

The role that Nehanda played during the first liberation war clearly shows that this was in reaction to the colonization that was taking place. It was in response to accelerated deforestation that she cried that the ancestors were not happy because areas where they used to hide and stay were plundered by the *white man* (commonly called "people without knees," because indigenous people were not familiar with seeing men dressed in trousers).

The most conspicuous way in which the antipathy of these mediums towards the new order was expressed was by the observation of a set of ritual prohibitions. These restrictions were understood to express the antipathy felt by the ancestors, not that of the mediums. It is the forces of nature themselves that are put at risk by the economic domination by the whites. Many spirit provinces contain pools of water sacred to the ancestors and protected by lions. These pools will run dry if a tin mug so much as touches their waters. Only a gourd or wooden bowl may be used to draw water from them. Such is the advance of white society into Dande that many pools which in the past were full even in the driest of dry seasons are today merely depressions. The ritual prohibitions were enforced when the mediums spoke in a state of trance, as well as in the course of their day-to-day activities (Lan 1985:139-159). In addition, from east of Dande came reports of mediums who opposed the construction of dams which would flood sacred pools.

During the liberation struggle in Zimbabwe guerrillas were never allowed to kill the wild animals in the bush, especially elephants and baboons. All things that grow wild in the bush, both game and uncultivated plants, are under the protection of the *mhondoro*. The forest, a hiding place for guerrillas, had been transformed into a resource which they drew on in time of danger or need. Wild animals and guerrillas were under the protection of the *mhondoro*. Lan (1985:226) suggested that by following certain ritual prohibitions the guerrillas gained acceptance as *autochthons*, the warriors of the past returned in new guise as quasi-descendants of the *mhondoro*. This was particularly effective because the political ideology of Dande derives from a conceptualization of the relationship between lineage and land over time. The lineage that has lived within a territory the longest is considered its owner; so it or its ancestors can ensure its fertility.

A gendered analysis of these beliefs is made by Gaidzanwa (1992) who focuses on the role of female spirit mediums. The most famous woman in struggles against colonization is Nehanda Nyakasikana, a female spirit medium who took a leading role in channeling resistance to the settlers. Nehanda's involvement in anti-colonial struggles is an indication of the spaces which existed for women in pre-colonial Shona society in the religious-political reality at a time when the distinctions between politics, religion and production were not pronounced. Nehanda was not a maternal symbol, and as a medium of a powerful spirit her spiritual-political identity overshadowed her identity as a woman.

This was to change after independence when Western liberal conceptions about women were mobilized to reconstruct and deliver the rights that women were perceived to have been struggling to gain. Nehanda was and still is renowned for her political-spiritual role, not for her role as a woman or a mother. Generally, spirit mediums were exempt from the demands made on ordinary men or women with respect to marriage and other roles. Some mediums did not marry, particularly female mediums who were possessed by male spirits. Thus motherhood was not the most salient or important role for spirit mediums in Zimbabwe.

Symbolically, the domestication of women is represented by the renaming of the largest maternity hospital after Nehanda Nyakasikana, the militant spirit medium who was executed by the colonial regime for her role in the resistance to colonization. The linking of Nehanda to a maternity hospital, rather than to a political movement, partly reflects the ignorance and misinterpretation of Zimbabwean culture by the politicians who were responsible for the new government (Gaidzanwa 1992:116).

In the religious sphere, pollution beliefs are evident, and women do not normally take a leading role in addressing ancestors and conducting spiritual ceremonies, unless they are religious specialists selected by the spirits of deceased people who possess the women. For example, in Shona culture young women still capable of bearing children are not allowed to brew ritual beer because they are regarded as impure, dangerous and polluting. Only post-menopausal women can participate in the brewing of ritual beer.

The Current Traditional Woodland Management Defined

In the past, values that maintained biodiversity were often woven into the fabric and inherited traditions of the people. It is interesting that most of the conservation practices that are used today have been in place since time immemorial. However, some of them have undergone some transformation to match the changing circumstances, and some practices governing access and use of resources were added during the colonial period. The existing rules and practices are listed below:

—Cutting of wet wood for firewood is strictly prohibited
—Dry wood and off-cuts from poles and carpentry can be used for firewood
—Sale of firewood and poles is strictly prohibited in order to protect the woodlands from plundering
—Cutting of all fruit trees and certain special species (like *Lonchocarpus Capassa* "mupanda") that have spiritual value is prohibited
—Permission for brick making is granted by the *Sabhuku,* or sub-chief
—People are only allowed to lop branches rather than cut standing trees

It is generally recognized that in Zimbabwe there are three classes of land tenure: stateland, communal areas and commercial land. According to Nhira and Fortman (1992:140), there are two systems of forest management in Zimbabwe which are not necessarily mutually exclusive: those management systems initiated, implemented and imposed by the state; and those management systems initiated and implemented by local communities and individuals.

In this essay the focus will be on the second system—by communities and individuals, with a special emphasis on the traditional systems of management. This type of management mechanism has been described by Nhira and Fortman (1992) as sacred controls, which are norms of tree use and protection based on folk or traditional religious beliefs and enforced by individual internalization of the norms, community sanction and by religious or traditional leaders.

In the communal areas of Zimbabwe some woodlands are protected and tree cutting is forbidden. Some of these areas are around gravesites for the common people and the chiefs. The size of these plots, which have existed since precolonial times, range from between twenty and eighty hectares. Woodland management in these areas is by default.

Zimbabwe has long been known for traditional religious practices, which J. M. Schoffelccrs (1979:5-6) has characterized as "profoundly ecological," and for issuing and enforcing directives with regard to a community's use of its environment. These are related to the management of trees and woodlands. He observed that traditional religious cults with ecological functions "are necessarily communal institutions involving the entire population of a geographic area in a system of common obligations."

The sacred controls are steadily weakening. One researcher (Matowanyika) found that 77 percent of his sample felt that the introduction of Christianity and Western ideas has been the cause of the breakdown of indigenous regulations. McGregor (1989:7-8, 39) noted that although, traditionally, woodland access was controlled, these controls were breaking down. "There are certain areas of woodland where cutting is prohibited and guarded by a lion spirit . . . or certain species are protected due to their significance in rituals."

Some trees cannot be used as firewood, e.g., *Pseudolachnosttylis maprounofolia*, which is used by herbalists who exorcise avenging spirits into the tree, and *mupanda* is said to attract lightning to the home if cut. Under stress these controls give way, and these trees are used. In explaining this change, some say they do not know of the old restrictions; others think that such things are only for old women, and others just refer to the problems they are having in acquiring wood. We even found cases of families burning exclusively the trees with customary prohibitions . . . McGregor 1989:7-8).

Some of the species such as *Ficus capensis* (muonde) *Afzelia quanzensis* and *Trichilia dregaana* (mutsikiri) are protected because they raise the water table. Most of the ficus species are essential for rituals, under whose shade ceremonies, such as the rain-making ceremonies, are held. The *Ochna pulchra* (muminu) are still not used for firewood as they are believed to cause family disputes. Religious ceremonies are still being held within these sites, however, and there is a general mobilization towards reviving the old taboos, especially after the 1990-1991 drought, the worst drought in living memory.

Immigrants and the government have often been blamed for the deterioration in the traditional means of control of sacred woodlands. Areas considered sacred are in hills and mountains. It was and is still believed those were areas where ancestral spirits rested or they were passageways for the *mhondoro* (ancestral spirits in the form of animals). These areas are traditionally called *rambatemwa,* which literally means "woodlands that cannot be cut." Remnants of these woodlands are still visible in some communal areas of Zimbabwe.

Impact of Gender and Tenure on Woodland Management

In the communal land tenure system there are no land titles. The Communal Land Act of 1982 vests ownership in the president. Therefore communal lands are state lands, and allocation, occupation and use of communal land is through the district council which grants occupation according to customary law. The customary law practice is that chiefs allocate usufructuary rights on pieces of land to adult married males for use by themselves and their families. This, in reality, means that women have access to land through their husbands or male relatives. Therefore men's access to land is primary; women's entitlement is secondary and entirely depends on the discretion of their male relatives.

The allocation of land based on patrilineal patterns is a fundamental gender-based disparity which when combined with differentials in gender roles affects gender relations and their impacts on the woodland resources. This type of land allocation has inherent weaknesses which automatically disadvantage women in terms of access to quality land and size of operational land units.

Until the passing of the Legal Age of Majority Act 1982, women could not contract or acquire property in their own right but remained minors for life. Even with the passing of this act, women in communal areas still get their land through the male relative. Exceptions are the free-hold areas where they are able to purchase land and in the resettlement areas where female adults with dependents can acquire land. At the community level this also means that women cannot make independent decisions with regard to the setting up of communal infrastructures, such as boreholes, grazing plans and even the decision to set aside indigenous woodlands and conserve them for future use.

Colonization brought changes into the dynamics of the domestic African systems and altered socio-economic relations all the way down to the household level. Household dynamics have played a key role in determining charges in gender relationships. According to J. K. Henn, all African political systems were based on the extended family as the fundamental socio-economic unit. The division of labor in the extended family household reflects its structure. The household head, sometimes in conjunction with the lineage head or clan chief, controled the use of land and other economic resources, such as tools or cattle. He also controled the labor of his family members. The household head allocated fields to wives, and sometimes required that a portion of the harvest go into his personal granary.

Where women had traditional usufructuary rights from their husbands, fathers or brothers, land reforms have transferred land to an almost exclusively male-oriented tenure system, and relegated women to landless agriculture laborers dependent for their subsistence on men. While customary law in Zimbabwe recognizes women's usufructuary rights and makes provision for the newly wed to be allocated a plot of land, widows become dependent on inheriting sons and are usually landless if they have only daughters. Divorced and separated women also become landless.

Lack of control over access to land, combined with the other limitations imposed on women by the socio-economic system, makes women not only victims but also agents of environmental degradation (Clones 1992:13). Hence, ineligibility for traditional credit, combined with lack of access to or control over cash from earned income, impairs women's capacity to acquire the necessary inputs to increase their productivity or to invest in maintaining and improving the fertility of their land.

Improving the technical skills of women across the entire spectrum of their activities should be reviewed as an investment in raising women's productivity today and in the future, via women's influence on the coming generation. It is vital when increasing knowledge to prevent deterioration of the fragile environment. Training in environmentally-friendly agriculture methods and access to technical information via extension services and other programs have not been available to African women farmers to the same extent as their male counterparts. This is particularly notable when one considers that women produce most of the food consumed at home.

The gender division of resources, knowledge, work and the products thereof, according to Rocheleau (1987), may reflect complementarity or coincidence of men's and women's interests in rural land use systems. The degree to which women in a given setting control resources may influence their ability to participate in forest development activities. Limits on certain resources may act as constraints to women's participation. Understanding the constraints and opportunities in a given situation is important for coming up with strategies to involve women in forestry activities and to ensure that women derive benefits from their participation.

A prominent gendered woodland resource issue that has not received direct attention is food security. Food security is endangered by undervaluing or neglecting women's work in agriculture and natural resources management. Biased statistics support policies that thwart women's work as food producers and natural resource managers. At the local level, food security is weakened by gender inequalities and sexual division of labor, where women have the main responsibility for supply of food, fuelwood and water, but lack the time and sufficient control over resources to be able to do this in a sustainable way.

Agriculture, forestry, energy and water supply are intimately connected ecologically through women's work.

Problems and Consequences of Deforestation

Deforestation, land degradation and watershed destabilization constitute significant environmental problems. For dry-land farming communities this translates into chronic problems with fuelwood, water and food supplies, as well as
diminishing returns to land and labor in household subsistence farming. More
acute problems may occur when environmental changes exacerbate the impact
of periodic droughts and famines.

Land degradation expands from physical degradation to encompass the life
support and livelihood needs of the rural poor. The collection of firewood is
increasingly becoming a time-consuming task which at an average occupies
between two and four hours for every trip, normally three to four times in a
week. Estimates show that in several deforested areas, women spend up to twenty
percent of their productive time collecting wood.

The most striking images engendered by the popular notions of women's
roles are those of women as *victims,* as *villains,* and as *fixers* in the process of
environmental degradation and the related decline in agricultural yields. As
victims women are depicted carrying heavy loads of fuelwood across devastated landscapes. As *villains* they are portrayed directly and indirectly as causes
of deforestation and over-population. Women as farmers, as fuelwood cutters
and consumers, as forest "invaders," as mothers, are seen as acting against the
national and global environment. Thus they become targets for environmental
education and regulatory action. Often such programs emphasize negative goals:
stopping cultivation of marginal lands, prohibiting women's access to forest
products, changing traditional methods of firewood use, and limiting family
size (Rocheleau 1989). As *fixers* social forestry research and development organizations have also recognized the potential power of women as agents of
agricultural resource management. However, in many cases, this has translated
into a narrow focus on women as free (or cheap) labor to work on social forestry projects in the community interest.

Case Study

The Association of Zimbabwe Traditional Environmental Conservation

Currently there are attempts by spirit mediums to revive the traditional ways of
managing woodlands. The fact that it is community and spiritual leaders who are
motivating environmental action is interesting, but not particularly surprising in the
light of Zimbabwean culture. Traditionally, chiefs have a close relationship with

the land and command a great deal of respect, while spirit mediums have much influence among the people because they are the link between the living and the ancestral spirits who are believed to preside over all community activities.

The Association of Zimbabwe Traditional Environmental Conservation (AZTREC) has been operating as a trust since 1988. AZTREC is currently involved in conservation projects in five districts in Masvingo in the the south and east of the country. With the assistance of the Forestry Commission, twelve projects were established in 1992, raising 60,000 seedlings of both exotic and indigenous trees and grass species, which are given free to villages. In rural areas, currently there are 437 woodlots in the area covering some 832 hectares of land. In addition, nearly 211 hectares of more extensive and permanent woodland have been planted with the help of AZTREC as a longer term solution to the high rate of desertification in the area.

AZTREC is currently working with a Kenyan NGO in a project to harness rain water in storage tanks for the use in homes and schools and to feed newly planted fruit trees. The Association of Zimbabwe Traditional Environmental Conservation is involved in the following activities:

Tree Planting

The objective of the forestation component of the program was to satisfy the requirements of the community by way of raising appropriate indigenous and exotic species. Tree planting is to meet wood product needs, such as for fuel, construction timber, fodder and medicinal purposes. The project has twelve nurseries throughout the province.

Woodland Management

Community awareness is achieved by involving communities through education and participation, drawing on tradition and customs that relate to the preservation of sacred places; e.g., *Mapa*, our traditional burial grounds for chiefs, and *Marambatemwa*, our natural sacred places.

Water Point Environmental Conservation

This project component has a number of activities including checking or reducing erosion and improving vegetation cover around water points and catchment areas. The community is involved in mapping their environmental problems and needs, followed by project planning for water point environmental conservation activities. Rehabilitation of catchment areas is done through the planting of indigenous grass, bushes, and trees along river banks and other catchment areas. Also waterproof tanks are constructed by individuals in the community. Trenches are then dug below iron gutted roofs so that rainfall water will be captured in the tanks.

Sustainable Agriculture

Here the project looks at ways of reducing external inputs and promoting the use of local resources. The project aims to achieve a situation whereby commu-

nity productivity is not hindered by lack of funds for buying fertilizers or pesticides, instead relying on local resources, i.e., pig manure, cow dung humus and
other agroforestry practices that entail intercropping. They will then be in a
position to be self-sustaining. To achieve this, the groups work together with
organizations, like Natural Farming Network. We are launching a permaculture
program funded by the British High Commission.

Women's Involvement

There are fourteen women's groups involved in these activities, and they all
have established nurseries. The nurseries are aimed at food security and maintaining indigenous technology which women have controlled on behalf of the
welfare of families.

The daily activities of the spirit mediums can be seen in the following description by Mrs. Lydia Chabata:

> She (the medium) is in charge of the Women and Environment Education
> and Activities. In this program, she supervises the tree planting in the
> nurseries and ensures the integration of women in these activities.
>
> She oversees three sacred places which are being protected as *Mapa* and
> *Marambatemwa* as part of woodland management. The sacred places are
> protected in order to preserve trees and grass species, used as breeding
> places for our fauna, but most importantly because it is our cultural custom.
> The sacred places are protected by spirit mediums, local authorities and
> chiefs.
>
> I am involved because I am also a spirit medium. My role is to motivate
> women's participation in management of sacred places. People are al-
> lowed to harvest woodland products from the sacred areas as long as they
> follow the procedures. That is, they first go to the chief's messenger who
> will pass on the request to the chief who will take it to the spirit medium
> in charge of that particular area. The feedback will follow the same channel
> from top to bottom.
>
> The ordinary woman has no say in the management of the forest. Only
> elderly women are responsible for sweeping the paths and carrying pots of
> beer if there is to be a traditional ceremony in that forest. Only places which
> were originally sacred places can be said to be a sacred place. No one has
> the right to designate any area to become a new sacred place. The practice
> of protecting sacred places will continue because there is now new
> awareness in most Zimbabweans to value our old traditional ways. The
> awareness campaign is now being implemented in schools, clubs, and
> almost everywhere.

Chabata also suggests some problems: "However, there seems to be
lack of conscience among the new generation in valuing most of the
taboos; for example, very few of them think twice about cutting down a
tree in a sacred place. The new generation should continue with the

practice in order to maintain our identity, for we can't be a nation without any culture" (Chabata, 1993, personal interviews with a spirit medium).

Strategies and Policies for Sustainable Development

In the broadest sense, strategies for sustainable development aim at *promoting harmony among human beings and between humanity and nature, and these center around the following issues:*
—Reduce or eliminate legal and social-cultural constraints to rural women having access to and use of scarce productive resources.
—Develop and/or diffuse labor-saving technologies by and for rural women, for use in the home and in business.
—Promote research on women's roles in such areas as soil conservation, irrigation and watershed management, shallow waters and coastal resources management, integrated pest management, land use planning, forest conservation and community forestry.
—Identify and employ rural women's indigenous technical knowledge on sustainable resource use.
—Determine the impact of environmental degradation on the livelihoods of women and on the well-being of their families.
—Identify more clearly and publicize the crucial relationships between population policies and practices and environmental sustainability.
—Increase the participation of rural women in the design of sustainable development programs and projects.
Prerequisite for changing the traditional development interventions to gender-responsive ones are awareness raising and training on gender issues at the policy-making level. A gender-responsive approach to sustainable development and natural resource preservation assumes adequate awareness of the gender issues at the policy-making level in the national capitals and/or by international agencies. To the extent that such awareness is absent, appropriate training or other measures to fill this gap become a necessary first step.

Both conceptual and practical policy issues must be decided in a gender-responsive approach. One major conceptual policy issue is the decision whether to emphasize projects exclusively addressing women's needs as a part of a development package or mainstreaming. The former approach, which is most often advocated by some women's groups as a necessary affirmative action to close the gap in gender disparities, has been questioned as possibly contributing to the perpetuation of gender disparities. However, both approaches could be used in a complementary mode rather than as alternatives.

There are distinct differences between men and women in their roles and responsibilities; constraints and opportunities in productive and income-generating activities; type and scale of productive activities (subsistence versus cash crops); education and knowledge of environmental matters. Because of these differences, plus women's unique reproductive and health-care responsibilities, it is to be expected that women have different priorities, different perceptions of impacts from development projects, different responses to fiscal incentives, and different utility functioning and consumption patterns. Integration of women in the development process requires their full participation and influence at all levels of the decision-making process, not just in development in the implementation and potential benefits.

Capacitation for women via education, training and experience is essential. Empowerment for women is here defined to mean the unrestricted opportunity to influence the decision-making process, to have unrestricted access to and control of resources and services, and to take power in discerning the benefits and obligations from a development project. Empowerment means the opportunity for equitable sharing in costs and benefits of the production process, in the opportunities and obligations for preservation of the natural resources, and in caring for the household.

Future Challenges

—Interventions to increase gender sensitivity, linking macro versus micro.
—Incorporating indigenous knowledge.
—Enhancing women's capacities as woodland managers.
—Reinforcing group mobilization and leadership.
—Diversifying household income generation and improving food security.

References

Agarwal, B. 1991. *Engineering Environment Debate Lessons from the Indian Subcontinent,* Michigan State University.

Blaikie, P. and Brookfield, H. 1987. *Land Degradation and Society,* London: Methuen.

Borkenhagen, L. M., and Abramovitz, J. N. 1991. *Proceedings of the International Conference on Women and Biodiversity,* Kennedy School of Government, Harvard University, October 4-6 1991.

Borooah, R.; Cloud, K.; Peterson, J.; Saraswathi, T. S.; and Verma, A. 1991. *Capturing Complexity, Women, Households and Development,* University of Illinois.

Bradley, P. N., and McNamara, K. 1993. *Living with Trees Policies for Forestry Management in Zimbabwe,* World Bank, Washington.

Brechin, S., and West, P. 1982. "Social Barriers in Implementing Appropriate Technology: The Case of Community Forestry in Niger," West Africa, *Humbold Journal of Social Relations,* Volume 9, No. 2.

Brechin, S.; Margin, W.; Shapiro, K.; and West, P. 1984. *Agroforestry in Developing Countries Economic and Social Policy Issue,* USAID.

Campbell, B. M.; Clarke, J. G. M.; and Gumbo, D. J. 1991. *Traditional Agroforestry Practices in Zimbabwe:* Agroforestry systems, Zimbabwe.

Campbell, B. M.; Vermeulen, S. J.; and Lynam, T. 1991. *The Value of Trees in Small-Scale Sector of Zimbabwe,* IDRC Publications.

Clones, J. P. 1992. *The Links between Gender Issues and the Fragile Environments of Sub-Saharan Africa,* The World Bank, Washington.

Correia, M. C., and Mvududu, S. C. 1992. *Women in SADC Forestry Sector Programme of Action Reid Collins and Associates,* Vancouver Canada; and Forestry Sector Technical Co-ordination Unit, Lilongwe, Malawi.

Dewees, P. A. 1989. "The Wood Fuel Crisis Reconsidered: Observations on the Dynamics of Abundance and Scarcity," *World Development:* 17:1159-1172.

Feldstein, H. S.; Flora, C.; and Poats, S. V. 1991. *The Gender Variable in Agricultural Research,* IDRC, Ottawa, Canada.

Forestry Commission 1990. *Deforestation and Afforestation Activities in Zimbabwe,* Harare, Zimbabwe, Government of Zimbabwe, International Institute for Environmental and Development 1992. *Environmental Synopsis of Zimbabwe* (ODA).

Gaidzanwa, R. 1992. *The Ideology of Domesticity and the Struggle of Women Workers: The Case of Zimbabwe,* The Hague, Netherlands: Institute of Social Studies.

George, Susan, 1992. *Debt Boomerang: How the Third World Debt Harms Us All,* London: Pluto.

Henn, J. K. 1986. *The Material Basis of Sexism: A Mode of Production Analysis With African Examples.* Boston University Press.

Kamau, I. N. 1989. *Agroforestry Technological, Innovations, Political, Ecological, Cultural Issues,* Michigan State University.

Lan, David, 1985. *Guns and Rain: Guerrillas and Spirit Mediums in Zimbabwe,* Harare: Zimbabwe Publishing House.

McGregor, J. 1989. *Coping with Deforestation: Local Strategies and State Policy in Zimbabwe's Communal Areas,* London, Commonwealth Science Council.

Merchant, Carolyn, 1992. *Radical Ecology: The Search for a Livable World* New York: Routledge.

Mies, M. 1986. *Patriarchy and Accumulation on a World Scale,* London: Zed.

Mies, M. 1988. *Women: The Last Colony,* London: Zed.

Mvududu, S. C. 1990. *Social Forestry for Rural Development: The Case of Women's Participation in Social Forestry Activities in Zimbabwe,* African Training and Research Centre for Women and United Nations Commission for Africa, Addis Ababa, Ethiopia.

Nhira, C. and Fortman, L. 1992. *Local Control and Management of Forest and Environmental Resources in Zimbabwe,* Harare: University of Zimbabwe Press.

Ranger, T. O. 1979. *Revolt in Southern Rhodesia, 1896-7,* London: Heinemann.

Rocheleau, D. E. 1987a. "Gender Resource Management and the Rural Landscape: Implications for Agroforestry and Farming Systems Research," Poats, S. V.; Schmink, M.; and Spring, M. 1987:149-169. *Gender Issues in Farming Systems Research and Extension,* West View Press, Boulder, Colorado.

Rocheleau, D. E.; 1987b. "The User-Perspective and the Agroforestry Research and Action Agenda," H. Gholz, ed., 1987:59-87. *Agroforestry: Realities, Possibilities and Potentials.* Martinus Nijhoff Doerdrecht.

Rocheleau, D. E. 1989. *Yours, Mine and Ours: The Gender Division of Work, Resources and Rewards in Agroforestry Systems,* ICRAF Nairobi.

Scherr, S. J. 1991. *Agroforestry Systems,* ICRAF Journal, Volume 15, Nos. 2 and 3, Nairobi.

Schoffeleers, J. M. 1979. *Guardians of the Land,* Gweru: Mambo Press.

Scoones, I. C. 1990. *Livestock Population and the Household Economy: A Case-study from Southern Zimbabwe,* Ph.d. thesis, University of London.

Van den Hambergh, H. 1993. *Gender Environment and Development. A Guide to the Literature,* Institute for Development Research by International Books. Utrecht, Netherlands.

Warner, K. 1993. *Patterns of Farm Tree Growing in Eastern Africa,* ICRAF, Nairobi and Oxford Forest Institute, Oxford.

Warren, Karen, 1987. "Feminism and Ecology: Making Connections," *Enrironmental Ethics* 9,1: 3-20.

World Bank, 1991. *Zimbabwe Agricultural Sector Memorandum,* World Bank, Washington.

Williams, P. J. 1992. *Women's Participation in Forestry Activities in Africa,* Project Summary and Policy Recommendation Environment Liaison Centre International, Nairobi, Kenya.

14

The Chisumphi Cult

The Role of Women in Preserving
the Environment

ISABEL APAWO PHIRI

The rate at which the environment is being destroyed is now the concern of every academic discipline. Religion is no exception. As observed by Schoffeleers, before the coming of Islam and Christianity to Central African societies, the people had their own philosophies in protecting the environment. These philosophies were reflected in the people's religion.[1] It is also an agreed fact among the scholars of the African Traditional Religions that in the African worldview, human beings exist in relation to the universe. That means there is a special relationship between God, deities, ancestors, human beings, and nature.[2] In the African traditional societies ecological concerns were shown in various ways, one of which was through territorial cults. Schoffeleers has said that

> Characteristic activities of territorial cults are rituals to counteract droughts, floods, plight, pests and epidemic diseases afflicting cattle and man [sic]. Put positively, territorial cults function in respect of the wellbeing of the community, its fields, livestock, fishing, hunting and general economic interests. Apart from engaging in ritual action, however, they also issue and enforce directives with regard to a community's use of the environment.[3]

The Chisumphi cult, which is the concern of this study, falls under the category of territorial cults. Detailed research of the cult has already been done from historical and theological perspectives. Y. Ntara[4] was the first Malawian to write on the cult in the fifties through his account of *Mbiri ya Achewa*. During the same period, W. H. J. Rangeley[5] and R. A. Hamilton[6] recorded in detail the historical organizational structures of the Chisumphi cult among the central Chewa and the Mbona cult among the southern Chewa. In the sixties additional research of the two Chewa shrines done by Thomas Price[7] was presented at a seminar held in the Centre of African Studies, University of Edinburgh. Commenting on Price's paper entitled "Malawi Rain-cults," George Shepperson noted the lack of an examination of the role of women in traditional cults.[8] J. M. Schoffeleers made significant contributions on the two rain shrines in a number of articles from a historical and theological perspective. In one article he carried out a comparative historical study of the two cults to show the different social and political organizations in which they operated.[9] All the studies have put emphasis on the historical developments, organization and fragmentation of the Chisumphi cult up to the 1970s. These studies appeared in a book that Schoffeleers edited entitled *Guardians of the Land*. In the introduction to this book, Schoffeleers showed concern about the lack of explicit study of ecological functions outside of accounts of ritual.[10] He went on to suggest that this could be "on one hand that all students of the cults have been most interested in their religious, political and historical aspects and on the other hand that their ecological functions are paradoxically not immediately evident. Yet the impact of territorial cults on the ecological system is such that, borrowing Rappaport's phrase, we may justifiably speak of 'a ritually directed eco-system.' "[11]

The aim of this research is to begin to fill the gaps by examining the contemporary role of women at and around the shrine in the use and protection of natural resources. This involved a socio-economic as well as cultural-religious analysis of the role of the cult in relation to the surrounding natural resources. The study also tried to find out whether the absence of a strong role played by the cult has an effect on the environment as experienced by women in the surrounding communities. Women have been singled out because, according to tradition, they are the ones who are responsible for fetching water, firewood and looking for everyday food. Therefore they are the ones who are affected more by the changes in the environment. Thus the overall aim of the present study is to investigate how women contribute to the destruction of the natural resources and whether or not African Traditional Religion provides usable resources to empower women as agents for sustaining the integrity of creation.

Background Information

The Chisumphi shrine is presently located in Kachikoti village, T. A. Pemba in Dedza district. It is 63 kilometers from Lilongwe city in Malawi. The traditional name of the place is Msinja. The major reason for choosing this shrine is because the historical and theological studies on the shrine mention the important role that was once played by "spirit wives." Ntara mentions that in the Proto Chewa period, all the Chewa shrines formed a network and were headed by "spirit wives" of the Chewa God known as Chisumphi.[12] The "spirit wives" were known as guardians of the land. The role of "spirit wives" continued during the period of Phiri clan.

Among the central Chewa, the most famous "spirit wife" was *Makewana*—mother of all the people—at Msinja. In fact Msinja was the center of the Chewa religion.[13] *Makewana* got her call by falling into a trance and delivering a message from Chisumphi to the people. The traditional role of *Makewana* was religious and political. Her political role came to an end first with the Ngoni attacks in the 1870s, and second with the coming of the colonial government in the 1890s. Since then the shrine has continued in a fragmented state and without much power. However, as reported by Schoffeleers, every time the country is affected by severe drought, there is an attempt to restore the shrine to its original status. For example, such an attempt was made in 1948. During the years 1992-1994 the country has experienced acute food shortages. It is the interest of this study to find out what the shrine keepers have tried to do in order to address the drought issue.

Tradition has it that once *Makewana*, the Keeper of the Shrine, was in office, she was supposed to remain single and dedicate her life to service at the shrine. There is a contemporary story which says that in the 1950s there was a young woman who was called by Chisumphi to become *Makewana*. Her original name was Mothela. Since the cult was in a deteriorated form and therefore not very influential, Mothela decided that she was going to maintain the title of *Makewana* but also get married. She conceived and gave birth to one child. Soon after delivery, she got sick. She began having hallucinations and her guardians began to see strange things in the house such as bright lights even though they did not have electricity. After a long illness, *Makewana* died. It was revealed through dreams to some people that she died because Chisumphi was not happy with the fact that she got married.

Since then the other women who were called to serve at the shrine refused to use the name of *Makewana*. Mkwinda, the next keeper of the shrine, regarded herself as a perpetual sister of *Makewana*.[14] She was a widow when she assumed the responsibility of looking after the shrine and died in 1992. Coincidentally that is the year that the whole country was badly hit by food shortages.

The current keeper of the shrine is Nandinesi Nabanda. She is a widow and had already reached menopause when she became the keeper of the shrine. While in the past, one became a keeper of the shrine through falling into a trance, the current one inherited the position from her mother, Mkwinda. She does not consider herself as *Makewana* or *Makewana's* niece but as a perpetual sister of the traditional *Makewana*. With this change of tradition, the name of *Makewana* as a female keeper of *Makewana* has fazed out. This change came about out of fear of what happened to the last *Makewana* and not because of the presence of a male chief known by the same name, as suggested by Schoffeleers.[15]

The story of Mothela seems to confirm the traditional belief that women must be single in order to serve God effectively. It could be possible that Mothela's death was not associated with her position at the shrine but was a result of complications connected with the birth of her child. However, in the African worldview when one has acted contrary to the demands of tradition and then dies, the common explanation is that death came about as punishment for disobedience.

Nandinesi Nabanda's Role as Protector of the Land

Nandinesi Nabanda considers herself as the protector of the land in two ways. First, through the annual rain-calling and first-fruit thanksgiving rituals. Second, by being in charge of the natural resources around the shrine. The role of a rain-caller involves the whole community of Kachikoti village. By observing the environment she can tell whether in a particular year there is going to be normal rains or delays or too much rain. A rain ritual is performed to hasten rain or stop it if there is too much.

Annual Rain-calling

In the case of rain-calling, the whole village is informed in advance so that couples can refrain from sex relations. This is because according to the beliefs of the Chewa the shrine is considered holy and sexual relations defiles the holy. On the actual day for the ritual, they start preparing very early in the morning. Traditionally, the female shrine keeper used to wear a dark cloth called *Biliwita*. It was supposed to symbolize and attract dark clouds. This cloth is no longer available. Therefore, she just wears ordinary clothes. She is the one who addresses Chisumphi and the ancestors at the shrine. In the case of the ancestors she does not mention any particular names. She also gives directions as to how the whole ceremony should be conducted.

Nabanda is accompanied by three groups of people. The first group is of girls[16] and sometimes boys[17] between the ages of six and eleven. The ages are significant because in the case of the girls they would not have reached puberty. The underlying belief here is that menstruation has a negative effect on the shrine. In fact all the women who were born and brought up in Kachikoti village have been to the shrine while they were within this age group.[18] This group has a distinct role to play. They wear ordinary clothes although in the past they also had to wear a dark cloth. They congregate at Nabanda's hut where their faces are covered with powdered charcoal and dotted with a paste made from maize flour. One girl carries porridge made from maize flour in a clay pot and the second girl carries a clay pot of water. The whole group sings rain-calling songs as they walk to the shrine with Nabanda. They continue singing as they go round the shrine. They are also responsible for cleaning the clay pots that remain at the shrine. They sweep in and around the shrine and pour the libation of porridge. After the ceremony they all go home singing and expecting rain to fall anytime. In the past, rain used to fall before reaching home. This has not been the case in the past ten years. The delays in rainfall in recent years are believed to be due to a combination of factors. Some of the factors include loose morals among the people, carelessness in cutting trees without planting indigenous ones and the will of God.[19]

The second group that accompanies Nabanda is that of three to four women who have reached menopause. Their role is mainly of supporting Nabanda in the shrine rituals. Traditionally the group of younger and older women who worked with *Makewana* were known as *Matsano*. This supports the tradition collected by Rangeley that *Matsano* were women who had not reached puberty or those who have reached menopause.[20] Avoidance of menstrual blood may also explain why they had to be only women who had reached menopause. The contemporary generation of women do not seem to remember that traditionally they were referred to as *Matsano*.

The third group is that of male officials. This includes the current chief, Kachikoti, his elder brother Mkale Julius Mabvuka Phiri and some counselors of the chief. Their contemporary duty includes looking after the shrine in conjunction with Nabanda. The shrine is just in the outskirts of the village. Before reaching the shrine, the chief addresses the spirits that are inhabiting the sacred tree which is closer to the village. The chief and his male group do not go all the way to the shrine. They stop a hundred yards from the shrine.

In the case of too much rain, the roof of the shrine is opened to allow light to go into the shrine. The roof of the shrine symbolizes rain-cloud cover. The action of removing some grass from the roof symbolizes chasing away the rain cloud. Therefore the rains are expected to stop. This exercise is expected to prevent the crops from rotting as a result of too much rain.

First-fruits Thanksgiving Ceremony

Once the rains have started and the pumpkin leaves have reached a good picking stage,[21] Nabanda calls for a thanksgiving ceremony. A day is chosen and announced for couples to separate. On the day of the ritual, each family brings to Nabanda one leaf of a pumpkin plant. The women of the family are the ones that take the pumpkin leaves to Nabanda. However if the women are menstruating, they do not go into the field to pick the pumpkin leaves. Instead they ask their daughters or female relatives to pick the pumpkin leaves for them. In the afternoon, a procession is made to the shrine just like in the rain-calling ritual. The only difference is that, instead of porridge, they take pumpkin leaves. This ceremony is repeated with the first green maize. It is a taboo to eat these two types of food before a thanksgiving ceremony has been performed. This ceremony is an acknowledgement that God is the source of food. God, the source of rain, provided the rain and therefore they show their gratitude by having a thanksgiving ritual.

Protection of the Natural Resources around the Shrine

Kachikoti village is surrounded by Dzalanyama Forest Reserve on the eastern side which is under the protection of the government. In fact, the government employee who protects the forest resides within the village. Between the village and the forest, there is Kanyungu Dambo with pools of water and communal grazing land. On the southeastern side there is the sacred grove where the shrine is located. To the north, there is the Diampwe River. Although the present shrine area is small, the sacred place extends to part of Dzalanyama Forest Reserve, and a section of the pool on Kanyungu Dambo. Each sacred place has a story as to why it is preserved.

Sacred Grove within Dzalanyama Forest Reserve

This area is referred to as the male side of the sacred place. Tradition has it that it was the residential area of *Kamundi Mbewe*.[22] He was a functionary of the shrine who used to perform the duties of a husband of *Makewana* during the initiation of girls.[23] The place is also referred to as *Pakabvumbwa* because there is a cave where the people of Msinja went to hide during the Ngoni raid of Msinja in the 1870s.[24] There is now conflict between the Department of Forestry and Shrine officials over the ownership of the place. The local people want to use the place for religious purposes but the Department of Forestry does not allow them because the sacred place is within the Dzalanyama Forest Reserve. Still the shrine keeper considers *Pakabvumbwa* as part of her area of influence. There is still a belief that there is a python that stays at that place and comes to eat the food offered at the shrine which is about a kilometer away. No one has seen the python, but they see its tracks the following morning after a ritual has been performed.

The women of the village buy firewood from the Dzalanyama Forest Reserve. For the younger women they buy firewood three times a week at the cost of 50t[25] per bundle. The older women buy firewood daily because their bundles are small. Since those who are sexually active cannot pass through the sacred place, it has now become a tradition that all women take a longer route to the place where the Forestry Department sells firewood. Before the Mozambiquean refugees came to settle at the village as well as the surrounding villages in the 1980s, the women of Kachikoti village used to spend an hour walking to and from the Forest Reserve to buy firewood. There has been population growth as a result of the presence of the refugees. The effect of that has been overuse of the section of the forest which was closer to the village. Now the women spend a quarter of each day to buy firewood.

Sacred Pool on the Kanyungu Dambo

Linden has argued that water symbolism is important in the theology of the Chisumphi shrine.[26] There is one pool on the dambo which is dedicated to Chisumphi. It is called *Dziwe La Anamwali*. Tradition has it that a long time ago six girls were going through an initiation ceremony in *Makewana*'s area. On the last day, very early in the morning, the girls with their sponsors went to one of the pools for a bath. They formed a line so that when each girl jumped into the water, she was followed by her sponsor. The last sponsor was surprised that all those who went before her did not come up to the surface. She therefore decided to hold on and see what was happening. After waiting for a long time and noticing that the others were not coming out, she sounded the alarm and the whole village of Msinja came to wait with her. By sunset there was a rainbow which appeared only on that particular pool. *Makewana* interpreted the presence of the rainbow as a sign that the girls and their sponsors were still alive but with Chisumphi. The place was declared sacred.

To mark the coming out of any initiates, the Chewa celebrate with a *nyau* (mask) dance. However since the disappearance of the six girls and the five sponsors *nyau* dance was banned in Msinja. Up to now *nyau* dance is not allowed in Kachikoti village.[27]

The mystical nature of the pool has continued to the present. After a while some people went fishing in the pool. The fish they caught had strings of beads around them just like the girls before they disappeared. This brought fear in the people. No one can draw water or fish from that particular pool. In 1993, it is reported that some men had a tobacco nursery near the pool but used water from another pool. The chief and Nabanda regarded that as disrespect to Chisumphi. Therefore they were fined two black chickens and one black goat. The two chickens were tied and thrown into the pool as living sacrifice to God. The goat was slaughtered at the pool. The blood dripped into the pool. The meat was roasted just beside the pool and was eaten only by the people who were there. The bones, skin and any remains were thrown into the pool.[28]

Despite the fact that two sides of Kachikoti village are surrounded by water, the women are facing fish and water shortages. Although some of the pools are not sacred, women do not go there to get water. There is so much fear of the place, especially by women. Furthermore, in the dry season the other pools dry up, except the sacred one which is not usable by the people. Recently, Diampwe River has been drying up faster than it did four years ago. This has been attributed to reduction in the rainfall. Since the water table has gone down, the one borehole which provided the village with clean water does not work anymore. As an alternative the women get their water from a two-meters-deep well which is just in the outskirts of the village. On average most homes in the village use six to eight buckets of water a day. This means the women have to wake up around four o'clock in the morning to fetch water. Since the lines are long and the water from the well is not enough for the whole village, it takes them an average of thirty minutes to one hour to get one bucket of water.

The scarcity of water has also meant problems in getting vegetables for daily food. Most of the women have a vegetable garden at one side of the dambo. Maintaining a vegetable garden is also a hassle because of the presence of cattle. The Department of Forestry has cattle which are left to graze freely in the dambo. Some of the people also own cattle. The population of cattle has increased and yet communal land for grazing has remained the same. This has led to overgrazing. Guarding the vegetable gardens to prevent the cattle from eating their vegetables is considered a woman's job. Therefore while guarding the vegetable gardens, the women prepare lunch for their families. When their daughters come back from school, they take over the guarding of the gardens so that their mothers can fetch firewood or more water for the home.

The Land Surrounding the Shrine

The shrine keeper makes sure that the trees around the shrine are never cut down. There is a story that a Ngoni chief, Kachere, sent some of his men to cut down one of the trees at Msinja to use in carpentry. The major reason was to challenge the sacredness of Msinja. Tradition has it that when they started cutting the tree, a voice was heard protesting. However, the people continued cutting. As the tree was falling there was a warning, a loud cry and blood came out of the tree. Everyone ran away. Soon after that Chief Kachere and all those who were involved in cutting the tree died. This served as a warning to all the people not to fell any trees around the shrine. The log is still there up to the present although most of it is rotten and was burnt by bush fire.

Bush fire has damaged most of the trees around the shrine so that there are now not more than twelve sacred trees. Most of the land is now under cultivation. The argument is that the people were allowed to cultivate near the shrine so that they can prevent bush fires from finishing the remaining trees at the shrine. Another possible reason could be that since there is an increase in population, there is also the issue of scarcity of land for cultivation. The garden closest to the shrine belongs to the shrine keeper and the chief. When a branch from a sacred tree falls down, it can only be picked up by the small girls who go to the shrine with the shrine keeper and the chief. It was reported that such kind of wood can only be used to warm up the people at night during a funeral. However, the keeper of the shrine reported that it can also be used for cooking by herself and the elderly women who accompany her to the shrine.

Conclusion

The discussion in this paper has tried to give a picture of the present state of the Chisumphi shrine in relation to ecology and women. It has shown that the shrine is still functioning. Rituals aimed at the preservation of the environment are still taking place. The places which were declared as sacred and therefore protected by the tradition of the shrine are still maintained. The tension that is there between the shrine officials and the Department of Forestry over the ownership of *Pakabvumbwa* is a complex one and needs attention from all the people who are interested in preserving natural resources and traditional religions.

The research has also shown that although this is a female-led shrine, it still observes traditions that affect women negatively. For example, a keeper of the shrine must observe celibacy; menstruation by women and sexuality of the people is seen as having a bad effect on the environment; picking of pumpkin leaves while menstruating is associated with unproductiveness of the land; married women who are sexually active cannot pass through the route to the shrine for fear of bringing misfortune to the community even though it is a short cut.

It was also observed in this study that some traditions have changed. The traditional names of female officials of the shrine have changed. The names of *Makewana* and *Matsano* have disappeared, although the roles in the preservation of the environment have remained. This is an indication that tradition is not static but dynamic.

If a comparison study was carried out to examine the economic status of Kachikoti village and other villages in Dedza, it could show that the women of Kachikoti are lucky because they do not walk very long distances to fetch water, firewood and look for food. While other parts of the country are seeking maize aid from the government, the people of Kachikoti village have enough to keep them going until the next rainy season. For the women of the village, they attribute that to the fact that they belong to a religious village and therefore they are blessed by God.[29]

The women of the village have also learned to view walking long distances to fetch firewood or standing in long lines for water as a social occasion where they can chat with their friends. However, this does not mean that they do not seek better or easier methods of acquiring firewood and water. What should be appreciated here is that they have turned a plight into a social gathering.

They do not look at having a personal tree plantation as a solution to the firewood problem because this has been viewed as a man's job. Those women who have their own plantations are criticized as wanting to become men.[30] Therefore, there is need to change this attitude so that women can begin to contribute to the preservation of the environment. Unfortunately, while the shrine keeper sees the need for planting trees as a solution to water and firewood problems, this is viewed as beyond the shrine's responsibility. It will require empowerment through conscientization programs for the shrine keeper and the women in the village to be able to contribute to the solutions of their environmental problems.

The problem of vegetable gardens and cattle is an acute one and needs immediate attention. One way of solving the problem would be for the women to come together and call for a meeting with the chief and the Forestry Department to discuss land being set aside for growing vegetables without disturbances from cattle. If the issues of growing vegetables, planting trees and maintainance of the borehole were accepted as community issues, and not just women's issues, all the problems raised in this study could be sorted out much faster.

Notes

1. M. Schoffeleers, "Introduction" in ed. J. M. Schoffeleers, *Guardians of the Land*. (Gweru: Mambo Press, 1979), p. 2.

2. E. Ikenga-Metuh, *Comparative Studies in African Traditional Religions*. (Onitsha:

IMICO Publishers, 1987), p. 263.

3. J. M. Schoffeleers, *Guardians of the Land*, p. 2.

4. See S.Y. Ntara, *Mbiri ya Achewa* (Lusaka: Northern Rhodesia and Nyasaland Publications Bureau, 2nd edit., 1950).

5. See W. Rangeley, "Two Nyasaland Rainshrines: Makewana, the mother of all people" in *Nyasaland Journal* (Vol. 2, 1962).

6. See R. A. Hamilton, "Oral Tradition: Central Africa" in ed. R. A. Hamilton, *History and Archaeology in Africa* (London: University of London, School of Oriental and African Studies, 1955).

7. See T. Price, "Malawi Rain-cults" in *Religion in Africa* (Proceedings of a seminar held in the Centre of African Studies, University of Edinburgh, April 10-12, 1964).

8. G. Shepperson, "Religion in British Central Africa" in *Religion in Africa*. (Proceedings of a seminar held in the Centre of African Studies, University of Edinburgh, April 10-12, 1964).

9. See J. M. Schoffeleers, "The Interaction of the M'Bona Cult and Christianity, 1849-1963" in ed. T. O. Ranger and J. Weller, *Themes in the Christian History of Central Africa* (London: Heinemann, 1975).

10. J. M. Schoffeleers, *Guardians of the Land*, p. 3.

11. J. M. Schoffeleers, *Guardians of the Land*, p. 3.

12. Chisumphi was one of the names used to refer to God among the Chewa.

13. This was confirmed by the current chief David Billiard Kachikoti during an interview held on August 17, 1994.

14. J. M. Schoffeleers, *Guardians of the Land*, p. 174.

15. Interview with Nandinesi Nabanda on August 17, 1994.

16. Nandinesi Nabanda remembers only girls playing this role. The current group of girls consist of Ezeliya Gama (9 years old), Marita Chikwembani (11), Lisineti Dzomba (9), Marita Ntekwe (10), Kalade Kadzalero (10), and Delezina Davide (9).

17. Interview with Nexion Kachime on August 17, 1994. He is a nephew of Chief Tsumbi, who has historical connections to the shrine. In fact the current chief, Kachikoti, was installed by Chief Tsumbi.

18. Interview with Namadesi, August 17, 1994.

19. Interview with Nabanda, Chief Kachikoti, Naziwaya, Flora Naphiri on August 17, 1994.

20. W. Rangeley, in *Nyasaland Journal,* Vol. 2, 1962, p. 36.

21. Pumpkin leaves are a common vegetable in Malawi. In this ritual they stand for all vegetables that women pick from their gardens six to eight weeks after the first rainfall.

22. Interview with Chiefs Ching'ombe Tsumbi and David Billiard Kachikoti on August 17, 1994.

23. W. Rangeley, in *Nyasaland Journal,* Vol. 2, 1962, p. 33.

24. Interview with Chief Kachikoti and Mkale Julius Mabvuka Phiri on August 17, 1994.

25. The current exchange rate is K7.7228 to US $1.00. K1.00 is equal to 100t.

26. I. Linden, "Chisumphi Theology in the Religion of Central Malawi," in ed. J. M. Schoffeleers, *Guardians of the Land*, p. 196.

27. Interview with Chief Kachikoti, Chief Msumbi, Nabanda and Naziwaya on August 17, 1994.

28. Interview with Chief Kachikoti and Mkale Julius Mavuka Phiri, August 17, 1994.

29. This belief was expressed in all interviews with both women and men. People

interviewed: Nandinesi Nabanda, Kazeka Naphiri, Lucy Nangozo, Margret Nambada, Nairi Naphiri, Esita Naphiri, Flora Naphiri, Naziwaya, Namadesi David, Chief Kachikoti, Chief Msumbi, Mkale Julius Mavuka Phiri, Nexion Kachime, Ezeliya Gama, Marita Chikwembani, Lisineti Dzomba, Marita Ntekwe, Kalade Kadzalero, and Delezina Davide.
   30. Interview with Namadesi David, August 17, 1994.

Bibliography

Bourdillon, M. *Religion and Society: A Text for Africa* (Gweru: Mambo Press, 1990).

Gwengwe, J. W. *Kukula ndi Mwambo* (Blantyre: Dzuka, 1975).

Hamilton, R. A. "Oral Tradition: Central Africa" in ed. R. A. Hamilton, *History and Archaeology in Africa* (London: University of London, School of Oriental and African Studies, 1955).

Ikenga-Metuh, E. *Comparative Studies in African Traditional Religions* (Onitsha: IMICO Publishers, 1987).

Linden, I. "Chisumphi Theology in Religion of Central Malawi" in ed. J. M. Schoffeleers, *Guardians of the Land: Essays on Central African Territorial Cults* (Gweru: Mambo Press, 1979).

Ntara, S. Y. *Mbiri ya Achewa* (Lusaka: Northern Rhodesia and Nyasaland Publications Bureau, 2nd ed., 1950).

Pachai, B. *The Early History of Malawi* (London: Longman, 1972).

Phiri, K. M., *Chewa History in Central Malawi and The Use of Oral Tradition 1600-1920.* Ph.D., University of Wisconsin, 1975.

Price, T. "Malawi Rain Cults" in *Religion in Africa: Proceedings,* Centre of African Studies, (University of Edinburgh, April 10-12, 1964).

Rangeley, W. "Two Nyasaland Rainshrines: Makewana, the Mother of All People" in *Nyasaland Journal,* Vol. 2, 1962.

Schoffeleers, M. J. "The Interaction of the M'Bona Cult and Christianity, 1849-1963" in ed. T. O. Ranger, and J. Weller, *Themes in the Christian History of Central Africa* (London: Heinemann, 1975).

———— and Roscoe, A. A. *Land of Fire: Oral Literature from Malawi* (Limbe: Popular Publications, 1985).

————. "The Chisumphi and Mbona Cults in Malawi: A Comparative History" in ed. J. M. Schoffeleers, *Guardians of the Land: Essays on Central African Territorial Cults* (Gweru: Mambo Press, 1979).

Shepperson, G. "Religion in British Central Africa" in *Religion in Africa: Proceedings,* Centre of African Studies (University of Edinburgh, April 10-12, 1964).

15

The Gikuyu* Theology of Land and Environmental Justice

TERESIA HINGA

Often, the environmental crisis in Africa has been wrongly presented as an inevitable product of the nature of the continent and its inhabitants. Famines are frequently depicted as products of drought proneness in the affected areas. Sometimes the view is proposed that Africa has too many mouths to feed and that the answer lies in more stringent birth control measures. Other times it is assumed that the crises bedeviling Africa today have to do with poor political leadership and possibly an inherent inability of the inhabitants of the continent to deal with the environment in a responsible way.

I would argue, however, that the current crisis has more to do with the historical developments on the continent, particularly after nineteenth-century colonization that saw the continent literally carved up and distributed among various colonial powers whose chief motivation was to exploit its rich material and human resources.[1] I would argue also that the process of colonization was informed by an ideology that was inherently racist and that as a result did not perceive any grounds for listening to the African peoples. At the same time, these African peoples had long wrestled with their environment and had developed values and ideologies that both celebrated and ensured a more balanced relationship with the environment, upon which they depended. I refer, for example, to the intimate relationship that pastoral groups had developed with the animals, upon whom they depended, and with the land that gave life to both human beings and animals. I refer, in particular, to the sense of respect for the environment as a source of life that often led the Africans to be disparagingly referred to as nature worshipers.[2]

---

*Gikuyu is sometimes written as Kikuyu. Gikuyu is the adjectival form and Agikuyu is the noun, which refers to the people who form this ethnic group.

Not only did the colonizers disregard the values and environmental ethics of the people they conquered, they also superimposed their own view of the human relationship with nature. In Africa, the Christian ethic of dominion, which is implicit in certain readings of the Genesis account of creation,[3] supported well the imperial ideologies that propelled the colonialist project. This combination allowed gross abuse of the environment at all levels, including the exploitation of mineral wealth, the wanton destruction of natural vegetation systems in favor of the monocultures of cash crops, such as coffee, tea, and tobacco, as well as the exploitation of the African human resources. The exploitation of Africans was particularly destructive since it led to a legacy of confusion, apathy, and a sense of alienation among the indigenous peoples. The fruits of this legacy are manifest are today in the perpetuation of the abuse of nature and of each other that sometimes reaches shocking levels in contemporary Africa.[4]

The environmental crisis in Africa has a variety of interwoven dimensions. I will focus on the issue of land and landlessness as one of the most crucial and controversial dimensions of the crisis, particularly from the perspective of justice. In Kenya, for example, this issue has led to bloody upheavals, as ever-increasing numbers of people lay claim to a seemingly less and less adequate resource. The issue of land and landlessness is therefore one that requires an urgent analysis in an attempt to gauge what has gone wrong.

Using the Agikuyu of Kenya as a case study, I will show how disregard for the traditional environmental ethics and the substitution of the colonial ethic of domination led to massive landlessness not only in terms of quantity, but also in terms of the quality of the available land. I submit that because of this quantitative and qualitative landlessness other problems have evolved, including in recent times the so-called "ethnic" clashes and the consequent loss of life, property, and the conspicuous displacement of peoples, leading to the emergence of the largely unprecedented phenomenon of internal refugees.

The Gikuyu Theology of Land: A Reconstruction

The Agikuyu constitute one of the fifty or so ethnic communities who live in Kenya.[5] The Agikuyu are primarily sedentary agriculturalists who make their living from tilling the land and keeping livestock. The Gikuyu theology of land can be reconstructed from an analysis of their oral traditions as well as religious and cultural practices that clearly show they had a more environment-friendly attitude than the colonial invaders.

Looking first at their theology of origins we note that the Agikuyu consider nature as belonging to the creator. According to their cosmogonic myth, *Ngai* (God) created nature and is therefore the ultimate owner and dispenser of it. This view is implicit in the very name for God, *Ngai*, which means "the great divider" of the universe.[6]

The Agikuyu also affirm that *Ngai* is not just a creator but also a provider for human needs. In his generosity he gives each group of human beings, wherever they are in the world, their fair share of the universe to use in order to meet their immediate needs. In this connection, we note that the Agikuyu often respond with gratitude to *Ngai* for giving them a good portion of the universe. According to one prayer of thanksgiving, the Gikuyu portion "lacks neither food, nor water, nor land to till."

Before the time of colonization, the Agikuyu clearly understood that *Ngai* alone had absolute rights over the environmental assets which he had created. Conversely, they, and by extension all other human beings to whom God had apportioned their rightful and fair share of the universe, had only usufructuary rights.

Because of this theological understanding, certain other pertinent ideals seem to have developed. The Agikuyu, among many other African communities, perceive the environment both as a gift to be enjoyed by divine favor and as a responsibility to take care of, since ultimately it belongs to the Creator. The sense of human responsibility for maintaining the balances of nature can be inferred in their religious responses to ecological disturbances and disasters. When, for example, the rains fail and drought prevails, the Agikuyu consider this an occasion to examine their consciences to find out where and how they have neglected their moral obligations to God, to each other, and to nature, a negligence that can lead to chaos, which may manifest itself in and through ecological disasters.

Kenyatta records the response of the Agikuyu when the rains fail:

> When the people, after preparing their fields for planting, see that the rains have failed and drought is prolonged, . . . the elders get together and summon the seers and ask them whether they have received any communications from *Mwene-Nyaga*[7] in connection with the causes of the drought . . . (Kenyatta, 1965:234)

This act of summoning the seers to diagnose where they have gone wrong and to prescribe an antidote is the Gikuyu way of acknowledging their accountability to God, an accountability considered to have consequences not only for them but also for the rest of the created order. It is interesting to note that their prayer for rain not only expresses their repentance for whatever they may have done to cause imbalances in nature, but also implores God on behalf of other creatures, thus showing the Gikuyu sense of responsibility for nature. This is demonstrated in the Gikuyu petition for rain that also pleads on behalf of their livestock. One prayer for rain as recorded by Kenyatta went thus:

> Reverend elder (*Ngai*), who lives on Kerenyaga (Mount Kenya) . . . You who make rain fall and rivers flood. We offer you this sacrifice that you may give us rain . . . People and children are crying . . . sheep, goats and . . . cattle are crying . . . (Kenyatta, 1965:237)

The sense of responsibility that the Agikuyu feel toward nature is also evident in the way they utilize it. Before planting in the soil, they routinely perform rituals signifying their awareness that the act of using the land is a privilege they owe to *Ngai*. When the crops are successful, the Agikuyu routinely offer prayers of thanksgiving to God and set apart some of the produce for God as a token of their gratitude (Kenyatta, 1965:242-247).

An analysis of the Gikuyu theology of land and nature shows a definite affirmation that nature is not to be wantonly exploited, but utilized with care and a sense of responsibility, precisely because it ultimately belongs to God, who also demands that human beings establish and sustain the created equilibrium.

The Gikuyu understanding of land as a gift from the creator, who alone has the absolute rights over it, has led to a development of a system of land tenure that intrinsically recognizes that no individual human being has the absolute ownership of land. According to the Gikuyu understanding of land tenure, as presented by Kenyatta, everyone is entitled to land, since God created land for all to use. Some people, however, may acquire a certain level of "exclusive" use of a specific piece of land by virtue of working on it and clearing it for agricultural purposes. Such a person has been named *Mwene Githaka*. An individual can also acquire land by legitimate exchange of goods or services, such as by "buying" land that has previously been cleared by someone else.

Nonetheless, the Agikuyu understand that though a person may be considered the "owner" of a piece of land that he has thus acquired, he is still not its absolute owner. Other family members have a right to the land by virtue of being kin or offspring. The laws of primogeniture militate against the head of household disposing of land at the expense of his dependents and descendants, even those not yet born. Even total strangers can access this land if they are in need of cultivation or building rights.[8]

Despite being described as the "owner" of land, in the traditional context such a person is in effect only a trustee or a steward, a status best described by the title *Muramati*. As such, he is obliged not only to take care of the land on behalf of other members of the family, but also to use his judgment to allow those in the community who do not have land of their own to have access to his land on a usufructuary basis. Such people may gain cultivation rights or building rights and use this opportunity to gain independence. These principles and ethics of land tenure are focused more on human need than on issues of ownership.[9]

Colonial Rule and the Emergence of the Land Crisis

The ethical and social ideals of the Agikuyu made it possible for them to have a balanced relationship with nature and with one another. With the coming of colonization in the late nineteenth century, however, these processes and ideals, which by and large were friendly to the environment and ultimately to the people that depended on it, were undermined and almost totally replaced by attitudes and ideals that enhanced domination, both of the people and the environment. This becomes clear when we look more closely at how colonialism impacted the continent.

It is important to reiterate that, in essence, colonialism was motivated by a desire to further the interests of the colonialists, apparently by any means necessary. Colonialism had as its defining feature the intent to exploit, to gain as much as possible by maximum use of the rich natural and human resources on the continent.

Thus, by definition, the colonialists did not prioritize the preservation and conservation of the resources of the continent. This included forest and wild game resources, mineral wealth and, of course, the land. The Agikuyu were particularly injured by colonial exploitation of the land. The colonialists abused and ignored the traditional Gikuyu ethic toward nature and land. Their unilateral assertion of control over the land without adequate concern for the indigenous peoples affected thousands of acres of the best land in Gikuyuland and created an acute shortage of land for the native peoples. Kanogo, one of the leading Kenyan historians, documents how the colonial enterprise turned many Agikuyu overnight into squatters on their own land, which they could no longer freely use or care for as demanded by God. In Kanogo's words:

> When the British declared a Protectorate over what came to be known as Kenya, Kikuyu settlements stretched northwards of Nairobi to the slopes of Mount Kenya . . . The settlers intended to appropriate the more highly cultivated areas, land that had already been broken in preference to waste and unoccupied land . . . [Colonial administrative] officers in charge of processing European applications for land usually gave settlers immediate authority to occupy land, with the only condition being that they pay the Kikuyu owners a meager three rupees per acre . . . By 1933, 109 square miles of potentially valuable land was alienated for European settlement . . . This indiscriminate alienation of African land rendered several thousand Africans landless . . . those who lost their lands in this way were urged to stay on to provide labor for the settlers . . . By July, 1910 there were approximately 11,000 Kikuyus . . . cultivating on land owned by the European settlers. Some of the squatters were the original owners of these farms. (Kanogo, 1987:11)

The painful reality of becoming squatters on their own lands was compounded by colonial exploitation of human labor with little compensation. The wage economy violated traditional understandings of labor as a method of producing wealth and materials for the improvement of one's family and community. The Agikuyu were reluctant to enter the wage economy, since cash for work was not only an inadequate compensation but was also an unfulfilling exercise since the wages earned went to pay taxes to run the colonial government rather than into their own pockets (Kanogo, 41-44).

Second, the colonialists introduced new ideas about land tenure that allowed individuals to own land absolutely and exclusively and to dispose of it at will. The individualization of land tenure had the immediate effect of rendering the Agikuyu landless in a quantitative way by turning the Agikuyu into squatters on their own land. It also significantly undermined community solidarity, which in traditional Gikuyu society acted as a check against lack of access to land even for the poorest in the community.

Besides literally confiscating the already developed land for its own exclusive use, the colonial government also restricted the use of undeveloped lands. The colonial government declared the unworked land "protected" reserves and required government permission for access to this land. The indigenous peoples were herded into disproportionately small areas of land summarily described as "native reserves," while most undeveloped but potentially usable land was declared "Crown" property by the British government. The resulting overuse and consequent deterioration of the little land available is apparent even today in the reduced productivity of the land occupied by the Agikuyu. As a consequence, the Agikuyu are now victims of landlessness in a *qualitative* way, in so far as the land that is accessible to them is overused and cannot sustain them.

The idea that the government could own land and disallow citizens at least usufructuary rights was unprecedented. The Agikuyu and other African peoples had always believed that use of the land—at least usufructuary access—was an inalienable right, regardless of one's status in society.

Moreover, the colonizers introduced patterns of land use that were ultimately inimical to the ecological balance. In search of material gain, most of the land taken over by the Europeans was put into cash crops such as tea and coffee, perennial crops that were ill-suited to the traditional patterns of land use that periodically let the soil lie fallow to restore itself. Thousands of acres of land in the richest parts of Kenya are still planted with these cash crops today, with no possibilities for crop rotation. One significant consequence is heavy reliance on chemical fertilizers to maintain suitable levels of soil fertility to maintain the cash crops.

It is also pertinent to note that setting aside so much land for non-food crops, usually intended for export, has led to the under-production of food crops and has resulted in frequent hunger and famine in areas where the first colonial settlers originally found adequate food supplies to use and to trade.[10]

The Gikuyu Response: The *Mau Mau* War and Its Legitimation

The realization of their plight led the Agikuyu to rise up in armed resistance against the colonialists and their exploitation of the land and its people. In waging the *Mau Mau* war of liberation, the Agikuyu felt they were fighting a just and holy war: they were fighting to defend their rights over the land that *Ngai*, God, had given them. It is interesting to note that, although the colonialists dismissed the Gikuyu war derogatorily as *Mau Mau*, defined as an irrational relapse of the natives to their precolonial "savagery," the fighters preferred to call themselves the Kenya Land and Freedom Army (Kanogo, 164). The Agikuyu perceived their goal as liberating themselves from the colonial political yoke and liberating the land from the illegal, abusive, and "sinful" occupation by the foreigners. The land and its reclamation was a constant theme of the hymns the fighters sang to encourage themselves in this very lopsided war.[11]

It is also noteworthy that the Agikuyu expected God to be on their side in this struggle, for their fair share of the universe was being usurped by the colonialists. Many of the hymns celebrate the victories of the guerrilla army over the more sophisticated weaponry and war skills of the colonialists. The victories were perceived as evidence that *Ngai* sided with the oppressed Agikuyu. One hymn celebrates the warriors' victory in a battle won in the name of *Mwene-Nyaga*:

> Friends, listen.
> Hear this story about Tumu Tumu Hill
> So that you may realize that Mwene Nyaga is with us and will
>   never forsake us
> We had great fighters in our army.
>
> Burunji gave his own life to save the lives of his comrades.
> He lit the fuse and threw the grenade
> and the enemy machine guns went dead.
> Such a great victory for our guerilla army!
>
>   (Kenyatti: 1987, 108)

The fighters perceived *Ngai* to be on their side because, despite their meager resources, the fighters were able to win significant battles against the oppressors. Even when the colonialists attempted to sabotage the struggle by destroying crops and livestock belonging to the Agikuyu, the fighters celebrated the fact that the powerful and just *Ngai* did not leave them hopeless. Instead, *Ngai* used nature to sustain the warriors so that, with *Ngai*'s blessings, they were able to sustain themselves with wild fruits and wild game. In one song the warriors sing:

> Olenguruone masses saw with their own eye,
> saw their cows and goats being penned away in kraals.
> The children also witnessed Olenguruone being destroyed
> And all the wealth and hopes of the masses smashed.
>
> Great were the cries of the Olenguruone children
> Because they were suffering under the rain and terrible cold.
> *Ngai* saw the enemy destroy the maize fields.
> He felt for the children suffering from hunger
> And blessed them with wild fruit and wild game.
> And he told them: Eat your fill.[12]
>
>   (Kenyatti, 52)

The thick forests on the slopes of Mount Kenya were also perceived as God-given hideouts from where the warriors could wage their predominantly gue-rilla struggle. The fighters clearly perceived this to be a just and holy war and *Ngai* was their best ally.

The hymns also give us significant insight into the Gikuyu theology of land. Many hymns refer to the Gikuyu cosmogonic myth cited earlier. They under-stood the war to be theologically legitimate insofar as the land was legitimately theirs. It was their moral obligation, therefore, to fight to reclaim what was rightfully theirs. As one hymn points out:

> *Ngai* gave us this country a long time ago
> When he was dividing the earth among nations
> And he said we should never give it up.
> But we were robbed of it by those colonial hordes that invaded our
>   country . . .
> *Ngai*, we shall get back our land . . .
>
> (Kenyatti, 28)

Women, Land, and Environmental Justice in Kenya

It is important to note that the colonial ideology of domination that led to the extreme abuse of the African environment also led to the gross abuse and exploita-tion of women, since colonial ideology and praxis were also very sexist. The colo-nial presence and ideology in Africa led to the radical patriarchalization of African societies, with the consequent disempowerment of women in all spheres of life. This fact is being documented increasingly by African women scholars as they seek to unmask the sources of their oppression and powerlessness.[13]

The Gikuyu situation exemplifies how colonialism led to the patriarchalization of African societies and the consequent disempowerment of African women. Kenyatta documents in vivid detail how the Gikuyu society was based on mu-tuality between the sexes. This applied both in running the affairs of the group and in working to produce goods and services for the community. He notes, for example, that women were not passive observers or slaves in the Gikuyu com-munity. Instead, women had a significant role to play in the political, economic, and religious life of the community. Kenyatta shows that the Gikuyu commu-nity was by and large an acephalous community, led by a system of councils convened to serve specific purposes in the community (Kenyatta, 179 ff.). Neigh-borhood councils administered justice in the local communities, women's coun-cils dealt with women's concerns, and ceremonial councils dealt with religious and ritual concerns of the community. As agriculturalists, the Agikuyu had developed divisions of labor that were complementary, without valuing the role of one gender over the other. Both men and women participated in the preparation of the land for planting, weeding, and harvesting, and even the building of shelter was a shared responsibility. There were some tasks, like that of waging war, that were more the preserve of men, for obvious reasons (Kenyatta, 52f).

Gikuyu women were far from the stereotyped picture painted, for example, by Evans Pritchards, who, as late as in 1955, spoke of "primitive" women who were voiceless chattels in the traditional social and political economies.[14] While this is not the place for a detailed critique of Evans Pritchards, it is important to note that colonialism led to the silencing and marginalization of Gikuyu and other African women, both in the colonial and in the neo-colonial social and economic context. While this was true in all spheres of life, I shall focus on issues of land.

First, the colonialists had a decidedly patriarchal understanding of the family. They assumed that African women were chattels of their husband, part of the property the men ostensibly owned, including land and animals.[15] Consequently, when the colonialists "negotiated" for land, they consulted only the men in the communities. This set a deadly precedent, particularly when colonial practice eventually became law. Most laws ignored the needs or rights of women.

Second, the colonialists introduced new attitudes and systems of land tenure that were contrary to the traditional ones. They assumed, for example, that land could be owned and disposed of by individuals, particularly by male individuals. The colonial system empowered individuals to own and dispose of land without considering the needs of others in the community. This individualization of land tenure greatly undermined women's usufructuary rights to land. Referring to the impact of the Land Registration Act effected in Kenya in the 1950s, one scholar laments the way this particular act diminished women's access to land:

> The colonial administration introduced in Kenya the concept of individual ownership, which was alien to the traditional communal ownership. The enactment of the Registered Land Act saw the introduction of absolute right over property . . . The Act was introduced because of the falling standards of agriculture in the African reserves, which were attributed to "defective tenure arrangements" in African society . . . One marked feature of the adjudication, consolidation and registration process of the 1950s was that women were not registered as owners of land. (Macharia, quoted in Khasiani:1992, 94)

Third, the colonialists introduced the idea that land was a commodity that could be acquired by the use of money. This radical commodification of land led to the restriction of land rights of those who did not have monetary power in the society. This would not have happened in traditional societies where even the poorest people had building and cultivation rights in the community. The commodification of land has particularly affected those women who fall victim of unscrupulous spouses or relatives who unilaterally sell the land and leave the women and their children destitute.[16]

Fourth, as noted above, the colonial government introduced the idea that land could be privately owned, regardless of whether or not the owner was actually using it. When the British came into Gikuyuland, they confiscated the land that had already been worked on by indigenous peoples, thereby declaring it settlers' land, and they also restricted future access to unworked land by declaring the rest of the land "Crownland," the property of the British government, even though the land was not actually being used. In this way, settlers were able to fence off and appropriate thousands of acres of usable land, without actually doing anything with it.

In the meantime, the relocation of indigenous peoples to small "native reserves," set a precedent for the contemporary practice of a Kenyan hoarding as much land as he can buy without any obligation to do anything with the land, other than to use it as collateral for massive loans from commercial banks that capitalize on the commodification of land. This practice has led to a severe shortage of land in the midst of plenty. It is not uncommon to find extensive "ranch farms," formerly owned by individual absentee colonialists, that have been taken over by individual African tycoons who have no use for them except to boost their egos. Meanwhile, the majority of Kenyans continue to fight over and to overuse the limited parcels of land that remain.[17]

These colonial and neo-colonial practices have directly affected women by grossly undermining their access to land. In a sense, women have become double victims because they also bear the burdens of a battered environment. As a United Nations report has lamented:

> Environmental degradation has already pushed great numbers of women into marginal environs where critically low levels of water supplies, shortages of fuel, over utilization of grazing and arable land and population densities has deprived them of their livelihood. (as quoted in Khasiani, 1992)

This deprivation has translated into frustration as women try to implement their inherent roles of mothering and nurturing life. The toll on women, who find it more and more difficult to feed their children in spite of many hours of hard work, is a painful reality that prevails on the continent.

Diffusing the Crisis: What Can Be Learned?

While women have often been passive victims of their circumstances, they have not completely lost their moral agency, though it has sometimes been ignored or muted, particularly by policy makers. It is noteworthy that women have been active and visible participants in the "holy" and just war for the physical reclamation of their land from the colonial powers. This is true not only in Kenya, but throughout the continent where wars of political liberation have been fought. In the Gikuyu case, women were active combatants in the Mau Mau war, and also supported the guerrilla army by supplying food and weapons (see Kanogo, 143). Indeed, the Mau Mau war was also a women's war for ecological justice to gain access to land.

The same kind of moral agency has manifested itself in the post-colonial and neo-colonial periods when women have continued to struggle actively for justice in all spheres of life, including political and economic spheres. In particular, African women have realized that they must fight for solutions to the environmental crises that affect them directly. In Kenya, for example, women have taken the initiative to fight for land reclamation in both qualitative and quantitative terms. This initiative has crystallized in the formation of many women's groups and organizations, which, in the spirit of traditional patterns of female solidarity, are empowering women to participate in diffusing the environmental crisis. Women are forming cooperatives to buy land, to build and improve their homes, to construct dams and water tanks to collect rain water, and even to pay school fees for their children.

One organization that has directly concerned itself with environmental degradation in Kenya is the Green Belt Movement, founded by Professor Wangari Maathai, a leading feminist and ecological activist. This movement has had tremendous success in mobilizing women at the grassroots level to participate in an aggressive reforestation program. The organization aims not only at reclaiming the quality of the land through planting trees, it also aims at reclaiming women's power by planting afresh the sense of self-confidence and pride in themselves nurtured in precolonial times by many African societies. This reclaimed self-confidence makes women better equipped to fight the multi-headed monster of injustice in Africa.

Conclusion: Toward Sustainable Solutions

Despite the many efforts of activists, NGOs, and international pressure, the environmental crisis continues to loom large in Africa and threatens to sustain African misery for many years to come. If any meaningful solutions are to be found, Africans must begin the process of self-reclamation and search urgently for new self-confidence. To the extent that they rediscover pride in their culture and in themselves, they will also begin to discover that the answers to problems that face Africa today will not come from outsiders, however well-intentioned and charitable they might be.

Such a critical reclamation of traditional values may lead Africans to rediscover one of the most fundamental ethical ideals concerning land and the environment: namely, that nature is given to us on trust to use responsibly—not at the expense of each other, but for the mutual enrichment of our co-trustees. The rediscovery that God is the absolute owner of the universe should caution us against the often fatal fallacy and illusion that human beings have absolute control over nature.

The fallaciousness of human control of nature is becoming palpably obvious from the way nature counters with a tremendous variety of disasters, many of which are linked to human abuse of nature. A recognition that we depend on nature should lead us to develop the sense of gratitude and respect for nature that was so palpable in traditional African societies. The rediscovery by Africans of a theology and ethics of the environment, as exemplified here by the Gikuyu case, should go a long way toward alleviating some of the problems we face because of environmental degradation and injustice.

Notes

1. For details of this exploitation see Walter Rodney, *How Europe Underdeveloped Africa* (Tanzania Publishing House, 1976).

2. See, for example, Kenyatta's apologetic rejoinder to those who accused the Agikuyu of worshipping nature (Kenyatta, *Facing Mount Kenya*, 1965:231).

3. See Genesis 1:26.

4. The sense of confusion, alienation, and apathy that seemed to overwhelm Africans in the wake of colonialism is well captured, for example, in Chinua Achebe's novel, *Things Fall Apart*. While we cannot exonerate those who commit acts of atrocity and violence in contemporary Africa, it is true to say that much of the chaos that manifests itself through civil unrest, coups, dictatorships, and civil wars is linked with the sense of things having fallen apart due to colonization. The challenge for contemporary Africans is not only to fight against colonialism but also to decolonize our minds in order to dismantle the legacy of destruction, death, and confusion that seems to characterize post-colonial Africa.

5. In this section, I rely quite heavily on Kenyatta's book *Facing Mount Kenya* (1965), which remains one of the most comprehensive accounts of the Agikuyu in pre-colonial Kenya. This book was first published in 1938.

6. See Kenyatta, 5.

7. *Mwene-Nyaga*, another Gikuyu name for God, describes God's holiness and mystery.

8. Ironically, it is this understanding of land tenure that initially led the Agikuyu to allow colonial settlers to settle in their midst as *Ahoi* and *Athami*. See Kenyatta, 45.

9. It is noteworthy that the Agikuyu were not unique in evolving a system of land tenure that ensured access to land as a basic right. For a similar system in another Kenyan community, see Ocholla-Ayayo, *Traditional Ideology and Ethics among the Southern Luo*, 1976:129-132.

10. Even where Europeans introduced crops such as maize and wheat, these functioned and still function as cash crops and are often ill-suited to the feeding habits of the people. For details of the connection between the introduction of maize and the emergence of frequent famine in Luo-land in western Kenya, see Cohen and Atieno, 1989:64.

11. For a detailed account of the significance of these hymns, see Kenyatti, *Thunder from the Mountain* (Africa World Press, 1987).

12. For a detailed historical account of the events that led to the Olenguruone crisis referred to in this hymn, see Kanogo, 115ff.

13. This is the position taken, for example, by Ifi Amadiume in her book, *Male Daughters and Female Husbands*. She dedicates one chapter to an analysis of colonialism and the erosion of Igbo women's power (see Ifi Amadiume, 1987:119ff).

14. See Evans Pritchard's essay, "The Position of Women in Primitive Societies and in Our Own." It is noteworthy that this lecture was given in 1955, a few years before Kenya gained independence largely through the impact of the Mau Mau war in which

Kenyan women were active participants! It is also noteworthy that the people described as "primitive" are Africans, since Evans Pritchards did his research among the Nuer and the Azande of the Sudan and the Luo of Kenya. For a Western feminist critique of this lecture and its implications for Western women, see Karen Sacks, "Sisters and Wives," 1982:36ff.

15. For details of this lamentable situation see Adhiambo Mbeo and Ooko Ombaka (eds.) *Women and Law in Kenya,* 1989:71.

16. The question of land and landlessness in Kenya is one of the key concerns in Ngugi Wa Thiongo's two books, *Devil on the Cross* and *I Will Marry When I Want,* in which he analyzes the neocolonial situation's impact upon Kenyan peasants who continue to be victims of injustice and oppression many years after Kenya gained its independence. He singles out commoditization and hoarding of land by a few and the consequent landlessness of the majority of Kenyans as key aspects of the injustice that common people endure in contemporary Kenya.

17. The acute shortage of land in Kenya which is largely due to the indiscriminate hoarding of the best parts of the country by a wealthy few has in recent years caused bloody clashes among Kenyan communities. These clashes have been erroneously labeled "tribal clashes," suggesting that the clashes are a consequence of innate hostility and enmity between the various tribes. This, however, has had the effect of camouflaging the real issues that are basically issues of distributive justice (or rather lack of it) in the country. For a detailed account of how the colonial situation rendered many of the ethnic groups, particularly the Agikuyu, landless, see Kanogo, *Squatters and the Roots of Mau Mau* (1987). For a discussion of the exacerbation of the situation in the postcolonial era (mainly due to the greed of a few) see Ngugi Wa Thiongo, *Devil on the Cross* (1982:99-118).

References

Amadiume, Ifi. *Male Daughters and Female Husbands* (London: Zed Books, 1987).

Cohen, William David and Odhiambo Atieno, eds. *Siaya: The Historical Anthropology of An African Landscape* (Ohio University Press, 1989).

Kanogo, T. M. *Squatters and the Roots of Mau Mau* (London: James Curry, 1987).

Kenyatta, Jomo. *Facing Mount Kenya* (1938; reprint New York: Vintage Books, 1965).

Kenyatti, Maina Wa. *Thunder from the Mountain* (Trenton, N.J.: Africa World Press, 1987).

Khasiani, S. A., ed. *Groundwork: African Women as Environmental Managers* (Nairobi: African Center For Technology Studies, 1992).

Mbeo, Adhiambo and Ooko Ombaka, eds. *Women and Law in Kenya* (Nairobi: Public Law Institute, 1989).

Ocholla-Ayayo, A. B. *Traditional Ideology and Ethics among the Southern Luo* (Uppsala: Scandinavian Institute of African Studies, 1976).

Rodney Walter. *How Europe Underdeveloped Africa* (Tanzania Publishing House, 1976).

Sacks, Karen. *Sisters and Wives: The Past and the Future of Sexual Equality* (Westport, Conn.: Greenwood Press, 1982).

Timberlake, Lloyd. *Africa in Crisis: The Causes, the Cures of Environmental Bankruptcy* (Washington, D.C.: Earthscan Paperback, 1985).

Wa Thiongo, Ngugi. *Devil on the Cross* (London: Heinemann, 1987).

———. *I Will Marry When I Want* (London: Heinemann, 1982).

Select Bibliography:
Third World Women, Theology, Ecology

Aquino, Maria Pilar. 1993. *Our Cry for Life: Feminist Theology from Latin America*. Maryknoll, NY: Orbis Books.

Balasuriya, Tissa. 1984. *Planetary Theology*. Maryknoll, NY: Orbis Books.

Bingemer, Maria Clara, and Ivone Gebara. 1989. *Mary, Mother of God, Mother of the Poor*. Maryknoll, NY: Orbis Books.

Boff, Leonardo. 1995 *Ecology and Theology: A New Paradigm*. Maryknoll, NY: Orbis Books.

Chung, Hyun Kyung. 1990. *Struggle to be the Sun Again: Introducing Asian Women's Theology*. Maryknoll, NY: Orbis Books.

Diamond, Irene, and Gloria Feman Orenstein. 1990. *Reweaving the World: The Emergence of Ecofeminism*. San Francisco, CA: Sierra Club Books.

Fabella, Virginia, and Mercy Amba Oduyoye. 1988. *With Passion and Compassion: Third World Women Doing Theology*. Maryknoll, NY: Orbis Books.

———, and Sun Ai Lee Park. 1989. *We Dare to Dream: Doing Theology as Asian Women*. Seoul, Korea: The Asian Women's Resource Center.

Galeano, Eduardo. 1973. *Open Veins of Latin America: Five Centuries of the Pillage of a Continent*. New York: Monthly Review Press.

Hallman, David C., ed. 1994. *Ecotheology: Voices from North and South*. Maryknoll, NY: Orbis Books.

Mueller-Fahrenholz, Geiko. 1995. *God's Spirit: Transforming a World in Crisis*. New York: Continuum Publishing Company.

Oduyoye, Mercy Amba. 1995. *Daughters of Anowa: African Women and Patriarchy*. Maryknoll, NY: Orbis Books.

———, and Musimbi Kanyoro. 1992. *The Will to Arise: Women, Tradition and the Church in Africa*. Maryknoll, NY: Orbis Books.

Plant, Judith. 1989. *Healing the Wounds: The Promise of Ecofeminism*. Philadelphia, PA: New Society Publishers.

Ress, Mary Judith, Ute Siebert-Cuadra, and Lene Siorup, eds. 1994. *Del Cielo a La Tierra: Una Antología de Teología Feminista*. Santiago, Chile: Editorial de Mujeres.

Ruether, Rosemary Radford. 1992. *Gaia and God: An Ecofeminist Theology of Earth Healing*. San Francisco, CA: HarperSanFrancisco.

Shiva, Vandana. 1989. *Staying Alive: Women, Ecology and Development*. London: Zed Press.

Tamez, Elsa, ed. 1989. *Through Her Eyes: Women's Theology from Latin America.* Maryknoll, NY: Orbis Books.

Journals

Con-spirando: Revista LatinoAmericana de Ecofeminismo, Espiritualidad y Teología, Santiago, Chile; Con-spirando Collective (three times yearly).
In God's Image, Seoul, Korea: Asian Women's Cultural Center (four times yearly).